⑪ 1|23

W9-CKQ-503

THE
SCANDALOUS
HAMILTONS

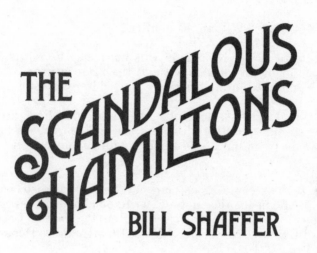

# THE SCANDALOUS HAMILTONS

### BILL SHAFFER

**CITADEL PRESS**
Kensington Publishing Corp.
www.kensingtonbooks.com

CITADEL PRESS BOOKS are published by

Kensington Publishing Corp.
119 West 40th Street
New York, NY 10018

Copyright © 2022 William R. Shaffer

All rights reserved. No part of this book may be reproduced in any form or by any means without the prior written consent of the publisher, excepting brief quotes used in reviews.

All Kensington titles, imprints, and distributed lines are available at special quantity discounts for bulk purchases for sales promotions, premiums, fund-raising, educational, or institutional use.

Special book excerpts or customized printings can also be created to fit specific needs. For details, write or phone the office of the Kensington sales manager: Kensington Publishing Corp., 119 West 40th Street, New York, NY 10018, attn: Sales Department; phone 1-800-221-2647.

CITADEL PRESS and the Citadel logo are Reg. U.S. Pat. & TM Off.

ISBN: 978-0-8065-4225-6

First Citadel hardcover printing: August 2022

10 9 8 7 6 5 4 3 2 1

Printed in the United States of America

Library of Congress Catalog Number: 2022934733

Electronic edition:

ISBN: 978-0-8065-4227-0 (e-book)

For my two loves:

CHRISTINE *and* CAROLINE

# CONTENTS

**Introduction** 1

CHAPTER ONE
**In the Woman's Power** 7

CHAPTER TWO
**A Woman's Ready Dagger** 16

CHAPTER THREE
**A Villainous Conspiracy** 32

CHAPTER FOUR
**Mr. Hamilton's Plight** 48

CHAPTER FIVE
**Mrs. Hamilton Weeps** 63

CHAPTER SIX
**Mrs. Eva Hamilton's Story** 86

CHAPTER SEVEN
**Mann or Hamilton?** 110

CHAPTER EIGHT
**Mr. Hamilton's Fate** 119

CHAPTER NINE
**Eva Begins Her Fight** 146

CHAPTER TEN
**Eva at the Footlights** 190

CHAPTER ELEVEN
**Mrs. Gaul's Queer Goings-On** 199

CHAPTER TWELVE
**Sequel to Tragedy** 212

CHAPTER THIRTEEN
**Let Him Be Forgotten** 225

**Epilogue** 245

*Notes* 247

*Image Credits* 277

*Sources* 279

*Acknowledgments* 295

*Index* 299

# INTRODUCTION

Had the Hamilton story that unfolds on these pages occurred today, it would merit blanket coverage on cable
news and provide ample fodder for a barrage of biting headlines on the front pages of the New York tabloids. Conspiracy
theories would be breathlessly tweeted from those laying
claim to inside information. Rumors and innuendo would be
passed along, *sotto voce*, at fashionable New York dinner parties—a perfectly tawdry tale involving a Founding Father's
descendant would be impossible to ignore.

During the Gilded Age, however, the only medium available
for "breaking news" was the newspaper. In 1889, there were
1,492 daily newspapers published in the United States—
an additional 14,787 monthlies, weeklies, and semi-weeklies
printed in America's largest cities and smallest towns fueled
the nation's insatiable appetite for news. There were nineteen
English-language dailies published in New York City alone,
joined by a host of others published in the native languages of
recently arrived immigrants. The largest New York dailies,
the *World, Tribune, Herald, Sun,* and *Times* had a combined
total of 475,000 daily readers—almost one newspaper for
every three citizens of New York. (The 1890 population of New
York City totaled 1.51 million people, the City of Brooklyn,
806,000.) Telegraph networks and the recently formed Associ-

ated Press allowed for news stories published in one part of
the United States to be transmitted across the country to run
simultaneously in editions nationwide.

The rise of yellow journalism in the last decades of the nineteenth century, epitomized by Joseph Pulitzer's *New York
World*, marked a turning point in the public consumption of
news. Publishers increasingly sought to capture the attention
of their audience by printing provocative headlines and titillating stories rife with hearsay and gossip. Articles that recounted violent crimes, attempted blackmail, prostitution,
alcohol-induced mayhem, morphine addiction, or a mysterious
death were lapped up by readers thirsty for even a hint of
scandal. The story of the tumultuous, five-year relationship
between Robert Ray Hamilton and the woman born as Evangeline Steele combined every one of these elements. For the
New York dailies, Ray and Eva were heaven-sent—an unex-
pected gift wrapped in truths, half-truths, and lies.

When the salacious details of the Hamilton story emerged
in August 1889, dailies were typically published as eight-page
editions, with eight columns per page. The front page might
feature up to twenty short articles laid out over those eight
columns, the sea of text broken up only by an occasional, small
illustration. For a story to command a full column on page
one, it had to be sensationally newsworthy. From the outset,
the Hamilton drama played out not only in full columns on
page one, but in multiple columns that continued onto the interior pages. The headlines used as chapter titles in this book
are representative of the many articles about the Hamiltons.

Why was such attention paid to Robert Ray Hamilton and
Evangeline Steele? In the nineteenth century the Hamilton
name was recognized by all Americans and almost universally
revered—akin at the time to the Kennedy name today. In
1804, the news of Alexander Hamilton being shot in a duel
with Aaron Burr produced the same level of shock as the news

of JFK's assassination in 1963. Fifty-eight years after Dallas, our interest is still piqued when we hear the Kennedy name in the news; so, too, with the Hamilton name long after that fatal event in Weehawken, New Jersey.

Members of the Hamilton family were listed in the *Social Register*, well known in political and financial circles, and many were members of Ward McAllister's "Four Hundred," the pinnacle of New York society (four hundred is the number of guests said to fit comfortably in Mrs. Astor's ballroom). Men like Ray Hamilton, born into the upper classes of the Gilded Age, traded stocks and real estate, entered into socially acceptable professions—the law, finance, medicine—and spent a fair share of their time with other members of their class idling in private clubs and fine restaurants. Their life of privilege was assumed from birth.

Conversely, Eva was raised dirt-poor in the northeast Pennsylvania coal country, the daughter of an alcoholic, itinerant logger. Women who were born into difficult circumstances, and who weren't afforded much of an education, had to scratch and claw for everything they obtained in life. If that scratching and clawing flirted with the law or social norms, so be it. They did what they had to do to get by.

And while Ray's name and identity were clearly defined at birth, Eva used multiple surnames over the course of her life—Steele, Parsons, Brill, Mann, Hamilton, and Gaul—and claimed at various times to be from New Jersey, Pennsylvania, or New York. This was easy to do during the nineteenth century. There were no such things as photo IDs, social security numbers, or background checks. You were, quite simply, whoever you said you were. The ability to invent and re-invent one's identity was particularly useful for a person who may have been inclined to engage in illegal or nefarious activities.

The newspapers had a field day contrasting Eva's hard-scrabble roots with Ray's inherited wealth and privilege.

Members of the working class who pored through newspapers like the *World* reveled in stories about the vulnerability of the rich and powerful—comforted in some way by the knowledge that even the privileged were susceptible to the vicissitudes of life, just like them.

Beyond following the blow-by-blow accounts of the events that transpired beginning in August 1889, readers were intrigued by Ray's and Eva's disparate socioeconomic backgrounds and how a man of his stature could become entangled with a woman regularly described by the press as a "bold adventurous." And one unanswered question hung over the entire drama: How could such a seemingly smart man be so stupid?

As Ray Hamilton left little record of his own judgment about the matter, it is difficult to conclusively determine his feelings about his life with Eva. What Ray did leave, however, was a lasting memorial in his own name, the Hamilton Fountain. It remains today at Seventy-Sixth Street and Riverside Drive in New York, more than one hundred years after it was set in place. Today, children splash their hands in the fountain's basin and local residents stroll past the outstretched wings of its crowning eagle, few of them knowing the long-forgotten Hamilton story and the fountain's raison d'être.

Attached to a lamppost adjacent to the fountain is a small plaque put in place by the New York City Parks Department that offers a brief biography of Ray Hamilton, explains the significance of ornamental fountains in early twentieth-century parks, and mentions a "public scandal involving Eva Mann, who he had secretly married, and who had used this alliance to raid his substantial financial holdings."

That one line piqued the curiosity of this author and instigated a search through court records, case files, personal correspondence, and archival material in an effort to learn more about this mysterious public scandal involving Robert Ray

Hamilton and the woman the Parks Department referred to as Eva Mann. While these materials certainly provide pertinent details about their relationship, it is through the dramatic newspaper accounts that ran nationwide during the last years of the nineteenth century that we learn of the public fascination with Ray and Eva and the white light of media attention that focused on the regrettable decisions made by these two ill-fated figures of the Gilded Age.

## CHAPTER ONE
# In the Woman's Power

On Monday, January 7, 1889, an unlikely couple crossed the Hudson River from Manhattan to Paterson, New Jersey, to be married. Robert Ray Hamilton and Eva Brill were improbable candidates to become husband and wife—during the course of their four-year relationship they had maintained separate lives and spent as much time apart from each other as they had together. A wealthy attorney and real estate investor, Ray also represented the fashionable Murray Hill District in the New York State Assembly from 1884 to 1888 and spent a great deal of time in Albany, only seeing Eva when he returned to the city on weekends.

When Ray was away, Eva associated with a dubious collection of friends and acquaintances who were far removed from the stature of her soon-to-be husband. The birth of their first child out of wedlock, three weeks before their journey to Paterson, provided the impetus for Eva to convince Ray to marry her. After four years, Eva's ambition to become Mrs. Robert Ray Hamilton was about to triumph over Ray's indifference to legalizing their relationship.

The Pavonia Ferry ran between Jersey City and Chambers Street in lower Manhattan. The wood-clad steamer bobbed through the chop of the Hudson on its fifteen-minute journey across the river, briefly slowing to square up to its Jersey City terminal before the engines revved, smoke belched from its stacks, and the captain made his final push into the pier. In warm weather, passengers lined the open bow front of the *Pavonia* to see the blocky silhouettes of factories and warehouses that lined the Jersey waterfront come into focus as the ferry neared the shore. On a cold January day, though, a bench inside the cabin would be the seat of choice for a couple seeking shelter from the winter winds that blew up the Hudson from New York harbor.

Ray and Eva's trek to Paterson, two stops inland from the ferry on an Erie Railroad branch line, ended at the Market Street Methodist Episcopal Church. The forty-year-old, russet-colored stone church in the center of town was topped by a hexagonal white steeple that rose to one of the highest points in the city. Neither Ray nor Eva were congregants of the Market Street church, but it was sufficiently out of the way as to not bring undue attention to the couple. The pastor, Reverend Edson Burr, (no relation to Aaron Burr) had never met Ray or Eva before they knocked on his door and asked to be married.

Reverend Burr held a Doctor of Divinity degree from Wesleyan University, was a staunch believer in the doctrines of his faith, and cherished every opportunity to preach the Gospel. Above all, he believed that a Christian minister had a responsibility to speak as a defender of truth. His obligation to the truth extended beyond the eyes of God—for a wedding to be legally recognized in New Jersey the state required that the truth be told by all applicants. Accordingly, Reverend Burr was duty-bound to gather pertinent information from the couple standing before him.

Boyishly handsome, Ray looked ten years younger than thirty-eight, his age at the time of the wedding. Thin and of medium height, he had jet-black hair and a full mustache that extended fully across his upper lip and connected with bushy sideburns. Ray wore the sharply tailored, narrow suits popular at the time, his jacket properly buttoned over a crisp white shirt finished with a Warville collar and a Windsor tie firmly knotted against his neck. He carried himself with the confidence and manners befitting a gentleman of his upbringing. Timothy Sullivan, a friend and colleague of Hamilton's in Albany, described him as "that thoroughbred dude."

Complying with Reverend Burr's directive, Ray registered as Robert R. Hamilton, a lawyer by profession. He noted his birthplace as New York City and that he was the son of Schuyler Hamilton and Cornelia Ray.

Eva's appearance belied her impoverished childhood in eastern Pennsylvania coal country. She wore fitted jackets that tapered at her waist over long, pleated tulip-shaped skirts, her chestnut blond hair swept up under a matching hat. Strands of pearls encircled her long neck, her ensemble accessorized with jeweled brooches and earrings.

Eva entered her full name in the registry as Evangeline L. Steele, age twenty-nine, birthplace Tunkhannock, Pennsylvania, and stated that she was the daughter of William Steele and Lida Cheevers. As the average age for marriage at the time was twenty-six for men and twenty-two for women, Ray and Eva were anomalous to the couples Reverend Burr normally joined in matrimony. He asked if either of them had been married previously, to which they both answered no.

Reverend Burr also had an obligation to ensure that two witnesses were present to attest to the nuptials. As Ray and Eva had traveled to the Market Street church alone—no family or friends accompanied them across the Hudson and no one met them upon their arrival in Paterson—Burr recruited his wife, Josephine, and his mother-in-law, Harriet Hill, to serve as witnesses to the marriage of these strangers from New York. With everything in order, Reverend Burr performed the ceremony, documents were signed, and the Certificate of Marriage was sent to the Bureau of Vital Statistics at Paterson City Hall.

If Ray had conformed to the expectations of his family and social circle, his wedding would have taken place at Calvary Church on Fourth Avenue in Manhattan, around the corner from Gramercy Park. The handsome Gothic Revival brownstone was home to congregants from some of the most prominent family names in New York: Astor, Roosevelt, and Vanderbilt as well as Hamilton. The ceremony and reception would have been chronicled in gushing detail in the newspapers, the guest list filled with names plucked from the pages of the *Social Register*. Ray's bride would have hailed from another prominent New York family; she would not have been a woman of undetermined character. By contrast, Eva would likely have been married by a country preacher in rural Pennsylvania with a few family members and a scattering of townsfolk in attendance, the reception organized around a pot luck and moonshine.

Ray, born in 1851, was the eldest of three sons born to General Schuyler Hamilton, a decorated veteran of both the Mexican-American and Civil Wars, and Cornelia Ray, daughter of wealthy New Yorker, Robert Ray. His younger brother, Schuyler Hamilton Jr., was born in 1853—the youngest son, Charles Apthorp Hamilton, born in 1858, died of natural causes at age seventeen. The grandfather of Ray, Schuyler Jr., and Charles was noted historian and biographer John Church Hamilton, and their great-grandfather was Founding Father Alexander Hamilton.

Much was expected from Ray, Schuyler Jr., their cousins, schoolmates, and friends. Their families produced politicians, statesmen, financiers, respected legal minds, and leading businessmen. They went to the best schools and married the daughters of other wealthy and socially connected families.

Ray's generation came of age in the 1870s and 1880s, just as the spectacular riches of the Gilded Age became manifest, visible to rich and poor alike.

Eva's father, William Steele, was a hard-drinking woodcutter who moved his family of six children from one logging camp to another to find work. Anthracite coal was king in the northeast corner of Pennsylvania when Eva was born. It was dug out of the Appalachian hills and used to fire the mills that forged the steel rails used by the railroads to haul carloads of coal out of the Wyoming Valley and across the country. The industrialization of America was on full display around Tunkhannock, but the fortunes gained from coal mining and the railroads didn't line the pockets of local laborers—it was the barons associated with the likes of Ray Hamilton who reaped the benefits of the backbreaking work performed by men like William Steele.

The Hamilton family had a long association with Columbia College, beginning with Alexander's enrollment at King's College in 1774. Exactly one hundred years later, Ray graduated from Columbia Law School and was admitted to the New York City Bar. Eva was educated in a one-room schoolhouse in a hamlet in Sullivan County, Pennsylvania, until she left school at age fifteen. The consensus in the community was that she wasn't going to be bright.

But even though Eva lacked much of a formal education, she learned at an early age that men, regardless of their class, were beguiled by her bright eyes, curvy figure, and a smile that betrayed just a hint of mischief. Ray Hamilton was no exception.

The newlyweds chose not to linger in Paterson after the ceremony, returning to Manhattan by the end of their wedding day. While Ray had agreed to marry Eva on short notice, he made no provision for them to live under the same roof. Ray lived alone on West Fourteenth Street and Eva lived in a boarding house on East Thirty-Third Street—an older widow, Anna Swinton, and her adult son, Joshua Mann, boarded in an adjacent room. Eva had left their infant daughter, Beatrice, in Mrs. Swinton's care while she traveled to Paterson for her wedding. When the newlyweds arrived back in the city, Ray went his way and Eva hers. Eva had no issue with this arrangement, as her new husband had made plans for them to begin an extended trip to California in March, with an eye to making their permanent home in San Diego.

San Diego had become more easily accessible to easterners via the transcontinental railroad four years before Ray and his new family set out on their journey. Only 5,000 people lived in the sleepy seaside town when the first California Southern trains arrived in 1885. The railroad brought an influx of new residents, including real estate investors like Ray Hamilton, who rushed in to buy prime oceanfront property. Dilapidated clapboard buildings were torn down to build hotels and shops, omnibuses began to operate on freshly paved streets, and the nearby Sweetwater River was dammed up to supply fresh water to a population that had swelled to nearly 30,000 residents.

Ray's real estate portfolio was extensive, but limited to New York City. Deeds of Surrender for properties that were owned by the Hamilton family were routinely swapped between the General and his two sons. Ray also held an interest in the Prescott House, an elegant, six-story hotel at Broadway and Spring Street and owned undeveloped lots uptown on Twenty-Ninth and Thirtieth Streets. He understood the influence of infrastructure on development and could afford to speculate.

Ray bought property as far north as Ninety-Third Street and Eighth Avenue when the success of the Ninth Avenue El, New York's first elevated train, spurred a building boom on the Upper West Side of Manhattan. And when the Brooklyn Bridge opened in 1883, connecting the City of Brooklyn with

New York, Ray purchased farmland on the far side of the bridge in Gravesend, speculating that the area was ripe for new housing. By 1889, his holdings throughout the entire city of Brooklyn consisted of thirty-two homes and thirty-one vacant lots.

The stunning, undeveloped coastline of southern California, though, presented development opportunities that were not possible on the more densely populated East Coast. But for all of the promise of riches that San Diego held out to a savvy investor, Eva surmised that Ray's actual intention for their trip was to shield their clandestine wedding and new baby from his family and friends. He had kept his relationship with Eva a secret from the outset and informed no one, not even his father and brother, of his marriage and fatherhood. By spending an extended period of time almost 3,000 miles away from home, Eva reasoned that Ray could plausibly return to the East Coast and explain that he had met her in California where they married and had a child.

Duplicity and connivance came naturally to Eva. Over the course of her lifetime, she concocted stories that changed depending on her audience, or the circumstances in which she found herself at any particular time. Facts were fungible; anecdotes were sometimes rooted in the truth and sometimes cut from whole cloth. Eva told some acquaintances that she was orphaned at a young age and adopted by the Steeles. To others, she said that her birth mother and father were wealthy and lived in Passaic, New Jersey. She described herself as an actress and a performer, but had no stage credits to support her claim.

The tapestry of fact and fiction that Eva had woven about her life was unneeded in San Diego. She arrived with a new husband, a new baby, and a new name—she knew no one in town and had no need to spin tales about her past.

Before their departure from New York, Ray and Eva had

hired Mary Ann Donnelly, a wet nurse, to accompany them on their journey west. In the late 1800s, it was common for wealthy families to hire a wet nurse either because of a mother's inability to lactate, or an unwillingness to feed her own child. The only real alternative to breast milk at the time was cow's milk—infant formula did not come into widespread use until the beginning of the twentieth century.

Wet nurses were often held in low regard by the well-to-do who hired them, as they came from lower social classes, eager to overcome their desperate circumstances. They were generally perceived to be "coarse, unruly and ignorant" and the physicians who recommended them to wealthy families admitted that they had "at least one virtue that overshadowed their many alleged vices—their milk saved babies' lives." During the course of the Hamiltons' stay in San Diego, Eva's relationship with her own coarse and unruly wet nurse, Mary Ann Donnelly, grew increasingly argumentative.

While Ray may have relished the fresh start for his new family in the West, Eva did not. Whether due to the change in climate, being so far from home, or adapting to her new role as a mother, she was unwell. Eva lost forty pounds and began drinking heavily. After only four months in southern California, a decision was taken to return east, summering at the Jersey shore before returning to New York at the end of August.

Lending credence to Eva's theory regarding Ray's real motivation for moving to San Diego, it wasn't until they had returned to the East Coast that Ray informed his father of his marriage and fatherhood. The General in turn passed the news on to Ray's younger brother, Schuyler Jr.

*Croton Landing N.Y.*
*Aug 7, 1889*

*Dear Ray,*

*I heard last night from father of your marriage and that I am an uncle. I am glad the lady is handsome and the baby sweet and pretty. I think they are the greatest comforts one can have in this life.*

*Sometime in the future if agreeable to you I would like to run down and see the family—I think my little niece will find a tender spot in my heart for her; what is her name?*

*Hope your wife and little one may add much happiness to your life, I remain*

*Your loving brother,*
*Schuyler*

*Send their pictures, especially if they are good looking.*

## CHAPTER TWO

# A Woman's Ready Dagger

**Monday, August 26, 1889**

It was an unseasonably cool start to the last week of August in Atlantic City, with the temperature reaching a high of just seventy degrees for the day. Rain was not expected, however, so as the sun rose above the grand hotels and quaint cottages that lined the seashore, the throng of seasonal residents lodged in guest rooms from Missouri to Massachusetts Avenues prepared to do what vacationers had done since trains started bringing Philadelphians to the Jersey shore in the 1850s: go to the beach.

The 10,000 year-round residents of this coastal resort town were joined each summer by 65,000 visitors who arrived throughout June, July, and August to idle their days away by the seaside. Some would spend their time fully immersed in the warm Atlantic surf, others wading in no farther than their ankles, all of them mugging for pictures or collecting seashells to have as keepsakes of their summer holiday at the shore.

Those who preferred not to contend with the sand and water could remain on the four-mile-long boardwalk that spanned the length of the beach, strolling to see and be seen. Tourist pamphlets recommended the boardwalk as a place to observe every aspect of the human character, declaring that a day spent on the crowded thoroughfare was worth a year in ordinary life. Some would choose to navigate the boardwalk riding in a novelty introduced to Atlantic City several years prior, the Rolling Chair. A modified wheelchair enclosed in a wicker shell, the Rolling Chair was popular with Nobs and Swells—moneyed vacationers who not only rented a chair for the day but hired a man to push them up and down the boardwalk as well.

The occupants of these two-person transports glided past the Windsor, Traymore, Dennis, and other grand hotels that lined the beach, observing the comings and goings of the well-to-do, occasionally stopping to say hello to friends or business associates who were also summering in Atlantic City. The streets just inland from the boardwalk were filled with quaint Victorian inns and cottages that featured steeply gabled roofs, cupolas, and long, shaded porches that wrapped around their shingled exteriors. These innkeepers offered accommodations on only one or two floors, providing an option for those vacationers who sought both a quieter respite and more privacy than could be found at the beachfront hotels.

The Hamiltons rented two rooms on the second floor of one of these inns on Tennessee Avenue—Noll Cottage—upon their arrival from the West Coast in mid-July. Ray and Eva occupied one room, Mary Ann Donnelly the other, with baby Beatrice shuttled between the two. For six weeks, the proprietress of the cottage, Elizabeth Rupp, bore witness to increasingly boisterous arguments between Ray and Eva, excessive drinking by both Eva and Mrs. Donnelly, and visits to Mrs. Hamilton from two strangers—an older woman and a younger man—on the several occasions when Mr. Hamilton had made overnight trips to Manhattan to attend to his business. To the presumed relief of Mrs. Rupp, the Hamiltons were scheduled to return to New York on the morning of August 26.

Both Ray and Eva were up before the sun on the morning of their departure, rising at 3:00 A.M. to pack. They were awake

only briefly before another argument ensued. Over the course
of their nearly four-year relationship, Ray and Eva had not
spent that much time together—for the most part, they only
saw each other the two or three days a week when Ray returned from Albany to New York City. But after being in each
other's company without a break for eight months, Ray had
grown weary of his wife. Eva's constant demands for money to
feed her insatiable appetite for clothes and fine jewelry only
added to the strain in their relationship.

The night before their scheduled departure, and after less
than a year of marriage, Ray asked Eva for a formal separation, offering her $5,000 per year in expenses and a promise
to provide for Beatrice in whatever way his infant daughter
needed. Ray told Eva that if she refused his offer, he would
return to New York alone and she would receive nothing. The
country girl who grew up in poverty and who had become too
accustomed to living in luxury, possessing the finery she
could only dream about in the backwoods of Pennsylvania, refused her husband's offer. Eva countered that if Ray followed
through on his proposal, she would make public what had
long been whispered about by his inner circle—that the silk-
stocking heir of one of the most famous names in America was
besotted with a prostitute.

Evangeline Steele was no stranger to the machinations of
men who were captivated by her charms. At age seventeen, a
salesman passing through Bernice, the small town where the
Steeles had settled, became enchanted with the beautiful Eva
and convinced her to leave her family and travel with him.
Anxious to see a wider world—Eva had never been more than
ten miles from her home—she left with him, against the
wishes of her mother. The couple stayed for four days in Oswego, New York, before the salesman took her virtue and then
abandoned her. With no money and her reputation compromised, Eva traveled a hundred miles south, alone, to Waverly,

New York, where she was taken into a brothel by a Mrs. Washburn and began her career in the sex trade.

From there, she moved to South Waverly and went to work for another madam, Mrs. Meade. A married, prominent figure in town became infatuated with the young Evangeline and began to demand sexual favors in return for not turning her in to the authorities. In addition to her physical attributes and charming demeanor, Eva also had a temper that could be displayed at the slightest provocation. Exasperated with the gentleman's demands, she got hold of a pistol and waited for him to come calling. On his next visit to Mrs. Meade's house, Eva aimed the gun between his eyes and squeezed the trigger. She missed a direct shot to his head but managed to blow off the better part of his right ear. Now wanted for attempted murder, Eva stole out of town and returned to Bernice to live with her parents, her previous whereabouts unremarked upon by her family.

She wasn't in Bernice long before Walter Parsons, the twenty-year-old son of the superintendent of the Bernice Coal Company, succumbed to Eva's allure. After a brief courtship, they ran off to Elmira and planned to be married. Walter's family got wind of their affair, found them, and whisked Walter Parsons away to live with relatives in Boston—as far away from the disreputable Eva Steele as possible.

After Walter's departure, Eva, now twenty-one years old, made her way to New York. While she may have moved to the city with little in terms of material possessions, she arrived with ambition, an awareness that men were easily drawn to her, and a means to support herself.

Prostitutes were commonplace in Gilded Age New York, plying their trade with little discretion. More than 40,000 girls and women worked in the business when Eva arrived in the city. Full-time prostitutes were joined by part-timers—factory girls, single mothers—even housewives who needed a few extra dollars a week to make ends meet. Showgirls and burlesque dancers were easily drawn to the trade as well. The barons, bankers, and stockbrokers who fueled the great expansion of wealth in the 1880s—gentlemen of Ray Hamilton's stature—preferred the refined brothels uptown, away from the tawdrier establishments near the piers surrounding lower Manhattan.

During Ray's bachelor days, the New York City Police Department stated that "startling as is the assertion, it is nevertheless true, that the traffic in female virtue is as much a regular business, systematically carried on for gain, in the city of New York, as is the trade in boots and shoes, dry goods and groceries." Physician and social reformer Elizabeth Blackwell noted, "shrewdness, large capital, business enterprise are all enlisted in the lawless stimulation of this mighty instinct of sex."

The most expedient path for women like Eva to leave the brothels behind and improve their lot in life was to be supported by a man of means—whether as a mistress to a married man, or as a reliable paramour to an eligible bachelor. She found the latter when Ray Hamilton stepped into a bawdy house on Twenty-First Street in 1885. Four years later, the $5,000 a year that Ray now offered was more than a pittance, and a far cry from the few dollars a session that Ray paid Eva when they first met. But that figure paled in comparison to the estate that Eva stood to inherit as Mrs. Robert Ray Hamilton should something unfortunate happen to her husband. She wasn't about to cede to his demand before leaving Atlantic City.

As the sun rose on the morning of their departure and the other guests at Noll Cottage made their way to the dining room for breakfast, Eva ordered Mrs. Donnelly to go out and buy a bottle of whiskey. The arguments and threats exchanged between the Hamiltons on that Monday morning were not new to the baby nurse, nor was Eva's request for alcohol. Bottle in hand, Mary Ann Donnelly chose to make a stop at the nearby Verona Hotel, one of the nondescript tourist hotels just off the boardwalk, before returning to Noll Cottage. One of the six-teen rooms at the Verona was occupied by Eva's friends from New York, Anna Swinton and Joshua Mann.

In the early summer, when the Hamiltons made the deci-sion to return east, Eva contacted Anna Swinton. The elderly widow was engaged in the dressmaking trade in New York and as Eva had lost forty pounds in California, she requested that Mrs. Swinton meet her in Atlantic City to alter Eva's en-tire wardrobe. Josh Mann accompanied his mother to the Jer-sey shore. The petite, sixty-year-old "Granny" Swinton, thin to the point of near-frailty, dressed in the plain, unpretentious clothes of a woman with no social ambition. A widow three times over, Granny had a daughter, Clara Kyrie, from her first marriage—Josh Mann was her son from her second mar-riage to a German bassoon player in the celebrated band of conductor Louis-Antoine Jullien. She married for a third time, to noted lithographer Frederick J. Swinton. When Swinton passed away, Granny lived off of his estate until the money ran out. With no means to support herself, she found work as a seamstress.

Josh Mann had never lived fully independently from his mother. A failed salesman, his limited mental capacity was exacerbated when he was kicked in the head by a horse sev-eral years earlier. His ability to think clearly was further com-promised by his propensity to drink from the time he woke up until he passed out at the end of the day. Even though Mann was a simpleton and barely functioning alcoholic, he pos-sessed a naïve charm that drew Eva Hamilton close, partially because she wanted to help him, and because he would do whatever she asked of him.

Mary Ann Donnelly had made Swinton and Mann's acquaintance in New York before departing with the Hamiltons for California—whenever Mr. Hamilton was away, the twosome appeared like clockwork at Eva's East Thirty-Third Street flat. Their routine continued in Atlantic City when Ray took his overnight business trips to the city.

When the nurse arrived at the Verona, she uncorked the bottle in Granny and Josh's room, poured a glass each for herself and Josh, and proceeded to tell them about the undoing of the Hamiltons' marriage, including Ray's offer of a separation agreement. While Josh and Mary Ann Donnelly were drinking at the Verona, Elizabeth Rupp went to the second floor of Noll Cottage, one last time, to plead for quiet from Ray and Eva. By the time she knocked and entered their room, though, the couple were a picture of marital bliss—Eva was sitting on Ray's knee in an armchair, her arms lovingly wrapped around his neck, the two of them smiling and laughing quietly to each other. The momentary tranquility was fleeting.

When Mary Ann Donnelly returned at 9:00 A.M., her breath bathed in alcohol and holding a whiskey bottle only two-thirds full, Eva summarily fired her for drunkenness and insubordination. The nurse exploded—"You she-devil!" she bellowed—accusing Eva of immoral behavior and intimating to Ray that Eva and Josh were more than friends. The volume of the shouting coming from the Hamiltons' room increased as Ray attempted to act as referee between the two volatile women. Eva, enraged by the nurse's accusations, picked up Beatrice's metal bathtub and flung it at Mary Ann, narrowly missing her head. The basin made a loud clanging sound as it bounced off a wall and spun to a stop on the floor. Ray implored Mrs. Donnelly to return to her room until he and his wife could resolve the situation.

Eva continued drinking throughout the morning, beside herself that Ray hadn't fully taken her side against Mary Ann Donnelly. In the adjoining room, Mrs. Donnelly drank from her own stash of brandy. Baby Beatrice slept soundly in her crib as Ray attempted to bring the conversation back around to the separation agreement with Eva. She finally admitted that she would not entertain any agreement that didn't start at a minimum of $6,000 a year.

Shortly before noon, the waitstaff at Noll Cottage busied themselves setting the dining room for lunch. Starched linens were laid across tables, wineglasses and silverware made a gentle clinking sound as they were set in place, and the aroma of roasted meat and fish drifted from the kitchen. As the first guests unfolded their napkins and studied their menus, the routines of everyone on the property came to a halt when the sound of heavy footsteps, crashing furniture, and, finally, a deep thud was heard from the second floor above them.

One of the waiters, who had little doubt about where the noise came from, rushed up the stairs and kicked in the door of the room occupied by the Hamiltons. Eva stood near the bed, gripping a double-edged knife with an elongated bone handle—what was known as a Mexican dagger. She was being restrained by Ray, partially wrapped in a bed sheet that covered his slashed and torn clothes. Mary Ann Donnelly lay crumpled on the floor, clutching her stomach, her dress and apron matted with blood.

After seething in her room for two hours after being dismissed, Mary Ann Donnelly had returned to the Hamiltons' room one last time—not to discuss the situation further with Eva, but to throttle her. She had grabbed Eva by the shoulders and pushed her backward as Ray tried in vain to separate the two alcohol-fueled antagonists. Eva grabbed Mary Ann's hair, Donnelly pushed back, and they ended up with their fingers in each other's mouths, careening heavily across the floor in an awkward, drunken tango. Eva broke free, grabbed the knife from Ray's partially packed trunk, and waved it wildly at both her husband and the nurse. Ray managed to

dodge Eva's slashes, but the heavyset, stumbling Mary Ann
Donnelly was not as fortunate. Eva's dirk plunged deeply into
the nurse's abdomen, missing her intestines by an eighth of an
inch.

The diners on the main floor of the cottage scattered upon
hearing Mary Ann Donnelly drop to the floor above them, and
an urgent call was placed to the Atlantic City Police Department. William Biddle was the first officer to arrive at 135
Tennessee Avenue. He pushed through the onlookers who
had already assembled on the street, stepped onto the shaded
front porch, and was directed to a back room on the ground
floor. Mary Ann Donnelly had been brought downstairs by
the cottage staff and was lying on a cot in a back room, blood
oozing from her stomach. Biddle asked if she knew who had
cut her.

Between gulps of air, Mrs. Donnelly spit out, "You know
who did it. It was that woman upstairs and I want her arrested. If I die, she'll hang for this." By Biddle's reckoning, the
woman was near death and he called for a doctor to be summoned immediately.

Mrs. Rupp directed Biddle up the stairs to the scene of the
incident. He walked into the bedroom, its furniture in disar-
ray, bed linens and clothing strewn on the floor. Robert Ray
Hamilton stood silently next to his wife. Biddle asked Mrs.
Hamilton if she had stabbed the woman downstairs on the cot.

Eva coolly responded, "I sent for you. I want that woman arrested. Her name is Mary Ann Donnelly and I will appear
against her at the police station." Biddle ignored her response
and repeated his question. This time Eva replied matter-of-
factly, "I did it and I'm sorry I didn't finish her."

Unclear of exactly what had transpired, Officer Biddle arrested both Ray and Eva Hamilton without incident and had
them placed in the small holding cell at the Atlantic City police station. Eva was held without bail; Ray was released on a

$600 bond and both were ordered to appear for arraignment the following day. News of the stabbing spread quickly, first by the guests at Noll Cottage, and then from the crowd gathered outside, to seemingly the whole of Atlantic City. Newspaper reporters from New York, Philadelphia, and Baltimore descended on the Jersey shore by nightfall. The *Philadelphia Inquirer* reported, "The sole topic of conversation here is the stabbing of the servant of the woman who calls herself Mrs. Hamilton, and many visitors who the cool weather would otherwise drive away are kept here by the exciting affair." Their stories were picked up by the Associated Press and splashed on page one of daily newspapers from coast to coast the next morning.

### Tuesday, August 27, 1889

Atlantic City's imposing City Hall stood two blocks north of Noll Cottage, at the corner of Tennessee and Atlantic Avenues. Framing the entrance to its four-story Romanesque façade, a clock tower rose another forty feet above the top-floor offices, capped by a steeply pitched copper roof. While Ray Hamilton spent Monday night in the comfort of the cottage, Eva slept in the City Hall jail. They were less than a quarter of a mile from each other, but the gulf that had opened in their relationship now far exceeded their physical distance.

The small courtroom in City Hall was normally used to adjudicate misdemeanors and petty crimes. It had no grand, raised dais for a judge to look down authoritatively upon the parties involved in a particular case—the presiding judge, Justice Albert W. Irving, sat at a small wooden table at the front of the room. Two additional tables, one for the prosecution and one for the defense, faced the judge, and a smattering of chairs for other interested parties lined the back wall of the room.

The morning after the stabbing, every inch of the cramped

courtroom was filled with the curious—nattily dressed vacationers in sharp suits and straw boaters stood cheek to jowl
with Atlantic City locals, all of them awaiting the arraignment of the progeny of one of the most well-known families in
America and his notorious wife. When the clock struck ten
o'clock, Justice Irving called the court to order.

Eva Hamilton was a study in contradiction when she was
led into the courtroom from a side door, appearing at once nervous, yet seeming to revel in the attention of the onlookers.
She wore a breezy summer ensemble of blue and white, remi-
niscent of a sailor suit, accented with diamond jewelry. The
normally dapper Ray Hamilton looked as if he had slept in the
clothes he was wearing, the gravity of the situation showing
on his haggard face. He bore little resemblance to a man who
lived a life of privilege. When Eva was seated next to him, he
treated her with complete indifference, hardly deigning to notice her presence.

Samuel E. Perry, a well-known attorney in Atlantic County
and former New Jersey state senator, represented the Hamiltons, assisted by Wendell Cherry. With the court in order,
Judge Irving called on District Attorney Joseph Thompson to
present the state's case. Ray was the first witness called and
confirmed that he was indeed Robert Ray Hamilton, age
thirty-eight, a member of the New York City Bar and the husband of the prisoner. Thompson turned his attention to the incident of the previous day.

"Were you present when this assault occurred at the Noll
Cottage yesterday afternoon? If so, please state what you
know about it."

"I was present at the time. The stabbing was done with a
dagger in the hands of my wife. The victim, Mary Ann Donnelly, has been employed by us as a nurse for the past eight
months. She accompanied us to California and back but was

discharged by my wife at nine o'clock yesterday morning—about three hours before the affair occurred. The reasons for her discharge I am advised by counsel to reserve for the present." After confirming that he and Eva had one child, eight-month-old daughter Beatrice, Hamilton was excused from the witness stand.

Officer Biddle and Mrs. Rupp stated their recollections of the events of the previous day. Dr. Howard Crosby, a physician staying nearby who had attended to Mrs. Donnelly at Noll Cottage, confirmed that her condition was still critical and that she may live another week, but also stated that he would not be surprised if she died within an hour. Sergeant Loder of the Central Police Station offered his testimony that Eva Hamilton admitted to the stabbing when she was brought into the station house, but claimed it was in self-defense, and that she had expressed regret over the incident.

The defense chose to not call any witnesses, opting instead to take the time to fully investigate the circumstances surrounding the incident and present their case at trial. The entire proceeding lasted less than an hour, and Eva was remanded to the Atlantic County jail at Mays Landing until a grand jury could be impaneled to bring full charges. Ray was released on his bond, with permission to leave the jurisdiction. Whether motivated by a vengeful desire to see Eva sent to prison, or a dose of compassion for his troubled wife, Ray chose to remain at City Hall until she was put on a train for the short ride to the county jail.

At two o'clock in the afternoon, a jailer called out "Time's up!" through the bars of Eva's cell. Constables William and Pettit flanked the prisoner as she leaned on Ray's arm for the short walk around the corner from City Hall to the Camden & Atlantic Rail depot, one block away on South Carolina Avenue. A porter from Noll Cottage trailed the entourage with a large valise filled with Eva's clothing and accessories—being kept behind bars was no reason to sacrifice one's sense of fashion.

The press, dutifully assembled outside of City Hall, whipped out their notebooks at the sight of Eva Hamilton being led away, furiously scribbling detailed notes of the procession. The somber couple ignored the reporters' shouted questions as they walked the length of the train platform. Ray had no intention of accompanying his wife to Mays Landing, but when she threw her arms around him and sobbed, "Goodbye, Ray!" it must have dawned on Hamilton that a potential newspaper story describing him as being so coldhearted as to abandon his wife in her time of need was to be avoided. He hurriedly bought a ticket on the platform and sat next to Eva for the twenty-minute ride to the county jail.

The train rolled out of Atlantic City and chugged through the dunes and scrub pines inland from the Jersey shore, stopping at Absecon and Ponoma before reaching Egg Harbor City and branching off to Mays Landing. A reporter managed to grab a seat in the same car as the Hamiltons and strained his ear just enough to overhear Eva tell Ray, "You know I told you before I left New York that if you did not discharge that nurse there would be murder committed. But don't worry about me, Ray. They won't keep me in jail long."

Ray, Eva, and the constables were met at the station by Sheriff Smith Johnson and escorted to the prison. The Atlantic County Jail in Mays Landing, designed by renowned Philadelphia architect Thomas Ustick Walter, stood two stories tall with a charcoal-color, slate roof. Ten windows, fitted with steel bars, flanked the blackened iron door. The façade was covered with large pieces of broken, gray-blue sandstone, fit like patchwork around the window and door openings. Eva began sobbing as they approached the bleak entrance to the prison. After one last embrace at the jailhouse door, Eva was led down the hallway to her assigned cell and Ray returned to Atlantic City on the next train.

Ray kept to himself on Tuesday evening, declining to see any callers while he sorted through a stack of telegrams that had arrived at Noll Cottage throughout the day. Friends from New York and colleagues from Albany offered condolences and whatever assistance they could provide:

*I extend to you my heartfelt sympathy and if I can be of service to you there or here do not hesitate to command.*

*Chas R. Hess*

*Can I be of any service? Send me now.*

*Joseph Murray*

*If there is anything in the world for me to do for you let me know.*

*Hugh Hastings*

Ray's father, General Schuyler Hamilton, wired from the Kearsarge House in North Conway, New Hampshire, where he was convalescing from an illness under the care of his second wife, Louisa. Ray's mother, Cornelia, passed away when Ray was sixteen years old and his father remarried in 1887. Schuyler Hamilton graduated from the U.S. Military Academy at West Point in 1841, upholding the Hamilton family tradition of public service, though his military career was interrupted over a forty-year period by injuries and bouts of illness. A man of moral rectitude and a stickler for order, the General avoided judgment of his oldest son for the moment, choosing only to plaintively express the sentiments of a concerned father:

*My dear son: Can I be of any service by coming to you?
Answer.*

*Schuyler Hamilton*

While Ray was on the train returning from Mays Landing,
Anna Swinton was on the opposite track—traveling alone to
visit Eva in jail. Granny arrived with a dinner basket, fresh
fruit, and a telegram addressed to Mrs. Hamilton. The emotional distress that Eva demonstrated on the train platform
earlier in the day had been replaced by rage about her incarceration. The tempestuous prisoner flung the food against the
wall of her cell and then stomped the remains with her foot for
good measure. She tore the telegram, still in its unopened en-
velope, to shreds, the scraps of bright yellow paper mixing
with the trampled food on the prison floor.

After Anna left the prison, curious reporters who had
staked out the Mays Landing jail quizzed her about her relationship with Eva Hamilton. She explained that she first met
Eva Brill nearly ten years before in a boarding house on West
Fifteenth Street. Anna Swinton piqued the interest of the assembled reporters when she declared, unprompted, that "my
son was undoubtedly Miss Brill's first and most devoted lover.
I knew he was with her frequently, but whether their relations were more intimate than I supposed they were—from
what I saw myself—I can't say. He was not the man to hold up
his end against Hamilton in a battle for a woman's love, as
Hamilton had good looks, wealth and influence behind him,
and for his wealth more than anything else I suppose, she
married the man she did, although she has today the warmest
feelings for my son."

Whether the veracity of Anna Swinton's story could be
proven, or whether Josh Mann and the former Miss Brill did
indeed have a prior relationship, the aging widow had added a

layer of intrigue to a tale that seemed to grow more curious
with each passing hour. And if the day had not already provided its fair share of titillation, a telegram addressed to Ray
Hamilton that arrived in the late afternoon at Noll Cottage
added to an increasingly perplexing puzzle. It was sent from
Reading, Pennsylvania, and arrived at the Western Union office in Atlantic City at 5:34 P.M. The local telegraph operator
transcribed the missive as follows:

*You can obtain very important information concerning*
*the child you testified that Mrs. Hamilton is the mother*
*of by presenting in person this message at Western Union*
*telegraph office Fourteen north Sixth St Reading*
*Pennsylvania where you can obtain address of written*
*advice at once if you desire interview.*

[NOT SIGNED]

## CHAPTER THREE

# A Villainous Conspiracy

Newspapers arrived on doorsteps across the nation on Wednesday morning, August 28, with the Hamilton affair featured on page one, just under the masthead.

## MRS. HAMILTON IN JAIL.

---

### THE STORY OF THE STABBING
### OF HER NURSE TOLD IN COURT.
*—New York Tribune*

## MURRAY HILL SHOCKED.
*—Rochester Daily Chronicle*

## A SENSATION STIRS UP THE TOWN
## OF ATLANTIC CITY.

---

### *An Aristocratic Woman in a Scrape.*
*—Austin Statesman*

## KILLED HER WITH A DAGGER.
*—Daily Chronicle, Aspen, Colorado*

# MRS. HAMILTON'S DIRK.

CAREER OF THE ATLANTIC CITY MURDERESS.
*—Los Angeles Times*

Curious readers from Philadelphia to Fresno pored over the details of the story with their bacon and eggs while Ray Hamilton remained at Noll Cottage, granted no newspaper interviews, and was not seen in public. (Contrary to some reports, Mary Ann Donnelly had not died.) Although he had the court's permission to leave Atlantic City until formal charges were brought against his wife, Ray chose to stay in the jurisdiction during the first two days after the incident. The initial batch of telegrams that arrived immediately after the stabbing were followed each day by bundles of mail that were delivered to his new, temporary residence at Noll Cottage.

Most of the letters were written by friends and colleagues, offering assistance in any way that Ray required. They came on letterhead from prestigious law firms in lower Manhattan: Ingraham & Allen, Morris & Steele, Jones & Rouschert, Varnum & Harris—and from Ray's fellow clubmen, written on the engraved stationery of the Union League and University Club.

Even the éminence grise of New York state politics, Hamilton Fish, took the time to write from his holiday at the Atwood House on Narragansett Pier in Rhode Island. The former New York governor, U.S. senator, and Secretary of State wished the young Hamilton well and offered to be of assistance, writing, "when a man is in trouble is the time for his friends to stand by."

Indeed, while Ray remained in seclusion at Noll Cottage, answering letters and avoiding the press, his well-connected network of friends in New York were not only standing by— they were already at work to clear his good name. As soon as the news broke about Ray's predicament in Atlantic City, several of his closest friends and fellow attorneys, Elihu Root, Samuel Clarke, and Charles Peabody Jr., agreed that something needed to be done—in addition to sending telegrams, they took action.

Elihu Root was a prominent lawyer and former U.S. attorney for the Southern District of New York. In private practice, he had represented Jay Gould, William Whitney, E. H. Harriman, and Chester A. Arthur, among others. Root stood alongside Arthur in the then vice president's Lexington Avenue parlor as a witness when Arthur was sworn in as president after the assassination of James A. Garfield in 1881. Meticulous and discreet, Root was so well respected that no one in the legal profession or law enforcement would turn down his request for help.

Samuel B. Clarke, an 1876 graduate of Harvard Law School, was a former assistant U.S. district attorney and Elihu Root's law partner.

Charles Peabody was, like Ray, a graduate of Columbia Law School. Upon his admission to the New York City Bar in 1875, he joined his father's prestigious law firm, Peabody, Baker & Peabody. He also served in the New York legislature, representing the Eleventh District for the 1876 term.

The day after the stabbing, the three attorneys contacted the one man who was the most capable of learning the truth about Eva Hamilton—the legendary Tommy Byrnes.

Thomas F. Byrnes was born in Dublin, Ireland, in 1842, the son of James and Rose Byrnes. The family immigrated to New York when Tommy was a young boy. He served in the Civil War with the 11th New York Volunteer Infantry Regiment (the Zouaves), became a New York City police officer in 1863, rose to the rank of captain in 1870, and became chief of the

NYPD Detective Bureau in 1880. Widely credited with modernizing the police department detective squad, Byrnes kept a collection of photographs of known criminals in a book on his desk—his rogues gallery—and was an artful practitioner of what became known as the third degree, a combination of physical and psychological techniques used to extract confessions from reluctant subjects.

A tall, beefy man with a thinning hairline and bushy mustache, Byrnes held his position during the reign of Tammany Hall in New York—the graft that flowed freely to city officials in the age of Tammany found their way into Tommy Byrnes's pockets as well. Even though Byrnes drew a salary of only $5,000 per year, he had amassed real estate holdings worth $500,000 and a bank account in his wife's name with $290,000 on deposit. To those who questioned his wealth, he explained that the sums were gratuities paid to him by Wall Street businessmen. In a book that Byrnes authored, *Professional Criminals of America*, he noted that "bankers, brokers, commercial and business men, and the public, were strangely ignorant concerning the many and ingenious methods resorted to by rogues in quest of plunder."

Although the stabbing in Atlantic City occurred more than one hundred miles from Byrnes's jurisdiction, when Root, Clarke, and Peabody contacted him, Tommy signed on to the effort. Though the records of Byrnes's gratuities were purposefully left unrecorded, given that the three gentlemen who sought him out were wealthy, well connected, and that their friend was involved in a story on page one of every newspaper in America, Tommy Byrnes likely added handsomely to his fortune with the Hamilton investigation.

On the morning after the stabbing, Byrnes met the attorneys at Root & Clarke's office on Broad Street in lower Manhattan while the Hamiltons' arraignment was taking place in Atlantic City. The threesome explained to the chief detective that they thought too highly of Ray to see his good name sullied by the accusations made against him—in no way did the known details of the situation square with the Ray Hamilton they had known for years. They knew little about his wife Eva and the two characters, Anna Swinton and Joshua Mann, that she associated with—the only piece of factual information that the three men could supply was that Ray and Eva's daughter, Beatrice, was born in Elmira in December 1888 while Ray was in Albany.

Tommy Byrnes quickly learned that Dr. Burnett Morse was listed as the attending physician on Beatrice's birth certificate and dispatched one of his best men, Sergeant Bobby Mc-Naught, on the next train upstate to track down the good doctor. Dr. Morse told McNaught that, yes, he had treated Eva Brill in December, but only for stomach cramps. He was adamant that she did not give birth to a child around that time, and in fact, there were no indications that she was likely to become a mother in the near future.

His questioning of Dr. Morse completed, McNaught called on various hotels and boarding houses in town, inquiring as to whether any of the proprietors knew of a woman who called herself Eva Brill, or anyone named Mann or Swinton. Multiple establishments provided the same answer—they weren't familiar with Anna Swinton, but Eva and Josh were well known. The managers not only acknowledged prior stays by the two visitors from New York City—they produced guest books showing the couple registered as Mr. and Mrs. Joshua Mann, husband and wife. The accusation leveled against Eva by Mary Ann Donnelly two days prior now appeared to be possibly more than the baseless, drunken ranting of a bitter nurse.

While Bobby McNaught procured affidavits from each of the proprietors in Elmira, Ray Hamilton remained behind closed doors at Noll Cottage and continued to answer the incoming correspondence. Anna Swinton and Josh Mann lingered at the Verona Hotel, taking their meals in their room, while Eva Hamilton awaited her fate at the Mays Landing jail. The four principal players in the unfolding drama, all ensconced in New Jersey, were unaware of McNaught's discoveries in upstate New York.

By Thursday evening, McNaught had dispatched his full report to Tommy Byrnes in New York. With evidence in hand, Byrnes instructed Root to wire Hamilton in Atlantic City on Friday morning and have him return to the city immediately. Upon receipt of Root's telegram, Ray left Beatrice in the care of Mrs. Rupp and boarded the next New York–bound train. To avoid a gauntlet of newspapermen awaiting Hamilton's arrival in the city, his friends arranged for Ray to stay in New Jersey at Charlie Peabody's brownstone on Park Avenue in Jersey City. He was shown into the front parlor by Peabody and was met by Root, Clarke, and Tommy Byrnes.

The chief detective didn't mince words. He explained to the four men that he could verify that Eva lied about giving birth the previous December and that Ray was not the father of the child christened as Beatrice Ray Hamilton. After pausing to allow sufficient time for that reality to be processed, Byrnes added that in all likelihood, Ray's marriage was illegitimate. The chief detective explained that while he was not in possession of a marriage certificate that recorded Eva and Josh Mann as husband and wife, the hotel guest books and affidavits from upstate New York clearly showed that, at the very least, a common-law marriage existed between the two.

Ray had met Josh Mann and Anna Swinton many times

over the course of his relationship with Eva and never questioned their friendship. Eva explained to him that Granny
Swinton had been kind to her when she first moved to New
York and that she felt a certain responsibility to look after
Josh. Eva never tried to hide the fact that small amounts of
the money Ray regularly gave her went to help support Josh.
While Ray may not have been thrilled to know that he was
supporting an alcoholic with no real future in life, Eva spent
the money that he gave her at her own discretion.

With Byrnes's revelation that Hamilton was, essentially, financing Eva and Josh's relationship, Ray's attitude about
Eva's two "friends" changed irrevocably. He had been deceived.
For a man of Hamilton's reputation and stature, there was no
greater embarrassment than to be played for a fool. His education and virtuous upbringing had been overwhelmed by
lust, his family name compromised by infatuation. The fact that
such damaging information was being revealed to Ray in the
presence of his close friends only added to his rising anger. He
became increasingly agitated as Byrnes detailed McNaught's
findings, bringing the conversation to a close by asserting that
if the details in the report could be verified, he wouldn't hesitate to have Eva and any collaborators prosecuted to the
fullest extent of the law.

With Ray Hamilton's approval to pursue any and all wrong-
doing perpetrated by Eva Hamilton and anyone else bound up
in her scheme, the chief detective expanded his investigation.
Byrnes believed that by cash or threat, he could get any criminal to "peach on his confederates," and that six hoodlums
couldn't plot a heist in New York without one of them being in
Tommy's pocket. Through his network of informants, Byrnes
learned that Ray Hamilton was not the only person involved
in the burgeoning scandal to leave the Jersey shore on Friday.
By coincidence or not, Anna Swinton and Josh Mann arrived

in Manhattan that same afternoon while Hamilton stewed at Peabody's home in Hoboken.

Tommy Byrnes ascertained that by Friday night, Swinton and Mann had checked into the St. Charles Hotel at the corner of Broadway and Bleecker Street. After four days of their real names being splashed in newspapers across the country, the mother and son registered as Mr. and Mrs. J. W. Brown and occupied a single room. Byrnes felt that he had enough evidence to arrest them immediately as co-conspirators in Eva's fraudulent scheme, but instead, he had them surveilled throughout the weekend to see if they led his detectives anywhere intriguing. By Sunday evening, Anna and Josh had done nothing to further pique Byrnes's interest, so he sent instructions to Bobby McNaught and his partner, Sergeant Hickey, to bring them in. McNaught and Hickey arrived at the St. Charles only to discover that the mother and son had given them the slip. The manager on duty informed them that Swinton and Mann had checked out, but left word at the front desk that they would return for their mail.

While Anna and Josh spent the weekend in the city evading the law, Eva spent her first weekend in prison at Mays Landing. More seasonal temperatures had returned to the Jersey shore by the end of the week, with sunshine, highs in the low eighties, and not a drop of rain in sight. As crowds of tourists thronged the boardwalk and packed the beaches, Eva sat alone, eighteen miles away, unaware that she had landed in Tommy Byrnes's crosshairs. Even without knowledge of Byrnes's investigation, Eva was disconsolate—her earlier confidence in an acquittal based on a self-defense plea had waned. She received no visitors and spent her days pacing the floor of her cell like a sentinel.

On Sunday morning, Sheriff Johnson's wife, Jennie, visited Eva and offered her a prayer book and hymnal. Eva declined, telling Mrs. Johnson with a wan smile, "I have no use for such books and haven't had for many years."

Eva ate little—sweetened coffee for breakfast, a dish of boiled rice for lunch, and a muffin for dinner—and letters she received expressing sympathy or support were glanced at with indifference and then tossed into a corner of her cell. The only note from a stranger that caught Eva's attention was one that included a box of Tutti Frutti chewing gum. She broke the seal immediately and chewed each little piece with vigor as she paced.

Eva did inquire with Mrs. Johnson as to the condition of Mrs. Donnelly—her first acknowledgment of the victim of her rage. Dr. Crosby had, in fact, removed Mary Ann Donnelly's stitches the day before at Noll Cottage, where she was convalescing. The doctor completed a certificate for the county prosecutor, Joseph Thompson, stating that he was of the opinion that the nurse was reasonably out of danger and expected to recover. Thompson opted to get a second opinion, calling in the county physician, Dr. Edward A. Reilly, to examine the nurse. If Reilly concurred with Dr. Crosby, Thompson was ready to reduce the charge to Atrocious Assault. New Jersey statutes called for a conviction on that charge of up to ten years of imprisonment—a lesser term could be offered at the discretion of the presiding judge.

On Monday morning, September 2, one week to the day after the stabbing, Tommy Byrnes was ready to move on Anna Swinton and Josh Mann. At noon, Anna returned to the St. Charles alone, ate lunch, and checked for mail. When she departed the hotel, two officers tailed her uptown to an apartment house at 335 West Twenty-Ninth Street, between Eighth and Ninth Avenues. Byrnes's informants had passed word that Josh Mann would be meeting her there later. In these kinds of situations, the chief detective preferred to arrest and interrogate suspects separately, eliminating the possibility of them knowingly corroborating each other's story. Accordingly, he directed Sergeants Hickey and Crowley to pick Granny up immediately and haul her in to the Central Office on Mulberry Street.

They dropped her off for processing and returned to West Twenty-Ninth Street. Two hours later, Josh Mann stumbled up the front steps of the apartment house, visibly and hopelessly drunk. Crowley clapped his hand on Josh's back, stating simply, "I want you." Mann offered no resistance and meekly followed the officers back down the stairs. When Mann arrived at the Central Office, both he and his mother were made aware that each other was in custody, but they were kept in separate holding cells.

Tommy Byrnes was a patient man. He believed that it wasn't always necessary to immediately question a suspect, but rather "to allow them the opportunity to reflect and examine the place where they are locked up." Accordingly, Swinton and Mann spent Monday night in their respective cells, separated by a concrete wall, reflecting. On Tuesday morning, they were taken to the New York City Halls of Justice and House of Detention—or as it was more commonly known, The Tombs.

The four-story, foreboding Egyptian Revival–style building occupied an entire city block, bounded by Franklin, Centre, Leonard, and Elm (now Lafayette) Streets. The Tombs was built in 1837 on the site of the former Collect Pond, a malaria-infested garbage dump from the city's colonial era that had been improperly drained and filled twenty years prior. As a result, The Tombs began to sink on its foundation not long after opening, and the perpetual dampness in the structure led to unsanitary conditions that existed for the life of the building.

After a visit to America that included a tour of The Tombs, no less an observer of deplorable surroundings than Charles Dickens wrote, "What is this dismal fronted pile of bastard Egyptian, like an enchanter's palace in a melodrama? Such indecent and disgusting dungeons as these cells would bring disgrace upon the most despotic empire in the world!"

The chief detective's strategy of biding his time and introducing Anna Swinton and Josh Mann to increasingly miserable conditions had its desired effect. By Tuesday afternoon, they both offered confessions. With mother's and son's statements in hand, Byrnes called reporters to his office early Tuesday evening, allowing them time to file their stories and for their editors to write the headlines that would dominate the next morning's papers.

Police reporters for the New York dailies had offices at 301 Mulberry, directly across the street from police headquarters. When news was slow, they hung around their clubhouse, had a drink, played cards, and swapped tall tales about their lives on the crime beat. When word came in of a newsworthy arrest, they grabbed their notebooks and beat a well-worn path up the stairs of the five-story, white marble central office to gather details from the officers who made the collar. But when a policeman crossed the street to announce that Tommy Byrnes wanted to see them, chairs pushed back from desks in unison, drinks were finished in one gulp, and unplayed cards were left on the table.

Byrnes only got personally involved in the biggest cases—when he summoned the press, reporters knew that they were about to get a major story. Beyond that, though, the chief detective was a master of stagecraft. The scribes never ceased to marvel at the way he fed them the details of a crime "like a dime novel recital." In the twilight of this late summer evening, Byrnes waited until all of the reporters had found a seat around his massive desk and then began to read extensively from Anna Swinton's confession.

The old woman began by stating that on or around November 10 of the previous year (1888), Eva called upon Mrs. Swinton to put her seamstress skills to work—she needed a layette made by December 15 and told Granny that it should be made with the finest fabrics and ribbons available. Naturally, Eva concocted a story, explaining that she and Josh were going to Elmira because a friend of Ray's had gotten a girl pregnant upstate and that the impending birth needed to be handled with the utmost discretion. After the baby was born, the newborn would need to be brought to the city and cared for until a permanent home for the infant could be found. Eva told Anna that she had agreed to take on the responsibility as a favor to Ray and would return to New York toward the end of December.

Anna Swinton was living on East Thirty-Third Street when Eva and Josh returned to New York on Christmas Day. They met her there, without the baby. Eva was surprised and irritated that Mrs. Swinton hadn't completed all of the sewing and embroidery for the layette, berating the old woman for not pushing hard enough to finish her work. They rushed out to a Jewish clothing shop on the Bowery that was open on Christmas to purchase a cap and cloak. Eva gave the packages to Mrs. Swinton and instructed her, "You hurry home and I'll go and get the baby." From where exactly, Eva didn't say.

The next day, Josh and Eva took a furnished flat on East Twenty-Eighth Street, staying there for one week, before moving again, to East Fourteenth Street. Once settled, Eva informed Ray that she had returned from Elmira with their daughter. It was here, in early January, that Ray Hamilton was introduced, as Tommy Byrnes explained with dramatic flair, to Baby No. 1. Mrs. Swinton said that Hamilton hugged

Eva and kissed the child, but was not exactly overcome with
emotion at the realization that he was a father. He also made
no plans for himself, Eva, and the baby to live under the same
roof.

Unbeknownst to Ray, the day after meeting his supposed
daughter, the baby girl became ill, and a doctor, William
Kemp, was summoned. Within forty-eight hours, the infant
had died—Dr. Kemp certified that the death was caused by
inanition (exhaustion), due to lack of nourishment. Because
Eva had made no provision for a wet nurse, had no ability to
lactate, and possessed a cluelessness about caring for an infant, the baby starved to death. The name given to Dr. Kemp
for the death certificate was Alice Mann, daughter of George
and Alice Mann.

Undeterred and lacking remorse, Eva contacted a local
midwife and moved ahead with her scheme. Unscrupulous
midwives operated what were known in New York and else-
where as baby farms. Babies born as the result of unwanted
pregnancies—by sexual assault or new mothers being under-
aged girls, women who were too poor to care for a child, or
those who may have been involved in a scandalous affair—
were abandoned to midwives, no questions asked. Unlike legal
orphanages administered by the state or a religious institution, midwives neither asked for, nor offered, documentation
about their young charges. Those infants fortunate enough to
survive were sold to anyone who crossed a midwife's threshold
and had the five or ten dollars cash necessary to purchase a
baby.

The unfortunate children, including those who may have
possessed a physical deformity or evident medical condition,
were often victims of infanticide. In 1879 a midwife in Philadelphia, known only as Janet R., was investigated by the Pennsylvania Society to Protect Children from Cruelty after the
SPCC received complaints from Janet's neighbors:

There is every reason to believe that (defendant) is engaged in "baby farming": she has now 2 or 3 babies on hand—within the last two months, 3 or 4 babies have been seen taken out of the house dead; the little coffins were placed in a private carriage, and rapidly driven away. There has been no sign of a doctor or undertaker attending the house—no crepe ever appeared on the door or shutters.

Oftentimes, there were, sadly, no little coffins. Babies were cruelly smothered in blankets, abandoned in alleys and left to die, or taken to the nearest body of water and drowned.

Before the first infant that Eva purchased was even buried, she bought a second baby from a different baby farm and brought that infant home to the East Fourteenth Street flat. Anna Swinton told Byrnes that this infant, too, became ill before Ray Hamilton even had a chance to see her. She became so ill, so quickly, that Swinton stated that she told Eva that "it would not do to send for Kemp."

Knowing that Dr. Kemp could alert the authorities after seeing two different babies that Eva claimed to be the mother of die within a few days, Baby No. 2 was taken to West Thirty-First Street to be examined by a different physician, Dr. Gilbert. This second baby died after one week and was buried as Ethel Parsons, daughter of Walter and Alida Parsons. Adair & Alfred, undertakers at 359 Fourth Avenue, buried both "Alice Mann" and "Ethel Parsons."

Eva had a problem. Although Ray had already met his daughter, Baby No. 1, he had not returned to Eva's flat since his initial glimpse of the newborn girl and was unaware that the baby he knew as his own flesh and blood had already been buried as Alice Mann. And that an infant bought as a replacement for his daughter had also died.

In order to keep her scheme from falling apart, Eva dispatched Anna Swinton to buy yet a third baby. The infant that

Anna returned with, Baby No. 3, sent Eva into a rage, as this new girl had dark hair and "looked like a Dutch baby." Eva sarcastically explained to Swinton that even Ray could spot the difference between a blonde and a brunette. Beyond the obvious physical difference, Anna Swinton told Byrnes that Eva had "an aversion to the babe at first sight. She couldn't like it, or even kiss it."

Eva took matters into her own hands and went out the next morning to find a newborn who could serve as a plausible replacement for Baby No. 3. When she returned to her flat, she ordered Mrs. Swinton to return the "Dutch baby." Anna balked, explaining that illegal baby farms did not, as a rule, have a return policy. Eva instructed Granny to tell the midwife that "she had no use for it, as the lady who adopted it had died."

Mary Ann Donnelly was hired to care for Baby No. 4, named Beatrice Ray Hamilton. It was this infant, purchased for ten dollars and plucked from anonymity, who accompanied Ray, Eva, and Mrs. Donnelly on their trip to San Diego, and then Atlantic City.

In explaining all of this to the assembled reporters, Byrnes added that Dr. Gilbert gave a statement to the police that when he attended to Baby No. 2, Eva and Anna Swinton urged him to do his utmost to save the newborn girl, telling him that a large moneyed estate hung on his ability to keep the infant alive. Anna told the doctor separately that it would be worth $100,000 to Eva if the baby lived.

The chief detective closed his remarks by noting that Ray had been convinced by his friends to appear as the complaining witness against Anna Swinton and Josh Mann on two counts, conspiracy and substituting children, and that Mr. Hamilton "will let the law take its own course."

With that, the reporters bolted down the stairs, squeezed en masse through the front doors of police headquarters, and raced back to their desks at 301 Mulberry. The idle chatter that filled the clubhouse during slow news periods was replaced by the din of clacking typewriters and sheets of paper being yanked from rollers. The race was on to file for the early edition of the next morning's paper and move the story across the wire.

## CHAPTER FOUR
# MR. HAMILTON'S PLIGHT

**Wednesday, September 4, 1889**

As dawn broke nine days after the stabbing of Mary Ann Donnelly, the most sensational headlines about the Hamilton affair to-date dominated page one.

### RAY HAMILTON DUPED.
*—Baltimore Sun*

### RAY'S BABY.
### *It Was Some Other Fellow's.*
*—Cincinnati Enquirer*

### EVA'S BABE WAS BOUGHT.
*—Boston Daily Globe*

### HIS EYES OPENED.

---

ROBERT RAY HAMILTON
THE VICTIM OF BLACKMAILERS.
*—Atlanta Constitution*

# A CONSPIRACY.

### SCHEME OF A DESIGNING WOMAN.
### —*San Francisco Chronicle*

Ray Hamilton could only read Anna Swinton's account of the events leading up to the birth of Beatrice with jaw-dropping astonishment. Her story, as related by Tommy Byrnes, ran completely counter to everything that Ray had taken on faith about his wife.

In April 1888, Eva announced to him that before the year ended, he would be a father. She wasn't actually pregnant but had determined that the only way Ray would marry her was if he felt a responsibility to do so—by informing him of her pregnancy, she reckoned that he would feel compelled to act in the manner she so desired. While Ray was never stingy with his money over the course of their four years together, Eva was well aware that if they remained unmarried he could leave her at any time and she would be back to where she was financially when they met. Marriage, however, legally entitled to her to dower rights—at least one-third of his estate—whether a marriage ended in death or divorce.

It was not unheard of for men of Ray Hamilton's stature to father children out-of-wedlock, but the women who birthed the bastard children of wealthy, oftentimes married men were normally paid a lump sum, including a discreet allowance for child support, in return for their silence. Eva saw an opportunity that far exceeded a one-time payment, however generous, and was determined to make herself over as Mrs. Robert Ray Hamilton.

The trick, of course, to the success of her scheme was concealing her alleged pregnancy from Ray. Even though they sometimes went weeks without seeing each other, there was bound to be a point after fourteen or sixteen weeks when they would meet and the physical manifestations of her impending motherhood would be evident. But Eva had a stroke of good fortune. Ray had decided against a run for reelection to the state legislature in the fall of 1888. As the autumn term would be his last in office, he planned to be in Albany full-time from the end of the summer recess until the State Assembly adjourned in November.

The last few weeks of Eva's alleged pregnancy would be easily accounted for. It was accepted practice for a woman to have a lying-in period—bedrest and minimal physical activity—as she neared the end of her pregnancy. This lying-in period could take place in a hospital, but often occurred in the private home of a family member. Eva would simply tell Ray that she planned on journeying to Elmira to be with her mother for her lying-in and then return to New York with their child when she was well enough to travel. Between Ray's time in Albany and Eva's alleged lying-in, her scheme made it unlikely that she would see Ray at all during her last trimester—from the beginning of September until just before Christmas.

The summer months, Eva's second trimester, were another issue. Ray would definitely be in New York and the hot, close weather that enveloped the city in July and August called for cotton or linen dresses worn without a jacket, making it more difficult to conceal a growing baby bump. The chance of seeing Ray on a regular basis throughout the summer was too risky. So Eva told him that as this would be her last summer unburdened by the responsibilities of motherhood, she wanted to travel to Europe. Alone. Without questioning her motives, Ray agreed to honor Eva's wish, booked her passage on the steamer *City of Berlin*, and gave her a thousand dollars to spend as she so desired. With the exception of an occasional rendezvous that might require a strategically placed blanket or shawl,

Eva stood a good chance of avoiding Ray for the last five months of her "pregnancy."

As the nation woke to the provocative headlines and pored over the sad and sordid details surrounding the Hamilton baby, Ray Hamilton remained in seclusion at Charlie Peabody's home in Jersey City. The reporters camped out near Peabody's Park Avenue brownstone clamored for a response from Ray regarding the explosive story. They got one that morning—not from Hamilton himself, but from Elihu Root's law partner, Samuel Clarke, acting as a spokesman for his friend Ray. Clarke affirmed Hamilton's commitment to seeing justice done, but declined to elaborate on Ray's emotions, his reaction to the specific findings by Byrnes, or the confessions of Swinton and Mann. The only reported detail that might offer a glimpse of Ray's mood was that the front of Peabody's house on Park Avenue "remained well darkened."

### Thursday, September 5, 1889

While Ray reeled from the published news stories that painted him as, essentially, a fool for falling for Eva's scheme, Tommy Byrnes pressed on. With Anna Swinton and Josh behind bars, their confessions in hand, Byrnes now concentrated his attention on the woman at the center of the conspiracy, Eva Hamilton. It wasn't enough for Byrnes that Eva was being held in New Jersey awaiting trial—he sought sufficient evidence to bring whatever charges he could muster in New York against Hamilton's wife.

As the nation digested the shocking news in Wednesday's papers, an unnamed German woman boarded an Atlantic City–bound train in New York, accompanied by two NYPD police officers, Bobby McNaught and Detective George McCluskey. The German woman was the midwife identified by Byrnes's detectives as being responsible for the sale of the last of four babies purchased by Eva Hamilton—the child now known as Beatrice Ray Hamilton.

The midwife told the detectives that the infant was quite recognizable, due to a "peculiar malformation of the baby's ears. They are abnormally large and protrude from the side of the head in a curious manner almost at right angles," adding that "this was the only objection which Mrs. Hamilton found with the ten-dollar baby at the time she bought it."

"I like it in every other way," Eva said upon receiving the newborn, "but I do wish its ears were not quite so large." She added, "Still, it's better than that flat-faced thing," in reference to Baby No. 3.

Upon their arrival in Atlantic City, McNaught, McCluskey, and the midwife walked the three blocks to Noll Cottage to meet Mrs. Rupp, who was still caring for Beatrice. When presented with Beatrice Ray Hamilton, the midwife declared without hesitation that the baby in front of her was the same infant she had sold to Eva Hamilton nine months prior. Satisfied with the midwife's positive identification, the officers led her out of Noll Cottage and bought train tickets to Mays Landing, where they hoped she could identify the baby's "mother" with the same certainty.

The threesome arrived to meet Mrs. Hamilton as evening fell, but the head jailer, Sheriff Johnson, was away for the night. The detectives consulted with Deputy Sheriff Frank Moore and Jennie Johnson, the sheriff's wife, regarding an interview with Eva Hamilton. Mrs. Johnson inquired with Eva, who agreed to see the visitors from New York. The midwife was unable to positively identify Mrs. Hamilton, though, owing to Eva's significant weight loss in the nine months since they had last seen each other.

When Sheriff Johnson returned to the jail the next morning and learned of what had transpired, he was livid. "I have all

along refused the Atlantic City reporters, some of whom are
my personal friends, access to the prisoner's presence. And
here was a lot of perfect strangers who in my absence and in
direct violation of my positive orders were allowed to see and
talk to this woman."

Jennie Johnson meekly explained that as the visitors were
not reporters, she felt that it was permissible to admit them to
Eva's cell. Deputy Sheriff Moore was fired on the spot for his
role in the decision, but the prevailing wisdom was that he
would soon be reinstated, owing to his long years of service
and the sentiment that he was very popular in the county.
Sheriff Johnson wasn't alone in his alarm about the interview.
Eva Hamilton's defense attorney, Samuel Perry, rushed up to
Mays Landing and upbraided his client for submitting to an
interview with the New York detectives and pleaded with her
to remain quiet, and see no one, until her trial.

McNaught, McCluskey, and the midwife returned to Atlantic City at dusk and spent the night before leaving for New
York the next morning. When they returned to Manhattan,
the midwife was shown a photograph of Eva Hamilton taken
around the time of the baby sale, from a photo album belonging to Anna Swinton that had been seized by the police. The
picture showed Eva standing ramrod straight, almost defi-
antly, in a richly embroidered dress and matching bonnet. The
midwife recognized Eva's rounder, fuller figure and said without hesitation, "That is the woman who got the baby from me
and gave me ten dollars."

As the detectives and midwife were returning to New York,
a train from Manhattan arrived in Atlantic City with another
party interested in the Hamilton affair. A lone gentleman
stepped onto the platform at eleven o'clock in the morning
and, like the officers and midwife the day before, went directly
to Noll Cottage. Edward Vollmer, an associate in Ray Hamil-

ton's legal practice, stepped into the foyer and without wasting time for pleasantries, handed Mrs. Rupp a letter.


LAW OFFICES OF ROOT & CLARKE
NO. 32 NASSAU STREET, NEW YORK

Sept. 4, 1889

Mrs. Howard Rupp:

Please let the bearer, Mr. Edward R. Vollmer, have my personal property in your possession, including trunks, clothes, gun case, box of saddles, &c. Yours truly,

ROBERT RAY HAMILTON


With no advance warning of Vollmer's arrival, Elizabeth Rupp refused to honor the note, and instead referred the attorney to Judge Irving's office at the City Hall courthouse. The judge reviewed the situation with Vollmer, musing that the letter meant that Ray Hamilton "will probably never set foot in this county again." He added, "We can do without him at the trial, and would rather have his six-hundred-dollar bail than himself." Irving escorted Vollmer back to Noll Cottage to inform Mrs. Rupp that it was okay—the gentleman could take Mr. Hamilton's belongings.

Once allowed by Judge Irving to enter Hamilton's room, Vollmer made quick work of his assigned task. Ray had given him a detailed list of his clothing and personal effects, as well as instructions to locate and pack up several pieces of Eva's jewelry. Vollmer was also to remove and return all photos from an album that had been left in their bedroom. Anything belonging to Eva, with the exception of the jewelry, was to remain untouched. Four hours after arriving in Atlantic City,

Ed Vollmer boarded a 3:40 train back to New York with two trunks, a valise, and a large box—all filled with the property of Robert Ray Hamilton.

While Judge Irving lingered at Noll Cottage as Vollmer packed up Ray's belongings, Mrs. Rupp had a separate issue she wished to discuss with the judge. The proprietress explained that she had agreed with Ray Hamilton to care for Beatrice in the aftermath of the stabbing—their arrangement continued after Ray departed Noll Cottage the previous week for Jersey City. She went on to say that she had visited Eva at Mays Landing to update her about Beatrice's well-being, and during the course of their conservation, Eva requested that Mrs. Rupp return with six morphine pills to help calm her nerves.

Judge Irving's response was clear and simple: absolutely not. He told Mrs. Rupp that "she would be likely to occupy a prison cell herself if she aided Mrs. Hamilton in her suicidal plans." Irving alerted the Mays Landing authorities and extra precautions were put in place to frustrate any desperate attempts by Eva.

While Mrs. Rupp was well acquainted with all manner of visitors descending on Noll Cottage throughout the summer, the curious arrivals of the last two days were anything but the usual check-in-let-me-show-you-to-your-room variety. And with Eva Hamilton's trial looming, the association of Noll Cottage with the Hamilton affair was far from over. But on this late summer evening, with temperatures returning to their normal high of near eighty degrees and vacationers still wading into the warm Atlantic surf, Mrs. Rupp's quaint inn was, for the first time in ten days, off of the front pages.

### Friday, September 6, 1889
A hundred miles from the relaxed environs of Atlantic City, a long line of curious New Yorkers queued up outside of The

Tombs on Friday morning, hoping to secure a seat for the arraignment of Anna Swinton and Joshua Mann—the first public appearance by the now infamous mother and son duo. The arraignment was scheduled to be held in the usual venue for such proceedings, Police Court, but owing to the public attention that the Hamilton affair had generated, the presiding judge, Justice Edward Hogan, moved the arraignment to the larger Court of Special Sessions.

In addition to its ability to house more spectators, the room possessed a gravitas lacking in the more plebian Police Court. Heavy curtains draped the two-story-high windows that looked out onto Centre Street and formed the backdrop of the courtroom. The presiding judge sat on a raised oak dais centered between the windows—the bench was flanked by fluted columns with brass lighting sconces that cast an incandescent glow onto the principal cast in the case before the court. An elevated witness stand was situated just below the judge's right side, in front of the prosecution and defense tables that were separated from the spectators by a low railing.

By the time the courtroom began to fill up after lunchtime on this late-summer Friday, temperatures had risen into the eighties, making the hot, sticky conditions that always existed in the dank, foreboding Tombs even more unbearable. A half dozen elderly women who were rumored to be friends of Anna Swinton's managed to finagle their way to the benches nearest to the witness stand and twittered in each other's ears before the proceedings began. All of the other spectators were men, and as the *New York Times* noted, "very poor looking men they were." The room was described by the *Times* as having the appearance of "the interior of a Bowery Theatre, with a particularly large and unattractive audience." The one exception to the motley assortment of spectators was the surprise appearance of celebrated actor and playwright, Billy

Florence, who was shown to a seat in the front row from which to observe the proceedings.

At 2:00 P.M., Justice Hogan took his seat on the bench and called the court to order. Anna Swinton and Josh Mann were somberly escorted to their seats at the defense table by Tommy Byrnes. They were represented by J. Stewart Ross and Alfred Ackert. Ray Hamilton followed the defendants into the courtroom accompanied by his attorneys, Charlie Peabody and Samuel Clarke. William T. Jerome, the city's assistant district attorney assigned to the case, brought the processional to a close.

As Ray Hamilton was the named individual filing the complaint, his signature on an affidavit was required before the proceedings commenced. D.A. Jerome surmised that a felony charge of conspiracy may be complicated to lay out in an arraignment hearing, but he wanted to ensure that Anna Swinton and Josh Mann remained in jail until they were bound over for trial. In an agreement forged with Ray and his attorneys, Jerome brought only an initial charge of grand larceny in the second degree.

Specifically, the charge stated that "on or about the 11th day of December, 1888, Eva L. Hamilton, his wife; Anna Swinton and Joshua J. Mann obtained from him the sum of $500 under false and misleading statements, to wit, that Eva L. Hamilton, then known as Eva L. Mann, was about to be delivered of a child of whom he, Robert Ray Hamilton was the father." The city could prove, Jerome stated, that "Eva L. Hamilton had never been delivered of a child, and there was never any reason to suppose that she would be." Both defendants pleaded not guilty.

The upheaval in Ray's life since the stabbing ten days before was evident in the Court of Special Sessions. He approached the front of the courtroom with a slow, plodding shuffle and seemed relieved to be able to sit down. He looked exhausted, his complexion pale and his normally bright eyes dulled by the barrage of headlines over the last ten days. As the party making the complaint before the bar, Ray was the first person called to testify. Over the course of the next two hours, every detail of his folly was mercilessly brought out. His education, reputation, and wealth were of no use on the witness stand—the tawdry details of his life with Eva were the only interest of the courtroom spectators.

After declaring that he was indeed Robert Ray Hamilton, age thirty-eight, and a member of the New York Bar, he began his testimony in earnest, answering every question posed by the prosecutor, Mr. Jerome, with certainty and without emotion.

"I met Eva four years ago in a house on Forty-Third or Forty-Fourth Street, I don't remember which, nor do I know the name of the proprietor. My intimacy with her was begun then." He went on to explain that he had seen her very little in the past year, 1888, as he was "busily engaged in my work in Albany."

In April of the past year, Eva informed him that before many months passed, he would become a father. "I believed her implicitly," he stated. In the fall of 1888, Eva told Ray that "the time of her maternity was near, and that she intended to live with a relative in Elmira until after the child was born." In early December, she wrote to Ray that she was in need of $500—Ray's understanding from her letter was that the money was needed for his child and he sent her a check without hesitation.

It was this transaction that brought about the charge of grand larceny. Ray concluded his direct examination by stating that although he had met Anna Swinton and Josh Mann previously, he did not tie them directly to the larceny charge until he learned of their confessions to Thomas Byrnes.

If the spectators in the courtroom were lulled into a state of listlessness by a combination of the stifling heat and Hamilton's dry, monotone answers to Mr. Jerome's questions, they were certainly brought back to attention when Mr. Ross began his cross-examination.

The sharply dressed Brooklyn attorney with a gift for oratorical flare shouted mixed metaphors and constructed a long-winded monologue that seemed to be, above all, for the benefit of hearing himself speak. But he did get Ray to admit that he had given Eva money on many occasions over the course of their four-year relationship.

"All she had to do was ask for it," Ray confirmed.

"Then why," Ross asked, "do you attach so much importance to this particular gift of $500?"

Ray replied that he found the amount excessive, and that in light of Swinton's and Mann's confessions, he considered the request fraudulent. Ross chose not to pursue the matter further, confident that he had made his point that the charge was without merit. Hamilton was dismissed and bound down from the witness stand with a much more noticeable spring in his step than when he entered the courtroom.

While Ray may have appeared to be physically relieved after offering his testimony, it stood to reason that extended excerpts of his account of his relationship with Eva would be printed verbatim in the newspapers. The impropriety of his relationship with his wife had been laid bare, the sheen of his well-mannered upbringing tarnished, and his dignity lay, very publicly, in tatters.

Detective Byrnes was called to the stand after Hamilton concluded and repeated, almost word for word, what he had told reporters earlier in the week. He did add that Mrs. Swinton told him that "if they get me talking I will make a scandal, and if Ray Hamilton prosecutes me I'll make it hot for him." Byrnes ignored Ross's histrionics during a brief cross-

examination, offering nothing in addition to what he had previously testified.

William Jerome, confident that the testimony of Hamilton
and Byrnes was sufficient to bind Swinton and Mann over to a
grand jury, called no further witnesses and rested his case.
Mr. Ross rose and lost himself in a jumble of words uttered at
the top of his voice, but finally got around to the fact that he
was asking for the charges to be dismissed.

"Not a scintilla of evidence," Ross claimed, "had been produced to show that either Josh or his mother had obtained
from Mr. Hamilton a dollar; that they never conspired to get
any money from him, that they had ever used any false pre-
tenses in obtaining from him, as charged, $500 or any other
sum, or that they ever did obtain that sum."

Justice Hogan endured Ross's harangue and announced
that he would render a decision at 11:30 A.M. the following
morning, on Saturday. At the end of the nearly four-hour
hearing, and with the intimate details of Ray Hamilton's recent life now made public, the reporters in attendance raced to
file their stories for the next day's papers.

### Saturday, September 7, 1889

Like the previous day, Tommy Byrnes led the two defendants
into the courtroom on Saturday morning to await the judge's
decision. Swinton and Mann were held in an examining room
until the judge appeared, the mother fighting back tears while
her son sat by her side and smoked cigarettes. Josh appeared
to be nervous—his small eyes darting from one side of the
room to the other, and his fingers trembled whenever he put
his cigarette to his lips.

As the clock approached 11:30, the appointed time for Justice Hogan's decision, Assistant D.A. Jerome entered the
room, followed by the strident Mr. Ross. Many of the spectators from the Friday hearing returned, including the group of

old ladies who "fluttered about the place like so many buzzards who had scented their prey from afar." One participant from the previous day, Robert Ray Hamilton, did not return for the ruling, choosing instead to spare himself of another visit to the wretched surroundings of The Tombs.

At exactly 11:30, Justice Hogan took his seat on the bench and announced to the court:

In the case of the defendants I have concluded to hold them—Anna Swinton and Joshua L. Mann—on the complaint of Robert Ray Hamilton, to await the action of the Grand Jury. There is no doubt in my mind that the crime of grand larceny has been committed and, under the circumstances, I am justified in believing that there is probable cause to hold the defendants in connection with it.

J. Stewart Ross stood to begin a long-winded discourse about how his clients had exposed Eva's scheme and maintained "that wicked woman is unquestionably guilty of every charge against her," adding, "I do think that my clients are absolutely innocent of the crime charged against them." Justice Hogan was unmoved by the counselor's oratory.

Prosecutor Jerome ominously reminded the court that "the defendants are held upon a very serious offense, a dangerous conspiracy—a conspiracy that would have been ultimately dangerous to life itself." He asked the judge to fix bail at $2,500 each, "in view of the large sums of money which have at various times passed into the possession of one or both of the prisoners."

An indignant Ross rose to vigorously oppose the proposed bail amount, declaring that he found it to be preposterous. He asked that bail be set at $500 and pounded on his desk so hard that Justice Hogan jumped in his chair.

Hogan waited until Ross returned to his seat and then fixed

bail at $1,500 each. He pointed at J. Stewart Ross and sternly told him, "If you begin to talk again, I'll make it $2500 or double."

The only representative from Hamilton's legal team to attend the hearing—strictly as a spectator—was Samuel Clarke. A reporter managed to ask him what he thought of the proceeding, to which he replied, "I am sick and tired of the whole thing! The necessary steps will begin at once to have the marriage of Mr. Hamilton to Eva set aside." Clarke emphasized that absolute fraud would be charged and he anticipated very little difficulty in having the marriage contract annulled.

When asked about Ray Hamilton's whereabouts and his current emotional state, Clarke answered only that he "was with friends, in their effort to liberate him, heart and soul."

# CHAPTER FIVE
## Mrs. Hamilton Weeps

*Monday, September 9, 1889*

After thirteen straight days on the front page of every newspaper in New York and countless others across the country, Robert Ray Hamilton awoke on Monday morning, September 9, undoubtedly relieved to not find his ordeal on page one. There were no salacious details about his wife, no breathless descriptions of court proceedings, and no reminders of his fall from the upper echelons of New York society. If indeed Ray was trying to be liberated "heart and soul" from his predicament, not seeing his name directly under a masthead while he had his morning coffee would be considered a positive development. There were no public sightings of the man at the center of so much recent attention, but bundles of mail continued to arrive in Atlantic City, at Peabody's house in Jersey City, and his law office in lower Manhattan.

More than fifty letters addressed to Ray Hamilton came from complete strangers, most of them with an offer, or a heartfelt plea, to take baby Beatrice into their homes.

*Newark. N.J.*
*Aug 29th 1889*
*Mr. Hamilton*

*Dear Sir, If you wish to put your little daughter in board*
*in a private family I will accept her as I am a lady of re-*
*duced circumstances and have two little ones of my own*
*who are 12 and 8 years of age. I have all chance a mother*
*needs to give the care to your little Beatrice as my*
*husband's income is very small. I thought I could help*
*along in that way. Hoping that this letter is understood*
*in the right way, I close and remain yours Respectfully*

*Mrs. P. Boll*

*P.-S.- I am related to some of the best families in New*
*York and if you should ask for references I could direct*
*you there.*

Annie Cliff of Chestnut Hill, Margaret Schuyler of Philadelphia, John Droley of Harlem (on behalf of his wife), and dozens
more made the same proposal as Mrs. Boll—all of them explaining that they were of reduced circumstances in one way or
another.

The mail that didn't offer a solicitation of care for Beatrice
offered instead a chance for redemption. Religious fundamen-
talists took the opportunity to remind Ray that "CHRIST
ALONE can save you," and that a good wife can be found, "In
the church or Sunday school, not in a Theatre or Ballroom."

Of all the letters and telegrams that had continued to arrive, however, there was no further communication from Ray's
younger brother or father. As the eldest of the Hamilton clan
and de facto protector of the family name, the General could
not have been pleased to see the name "Hamilton" included as
part of larger headlines on front pages that read "A Bogus

Baby Furnished as the Hamilton Heiress," or "How Robert Ray Hamilton was Deceived and Robbed." Whatever the General may have been thinking, though, his thoughts were kept privately in New Hampshire, where he continued to convalesce.

Any consolation or advice provided to Ray during the run-up to Eva's trial in New Jersey came from his friends and colleagues—the extended Hamilton family remained on the sidelines in the dramatic turn in the life of their son, brother, and cousin.

### Thursday, September 12, 1889

Ray's three-day streak of living outside of the glare of the press came to end on Thursday when it was reported that he had surreptitiously arrived in Atlantic County. Summonses to members of the Grand Jury had been issued "for the purpose of hearing testimony and preparing an indictment in the case of Mrs. Robert Ray Hamilton."

As the case was scheduled to be called on Monday, September 16, Hamilton undoubtedly wished to be briefed to the fullest extent possible regarding the status of the prosecution. Hamilton didn't bother to stop in Atlantic City—instead he traveled directly to Mays Landing and checked into Norcross & Veale's Champion Hotel. The handsome, four-story hotel sat behind a low, wrought-iron fence directly opposite the courthouse and jail and was perfectly suited to Ray's needs with a parlor, reading room, saloon, and dining room offering a bill-of-fare to rival any New York restaurant. The bar was well stocked with the finest wines and liquors, both foreign and domestic. For two days, Ray met with representatives of the Atlantic County's sheriff's office and was not once seen outside of the hotel premises.

When Hamilton left Noll Cottage at the end of August, it was widely assumed by the local authorities that he would forfeit his $600 bail and never be seen in Atlantic County again. But after Ray had boarded a train back to New York on Thursday after his meetings at the Champion, Sheriff Smith met with reporters to confirm that Mr. Hamilton would be back in the courtroom on Monday morning and was "prepared to answer any questions the court may see fit to ask."

Baby Beatrice had remained in Atlantic City since the stabbing on August 26, still under the care of Elizabeth Rupp, the proprietress of Noll Cottage. By his own actions, Ray had showed little enthusiasm when his "daughter" was born—now that it was public knowledge that Beatrice was, in fact, *not* a blood relation, his desire to be near her waned. Although the infant bore the name Hamilton, and was legally considered to be his daughter, he left Atlantic County without paying her a visit.

While Beatrice was too young to perceive Ray's inattention as a snub, the same was not true for Eva Hamilton. Within hours of her husband's arrival in town, Eva learned that Ray was staying one block from the Mays Landing jail. Excitedly, she had multiple notes sent across the street to his hotel asking that he come see her. When he refused to acknowledge her invitations "she became bereft of reason." She went so far as to accuse the jailhouse messengers of failing to deliver her letters and deceiving her. Assured that her messages had indeed been delivered, Eva launched a tirade, berating the jailhouse officials and appeared to be more disturbed by Ray's failure to call than she did by her approaching trial.

The empathy Ray had shown by accompanying Eva to Mays Landing after her arraignment and his appearance at that time as a concerned husband—those feelings were gone. After all of the revelations about his wife, Anna Swinton, and Josh Mann had been made public by Tommy Byrnes, and all of the public humiliation that he had endured in the previous two weeks, Ray Hamilton had clearly returned to Mays Landing with one goal—to see Eva prosecuted to the fullest extent of the law.

To no one's surprise, on September 16, the Grand Jury handed down an indictment, charging Evangeline Hamilton with one count of Atrocious Assault in the stabbing of Mary Ann Donnelly. The court wasted no time placing Eva's trial on the docket, scheduling it to begin two days later, on Wednesday, September 18.

## September 18, 1889

The *New York World* dramatically framed the outset of Eva's trial:

> Mrs. Robert Ray Hamilton appeared in the Atlantic County Court House today to answer a charge which, while of no great significance, brought to light one of the most astounding stories of conspiracy, of turpitude, of plot and counterplot ever revealed outside the realm of improbable fiction.

The brick courthouse at Mays Landing was large enough to seat sixty spectators, separated from the attorneys' tables by an oak railing. Judge Alfred Reed sat on a raised dais flanked by two doorways—one that led to his chambers, the other to an anteroom connected to the jail. A curved witness box was attached to the judge's dais on his right side, adjacent to twelve jury chairs. As soon as the courthouse opened that morning, spectators squeezed through the front door of the courthouse to secure a seat for the much anticipated trial. By mid-morning, the overflow crowd filled the foyer leading into the Mays Landing courtroom, and the stairs leading to the second floor of the building became impromptu seats for those who arrived just before the start of Eva's trial, scheduled to begin at 11:00 A.M.

A few minutes before the appointed hour, a clerk clanged a bell to announce that court was in session; Judge Reed emerged from his chambers, and the prospective jurors, witnesses, reporters, and spectators, including some local farmers who came into town to see the show, all settled into their seats.

Samuel Perry sat at the defense table, organizing the files he had assembled to mount his defense. Assistant Prosecutor Clarence Cole busied himself at the State's table, while Prosecutor Thompson used the dagger that had been previously lodged in Mary Ann Donnelly's abdomen to sharpen a lead pencil. At eleven o'clock sharp, Thompson rose and called "The State versus Hamilton."

Eva Hamilton was brought into the courtroom by a sheriff and escorted to her seat next to Mr. Perry. She was dressed more for high tea than she was for a trial, wearing a black dress trimmed with white satin and a flowing Directoire coat. The coat gracefully enveloped her figure, and a Gainsborough hat trimmed with ostrich plumes completed her ensemble. Reporters noted that her eyes, "which are wonderfully bright and expressive, showed perceptible traces of tears." Mary Ann Donnelly and Elizabeth Rupp entered the room after the defendant was seated, followed by Ray Hamilton. He took a seat next to Mrs. Rupp and made no attempt to look at his wife.

Judge Reed wasted no time in calling prospective jurors— four men were selected within the first ten minutes of *voir dire*; none were rejected by either the State or defense. Eva kept her gaze fixed on the men who would decide her fate, and perhaps realizing the speed in which the proceeding was moving, she began weeping. After another four jurors were selected in the next ten minutes, Eva began to sob more dramatically than before. The ostrich plumes on her hat swayed back and forth as she trembled before the jurors. If Eva's tears were a deliberate act to delay the proceedings or to influence the prospective jurors yet to be called, they didn't work. The last four jurors were seated by 11:30—the entire process took only thirty minutes, including the appointment of Samuel Reeves as jury foreman.

The State immediately called its first witness, Dr. Howard Crosby, the physician who had treated Mary Ann Donnelly after the stabbing. He matter-of-factly recounted the size and location of the wound and when shown the dagger, he acknowledged that such a knife could produce a wound of the type and size he had described. He added that the nurse was now out of danger and that a full recovery was expected. When Dr. Crosby stepped down from the witness stand, the dry, emotionless portion of witness testimony in the Hamilton trial ended, as the next witness called was Mary Ann Donnelly.

The nurse was said to "look shabby in her black dress that hung in limp folds," but she had a gleam of defiance in her eyes as she was sworn in and took her seat in the witness chair. Mrs. Donnelly stared directly at Eva Hamilton, who concealed her face behind a fan when the nurse began her testimony.

Mary Ann Donnelly stated that at 6:00 A.M. on the morning of August 26, Eva summoned her into the Hamiltons' room at Noll Cottage to unlock her trunk, as they were due to return to New York that morning. Mrs. Donnelly entered to find Ray Hamilton partially undressed—his clothing appeared to have been torn—and she modestly withdrew from the room. Donnelly noted that Eva was furious and demanded that the nurse return and unlock her trunk at once.

Mrs. Donnelly testified that when she reentered the room after several minutes, Mr. Hamilton had a bed sheet wrapped around his torso and that he and his wife were arguing—Mrs. Hamilton insisting that they return to New York as planned and Mr. Hamilton refusing to agree to join her. A bellman had been called upstairs twice by Mrs. Hamilton to take their trunks downstairs, only to be turned away both times by Mr. Hamilton. Now completely agitated, Eva ordered Mrs. Donnelly to go outside and locate a police officer to have her husband arrested. She also took five dollars from Ray's trousers and told the nurse to pick up a quart of whiskey while she was out.

An impatient Judge Reed interrupted the nurse and implored her to proceed to the actual stabbing. Thompson didn't ask about, nor did Mrs. Donnelly volunteer anything about, her side trip to the Verona Hotel that morning and her drinks with Josh Mann.

Mrs. Donnelly stated that she chose not to summon a police officer, so as to not embarrass Mr. Hamilton, but she did return with the whiskey. When she did so, Mrs. Hamilton called her a vile name (which Mrs. Donnelly declined to repeat in court) and grabbed the nurse by the hair. The nurse stated that she threw Mrs. Hamilton onto the bed, grabbed Eva's hair with one hand, and jammed the fingers of her other hand into Eva's mouth, demanding that Mrs. Hamilton retract the epithet. Mr. Hamilton separated the two women and ordered the nurse to leave their room at once.

Ray and Eva continued arguing while Mary Ann Donnelly silently fumed in her own room and drank two glasses of brandy. As the noon hour approached, she marched back into the Hamilton's room to again demand a retraction from Eva. She found Mrs. Hamilton with one hand around Ray's throat and the other holding the dagger dangerously near to her husband's heart. When Mrs. Donnelly saw that Ray's trousers were slashed from the knife, she ran to his defense. Just as she reached him, Eva released her grip on her husband, swung around, and plunged the knife into the nurse's abdomen.

Thompson paused to let the nurse's dramatic account of the stabbing linger with the jurors. He picked up the dagger and asked Mrs. Donnelly if this was the weapon that Mrs. Hamilton wielded in the attack. She first turned her head away, stating, "I don't want to look at it." After a brief hesitation, the nurse nodded and said, "Yes, that's it. She took it out of the bottom of the trunk which I had packed."

Thompson had no further questions.

An attorney of Sam Perry's caliber surely surmised that his only chance for an acquittal was to mount a credible case that Eva Hamilton acted in self-defense on August 26. Calling Eva as a witness was risky, and Ray Hamilton's integrity and standing would be difficult to call into question. Of the three principal players involved in the events that occurred at Noll Cottage, it was Mary Ann Donnelly who provided Perry with the clearest opening. To cast a reasonable doubt in the minds of the jury, the veracity of her claims would need to be called into question and her reputation brought into the light.

Perry rose to begin his cross-examination, posing his questions to the nurse in a calm, measured tone.

"Are you married?" the counselor asked.

"Yes, I'm married."

"Husband living?"

"Yes."

"When did you last see him?"

Donnelly bristled at the question. "I won't answer you." The judge informed her that she did not have that option.

"In March of this year."

"And when was the last time you lived with him as a wife?"

"It's been over a year."

Mrs. Donnelly made a point of stating that she left him—he did not leave her. Perry asked her if the rumors that she regularly fought with her husband, and that she had once struck him in the face with a hatchet, were true. She answered no to each question. He then asked if it was true that she had ever been previously discharged from her service as a baby nurse for fighting. Again, she answered no.

"You were a wet nurse for Mrs. Hamilton, were you not?"

Mrs. Donnelly answered in the affirmative, but Perry chose not to ask about any children that she was a mother to, or how long she had been employed as wet nurse before going to work for the Hamiltons. (Donnelly never publicly spoke about any children of her own). Perry instead began to question Mrs. Donnelly's drinking habits.

The adverse effects of alcohol consumption while breast-feeding had only begun to be studied in the latter part of the nineteenth century, but Perry was less concerned about any potential harm done to Beatrice than he was about how alcohol may have played a part in Mrs. Donnelly's confrontation with Eva on the morning of the stabbing.

The nurse admitted that she occasionally drank whiskey, but never enough to "send her over the bay." Perry asked about her departure from Noll Cottage on the morning of the twenty-sixth, and if she made any other stops in addition to buying the quart of whiskey. Mrs. Donnelly answered, yes, that she had also gone to the nearby Verona Hotel to meet Anna Swinton and Josh Mann to tell them about the row taking place between Mr. and Mrs. Hamilton. She then admitted that she drank whiskey with Josh Mann and some brandy "with herself."

Perry asked her if she was drunk on the morning of the stabbing.

"Well, I wouldn't say I wasn't sober," Donnelly replied.

"You drank brandy in the morning and didn't you have several rounds of whiskey with Josh?"

"No, sir. We never go round it. Can't a lady take a sip of whiskey at seven in the mornin' and half a wine-glassful of brandy at noon without getting drunk?"

Perry asked if was true that she had once kept Beatrice out for an entire afternoon while she got drunk. She admitted to keeping the baby out but insisted that she had not been drinking that day.

She also denied ever threatening Mrs. Hamilton with bodily harm. Perry concluded his cross-examination by asking Mrs. Donnelly if Eva Hamilton said anything when the nurse entered the Hamilton's room for the third time that morning.

"She hollered, 'Murder! Police!' I guess she thought I was going to murder her."

Perry let Donnelly's response hang in the air for a moment, and after a sufficiently dramatic pause, he asked, "Going to what?"

"I guess she thought I was going to murder her," she repeated. With those words still lingering with the jury, Mary Ann Donnelly was excused from the witness stand.

Perry had to have felt good about what he was able to get Mary Ann Donnelly to admit to under oath. An unpleasant disposition, coupled with a confessed fondness for drink, gave Perry, at the very least, a platform on which to build a case of self-defense. Whether Donnelly's testimony alone would be enough to sway the jury was an open question—Perry's strategy required another witness to further cast a reasonable doubt in the minds of the jurors. He planned to call Robert Ray Hamilton.

Before doing so, however, he quickly recalled Dr. Crosby to the stand. As the State's witness, Crosby had already described the clinical condition of Mary Ann Donnelly when he arrived at Noll Cottage. But under Perry's questioning, the doctor further testified that "Mary Ann Donnelly was decidedly under the influence of liquor" when he first saw her. He added that "it was noticeable both by the scent and her actions."

Necks craned and an audible "Ah!" was heard in the courtroom when Samuel Perry called Ray Hamilton to the witness stand. As the normally unflappable Hamilton took his seat, he nervously wrung his hands and bowed his head, the gravity of the situation evident in his demeanor. Given Hamilton's public pronouncements about his desire to see justice served, as well as his testimony in New York related to the fraud and conspiracy charges, Samuel Perry may well have assumed that the State would have been eager to call Ray as a witness.

But when Prosecutor Thompson issued his list for subpoenas to the court, he declined to include Ray Hamilton as a witness for the prosecution. Perhaps thinking that there was more to Hamilton's story than may have been presumed, Perry didn't hesitate to issue a subpoena for Ray to testify on behalf of the defense.

In a low but unfaltering voice, Ray began his testimony. Contradicting his nurse's earlier account, he confirmed that while in California in April, Mary Ann Donnelly left the baby out for an entire afternoon and insisted that the nurse did indeed return home drunk. When Mrs. Hamilton, who Ray only identified as "the defendant" for the entirety of his testimony, told Mrs. Donnelly that she would likely be discharged, the nurse threatened Mrs. Hamilton with bodily harm. The start of Ray Hamilton's testimony could not have gone better for the defense.

Ray then began to recount the events of the morning of March 26. He stated that he and Eva had previous conversations about a formal separation—he was willing to provide her a $5,000 per year allowance, but given Ray's annual income of $40,000, she insisted on more money. Eva wished for both of them to return to New York on August 26 to speak to an attorney about their situation, but Ray refused for them to leave together.

Frustrated that her husband was still in bed while she prepared for their hoped-for joint departure, Eva tore his coat in a fit of anger. She then leaned over the bed and tore open the night shirt he was wearing and said that if he wouldn't get up, "she would fix it so I wouldn't stay in bed."

Ray stated that he momentarily grabbed her wrists, nonchalantly adding that Eva also struck him across the face with her parasol. Their argument continued throughout the morning—shortly before noon, Mrs. Donnelly rushed into the room wishing to hand Ray two letters (he did not disclose their contents in court). Eva was appalled at the nurse's forward nature and summarily dismissed her. The nurse lunged at Eva, shouting, "Let me kill her!"

Ray stated that Mary Ann Donnelly called the defendant a vile name and questioned the legitimacy of the Hamilton's marriage.

He forced the nurse out of the room, but it was "hardly a minute before Mary came rushing up again. I tried to stop her but she reached the defendant and struck her on the head with her left hand. The defendant struck around me with the knife, cutting my trousers, and then cut Mary."

Perry had no further questions and D.A. Thompson declined to cross-examine Ray Hamilton. He was excused from the witness stand and kept his head down, eyes glued to the floor, as he solemnly crossed the courtroom and returned to his seat next to Mrs. Rupp, offering not so much as a sideways glance at his wife.

Dr. Daniel Ingersoll, who treated Eva Hamilton two days after the stabbing, testified to the fact that she had a black eye, cut tongue, a skinned eyelid, a bruised and lacerated arm, and additional bruises on her hips and knees as a result of her fight with Mary Ann Donnelly.

Elizabeth Rupp made a brief appearance on the witness stand and essentially corroborated Ray Hamilton's account of the incident. She stated that she had entered the Hamilton's room twice to help break up the argument, but to no avail. The only new information added to the established sequence of events was that she snatched baby Beatrice from the room and brought her downstairs to keep the infant out of harm's way.

The trial had reached a point where Samuel Perry had a decision to make—whether to put his client, Eva Hamilton, on the witness stand, or to rest his case. Mary Ann Donnelly's credibility was certainly suspect, and Ray Hamilton had said nothing to egregiously contradict a self-defense argument. If Eva could retain her composure and back up her husband's version of events, Perry could go to the jury to discredit Mary Ann Donnelly's account of the stabbing with not one, but two, rebuttals of the State's charge of Atrocious Assault.

On the other hand, if Eva got on the stand and concocted her own version of the story that stood in conflict with what the jury had already heard, her cause could be hurt by muddying the waters. Perry rolled the dice and called Mrs. Eva Hamilton to the stand.

Eva played the part of an ingenue as she stood at the defense table and removed her coat to display her shapely figure. She dramatically turned her tearful eyes toward the jury box as she made her way to the witness stand.

Perry started by trying to establish that Eva lived in constant fear in the presence of Mary Ann Donnelly. She began to speak hesitantly, in a low voice, but "she soon showed in a marked manner what a vindictive and fickle nature she possesses."

"I was always afraid of Mary," Eva began. "I could never say that, except in my soul, as Mr. Hamilton always upheld her. She made threats against me and told how she had once mauled another woman so badly that the other woman was picked up for dead."

When asked to elaborate on the nurse's threats, Eva said, "She told me that she would cut my heart out and show it to me."

Eva then went on to describe the stabbing as she remembered it, verifying most of the details already elucidated by Mary Ann Donnelly and Ray Hamilton. Her version differed only in that Eva claimed the nurse had her pinned on the bed when the stabbing occurred, and that Eva was merely trying to push the nurse off of her. "I didn't know that she was cut at all, until the policeman came."

Having no further questions for his client, Perry took his seat at the defense table while Eva remained on the witness stand for her cross-examination by Prosecutor Thompson. The feeling in the courtroom was that Perry had made a strong defense for his client and a favorable impression on the jury. The prospects for Eva's acquittal had brightened considerably.

Perhaps Thompson, too, felt the swing in momentum toward the defendant and ignored the sequence of events that had already been told three times. Instead, he immediately bore in on the defendant's credibility.

"When did you first meet Mr. Hamilton?" Thompson began.

Samuel Perry rose immediately and objected. Given all of the rumors about Eva circulating in the newspapers and the published testimony in the Swinton and Mann case in New York, his attempt to shut the prosecutor down before Thompson could gain any traction in an attempt to impugn Eva's character was to be expected. Judge Reed allowed the question to stand.

Eva hesitated for twenty seconds before answering, while Ray Hamilton bent forward, placed his elbows on his knees, and dropped his head between his hands. In a nearly inaudible voice, Eva continued her testimony.

EVA: I don't know, I met him some years ago.

THOMPSON: Where?

E: At a friend's house.

T: Where?

E: I don't remember. I think it was a Mrs. Brown. A Miss Baker was with me. Mrs. Brown was her friend.

T: Had Mrs. Brown a husband?

E: Yes, sir.

T: Did he live with her?

E: Yes, sir.

T: When did you next meet Hamilton?

E: On the street, I think.

T: And next?

E: At my boarding house.

T: Where was that?

E: I don't remember.

T: Are your mother and father living?

E: No, sir.

T: How did you support yourself before meeting Mr. Hamilton?

E: By money left by my father.


Eva's answer elicited raised eyebrows in the courtroom, as the newspapers had published numerous accounts of Eva's upbringing in rural Pennsylvania as one of six children of an itinerant logger. Thompson kept up the barrage.


T: Where did your father live?


Again, Perry rose to object—if for no other reason than to slow down the onslaught of questions—but was overruled by Judge Reed.

E: In Sullivan County, Pennsylvania.

T: Had you any sisters or brothers?

E: I had a foster brother.

T: How long have you lived in New York?

E: Two years before meeting Mr. Hamilton.

T: What is your relationship to Mrs. Swinton?

E: None. She is not related to me. I met her six or seven years ago at a boarding house. Number 10, East Twenty-Eighth Street. She had a child or grandchild with her. Don't know whether he was her son or not.

T: What is his name?

E: Joshua Mann.

Thompson now moved to the crux of his line of questioning.

T: How old was your child when Mary Ann Donnelly came to you?

E: Three months.

T: Where was your child born?

E: The northern part of Pennsylvania.

T: What town?

Eva became very distressed and asked Mr. Perry if she had to answer the question.

Judge Reed interjected, "Why?"

"It might do me very much harm."

The judge explained, "You have a right to decline on the ground that it might incriminate you in another case."

"I do decline on that ground."

Thompson bluntly asked his final question. "Are you the mother of that child?"

Eva again looked pleadingly at her attorney, as her "assumed truthfulness had left her instantly." Perry rose to state that his client refused to answer this question on the same ground as the previous. Ray Hamilton never lifted his eyes from the floor during the entire exchange about Beatrice. When Eva was permitted to step down she was in a state of near-collapse.

It was now 4:30 in the afternoon, and the testimony that filled a long, intense day in the courtroom had come to a close. Judge Reed informed the court of his desire to get the case to the jury as expeditiously as possible and that the attorneys should be prepared to make closing statements at the opening of court the next morning. With a bang of the judge's gavel, court was adjourned for the day.

As spectators queued up to leave the courthouse and reporters rushed past them to file their stories, Eva Hamilton was met by a sheriff to be escorted back to her cell for the evening. She looked longingly toward Ray Hamilton, hoping to catch his eye in the crowd of people leaving the courtroom, but her gaze went unnoticed. After four tumultuous years together, and the last ten months as husband and wife, Ray Hamilton left the Mays Landing Courthouse without so much as looking at his wife.

### Thursday, September 19, 1889

Court was scheduled to begin at 9:30 on Thursday morning, but a train from Atlantic City carrying the judge and attorneys to Mays Landing was delayed due to a derailment of a freight train ahead of them on the tracks. The local farmers who had returned to the courtroom from the previous day "showed some signs of impatience by whisperings and making guttural sounds peculiar only to the residents of South and West Jersey."

It wasn't until 10:40 A.M. that the entourage arrived and

Judge Reed called the court to order. All of the principal play-ers from the day before were present, save one: Robert Ray Hamilton. At the conclusion of testimony on Wednesday, Hamilton and his associate, Ed Vollmer, departed Atlantic City immediately and returned to New York.

Once the jurors were seated, the judge announced, "Sheriff, bring in the defendant." Informed by the sheriff that Mrs. Ham-ilton "begged to be excused from appearing on account of seri-ous illness," Judge Reed ruled for the case to proceed with or without the defendant in attendance, and for closing argu-ments to be presented to the jury.

Samuel Perry went first. He implored the jurors to ignore whatever salacious stories about his client that they may have read in the newspapers and to focus purely on the testimony given in court. Perry spoke at length about Mary Ann Don-nelly and claimed that the testimony showed that the nurse was clearly the aggressor on the morning of August 26. The nurse was "hot-tempered and frenzied with brandy" that morn-ing, Perry said, and she had murderous intentions directed to-ward Mrs. Hamilton.

"Was Mrs. Hamilton justified in striking the blow in self-defense?" Perry asked. "Is there anyone in this room, placed, as Mrs. Hamilton was, on the bed in the desperate clutches of a drunken nurse, who would not take a similar opportunity to protect their life? Gentlemen of the jury, consider well the facts in the case and give my poor, forsaken client the full ben-efit of the aggravating circumstances which compelled her to commit the act for which she is held."

Perry sat, and Joe Thompson began his closing remarks by highlighting the impending separation between Ray and Eva Hamilton and their argument over his proposed allowance of $5,000 per year. He noted the discrepancies in the testimony of husband and wife and pronounced Eva's answers to be "a tissue of lies from beginning to end." He continued by assert-

ing that had it not been for the timely entrance of Mrs. Donnelly into their room, "Mr. Hamilton's life would probably have
been taken." He concluded, somewhat ominously, by stating
that "Mrs. Hamilton is a fortunate woman in not being called
upon to answer a charge of murder."

After a mid-day recess for lunch, Judge Reed returned to
the bench at 2:00 P.M. to give instructions to the jury. The
*Philadelphia Inquirer* noted that "it was apparent to everyone that Judge Reed was against the defendant. Although
the cynical smile which he had worn during Counselor
Perry's peroration had disappeared, it was succeeded by an
unsympathetic seriousness that boded ill for the fair but frail
wife of Robert Ray Hamilton." The *New York World* reported
that "it would be fair to say that the charge of the presiding
judge partook more of the nature of an argument than it did of
a simple laying down of points of law and review of the evidence."

"The whole matter hinges on the plea of the defense," Judge
Reed began. "The blow may have been struck in self-defense,
but when a deadly weapon is used in self-defense it materially
alters the case." He instructed the jury to "set aside all the
facts which led up to the cutting," and focus solely on the question of whether the blow was struck by Mrs. Hamilton in order
to save her own life. If the jury felt that the knife-thrust was
not malicious, they could return a verdict of assault and bat-
tery, but "if they viewed the matter from the standpoint that
she reached around to stab the nurse, then there was no reason why they should not return a verdict in accordance with
the indictment."

Perry implored the judge to instruct the jury more fully
about the threats made by Mrs. Donnelly before entering the
Hamiltons' bedroom for the third time. Judge Reed made a
perfunctory acknowledgment of the Donnelly testimony, but

Perry practically begged him to elaborate for the benefit of the jurors. The judge cut him off, stating, "I've charged all that I am going to charge."

While the jurors were sent into a separate room to deliberate, the spectators in the courtroom were entertained by a case called before Judge Reed involving the custody of a dog. The dog hearing was suspended before it reached a resolution, though, when Jury Foreman Reeves sent a note to the judge only one hour after receiving the case, stating that they had reached a verdict. Judge Reed called for Eva Hamilton to be immediately brought across the street from the jail, regardless of her present condition.

Sheriff Johnson escorted a nervous and trembling Eva Hamilton to her seat at the defense table. She gave a "hasty glance around the room as though looking for a friend, but with the exception of the sheriff's wife, no friendly face met hers." Samuel Perry smiled at the jury as if expecting a victory and whispered in Eva's ear while everyone took their places.

"Gentlemen of the jury," asked the court clerk, "have you agreed upon a verdict?"

Samuel Reeves rose and announced, "We find the defendant, Evangeline Hamilton, guilty as she stands indicted." Eva stared at the jurors in disbelief for a moment and then her head sank to her chest.

Samuel Perry asked the court to poll the jury. Each juror stood in turn, looked squarely at Eva Hamilton, and announced, "Guilty." Eva betrayed no emotion as the word "Guilty" was repeated twelve times, "her calmness worthy of that of an ancient stoic." Judge Reed briefly retreated to his chambers, then returned to the bench within minutes.

"Evangeline Hamilton. Stand up," Reed sternly commanded.

Her attorney stood beside her, holding her by the elbow as she listened to the judge.

You have been convicted of a grave charge. That of atrocious assault upon Mary Ann Donnelly, the extreme penalty of which is ten years. But there are extenuating circumstances in this case, and the sentence I am about to impose should be considered lenient in a case of conviction of atrocious assault. I sentence you to two years in the State Prison at Trenton and you shall stand committed until the costs of the case shall be paid.

Eva slumped into her chair upon hearing her sentence, silent, staring straight ahead. When Samuel Perry momentarily left her side to file paperwork at the bench, she turned to the reporters who had clustered behind her. She hurriedly told them that Anna Swinton had nothing to do with the conspiracy case in New York, that Ray had been "criminally intimate with Nurse Donnelly," and that Beatrice "was the child of a friend of hers in New York, and that Ray knew it and had known it at the time she got the baby."

She also noted that "she thinks a good deal about the baby and is anxious to have it cared for." Before she could continue, Sheriff Johnson pushed his way through the reporters and led her back to the Mays Landing jail, where she would remain until her transfer to Trenton State Prison on Saturday morning.

Outside of the courthouse, New York City police detective George McCluskey walked to the train station to begin his return to Manhattan. Tommy Byrnes had been kept apprised of the testimony throughout the day on Wednesday and sent McCluskey down to Mays Landing on Thursday morning, as Byrnes had expected Eva to be acquitted on the charge in Atlantic City. McCluskey was to pick her up and bring her to New York to face the conspiracy charge along with Swinton and Mann—those plans were thwarted when the New Jersey jury returned a guilty verdict.

A reporter who returned from Mays Landing to Atlantic City after the sentencing caught up with Elizabeth Rupp at Noll Cottage to inquire as to the whereabouts of baby Beatrice. Mrs. Rupp confirmed that the infant was still with her and that Mr. Hamilton told her that he would decide within the next two days about his long-term plans for her care. She added that Hamilton told her before he left that "he would never set foot in Atlantic City again, as it would recall many incidents that were painful to him and which he wished to blot from his memory."

## CHAPTER SIX
# MRS. EVA HAMILTON'S STORY

The news of Eva's conviction, like everything else about the Hamilton saga, was splashed across the front pages of the nation's newspapers the morning after Judge Reed pronounced his sentencing of the "bold adventuress." Ray's father, still in North Conway, New Hampshire, penned a letter to his son as soon as he learned the news coming out of Mays Landing.

*The Kearsarge*
*North Conway, N.H.*
*Sept. 20, 1889*

*My dear Ray:*

*I congratulate you on the sentence of Eva to the penitentiary for (2) two years. My wife heartily unites with me in well wishes. Your whole deportment under your great trial is deemed unexceptionable.*

>*Your Affectionate Father,*
>*Schuyler Hamilton*

*We expect to leave here on Tuesday next for N.Y. City. I will telegraph you on that day.*

The younger Hamilton must have felt a palpable sense of relief upon reading his father's letter. It was possible that the General might offer a forceful recrimination of his son's behavior once they were reunited, but for the moment at least, the patriarch of the Hamilton family was squarely in his eldest son's corner.

Ray kept a decidedly low profile upon his return to New York after the trial. He gave no interviews; was not spotted entering the Union League, University Club, or Delmonico's to celebrate Eva's conviction; and kept his place of residence unknown to the public. Try as he might, though, Hamilton couldn't keep his name out of the news.

After the trial, Elizabeth Rupp closed up Noll Cottage for the season and returned to her year-round residence in Philadelphia with her husband and three children. Baby Beatrice was still in her care. On September 26, after nearly a month of observing and understanding the workings and power of the newspapers, Elizabeth Rupp granted an interview to the *New York Times* directed to an audience of one: Robert Ray Hamilton.

"Before he left Mays Landing," Mrs. Rupp began, "Mr. Hamilton told me if I needed any money to address him through his New York lawyer, and let him know what I wanted. I did write, telling him that I thought $1000 was not too much to ask for all the trouble I had been put to through the scandal and the loss of my business, but I did not hear from him until yesterday afternoon, an hour or so before I started from Atlantic City."

"What did he send you?"

"What did he send me? Why, a check for $250, which is nothing more or less than an insult. If I had asked for $4000 or $5000 it would be different, but I only ask for $1000 which I think isn't too much from a man like him who has plenty of money. I don't think he ought to wait for me to ask him."

She continued, "I will keep the baby until Mr. Hamilton tells me what to do with her. He told me several times that he intended to provide for Beatrice, and I am willing to keep her just as long as Mr. Hamilton wants me to, because both myself and the children are greatly attached to her."

Elizabeth Rupp ended the interview by telling the reporter that she heard that Mary Ann Donnelly "will appear among the freaks at a museum in New York for a few weeks and be paid $75 per week."

Indeed, Mrs. Rupp had heard correctly. On October 4, an advertisement in the Amusements section of the *New York Evening World* announced:

## GLOBE MUSEUM
### 298 BOWERY.

### NURSE DONNELLY,
Having recovered from the Murderous Assault of

### EVA RAY HAMILTON

is now holding receptions in our Curio Hall.

### OPEN FROM 11 TILL 10. ADMISSION 10c.

For several weeks after her recovery, Mary Ann Donnelly appeared on stage at the Globe Museum in lower Manhattan, one of the most notable of the popular dime museums that regularly showcased people with physical deformities and curiosities from the natural world.

Mary Ann Donnelly appeared on stage wearing a white gown with narrow pink stripes and a lace cap. She displayed the dress and petticoat she was wearing on the day of the stabbing, holding it up so that the crowd could plainly see the long slits produced by Eva's dagger. Audience members were free to ask questions of her about the Hamiltons or the details of the incident at Noll Cottage. The whiskey bottle that she, Josh, and Eva all drank from on the morning of the stabbing sat on a table next to her. Mrs. Donnelly told a reporter that "she was greatly embarrassed at the staring eyes that rested upon her," but that the $150 per week that she was being paid was too great a sum to ignore.

### September 27, 1889

Eight days had passed since Eva Hamilton's conviction, but she remained at Mays Landing, in the more comfortable surroundings of the county jail. Jennie Johnson had taken a liking to the convict, and with Sheriff Johnson's acquiescence, she was moved into an attic room in the sheriff's residence, adjacent to the jail. She ate dinner each night with Sheriff Johnson, Jennie, and their two young sons, Alfred and Enoch. Both Alfred ("Alf") and Enoch ("Nucky") would succeed their father as Atlantic County sheriff—Alf retained the position when his younger brother "Nucky" became Atlantic County treasurer and oversaw the political machine and vast corruption in Atlantic City during prohibition.

While there was no rush to send Eva off to the decidedly harsher confines of Trenton State Prison, a state law stipulated that a prisoner must be transferred to Trenton no more than fourteen days after their sentencing. In Eva's case, no later than October 8.

Ray Hamilton quietly arrived at Mays Landing on September 27 to visit his wife, a meeting that was dutifully splashed in the newspapers the next morning. The *New York Times* ran a one-paragraph story at the bottom of the front page under the bland headline, "Mr. Hamilton Visits His Wife." They reported that Eva "is said to have telegraphed him that she had proofs of her innocence of the charges against her."

The *Evening World* led with a more dramatic approach:

> The hovel-born adventuress in prison here
> has made good her boast: "Let me see Ray
> Hamilton for twenty minutes and I'll win
> him back again." She has captured what
> she never lost, the heart of a man she has
> deceived so basely. She owns him body
> and soul and his enthrallment is as com-
> plete today as it was when he first came
> under the magic of Eva Steele's spell.

Given Ray's disgust with his wife's stories and lies, and his
vow to never again set foot in Atlantic County, it is unlikely
that he made the journey to hear Eva's latest rantings about
what had transpired in the last year, or to fall once more
under her spell. More likely, Ray arrived at Mays Landing to
explain his plans for the care of Beatrice and to give Eva a
chance to see her "daughter" one last time before she was
taken to prison. Regardless of Ray's motivations or intentions,
when he visited his estranged wife on September 27, it was
the last time that he and Eva Hamilton ever saw each other.

### September 30, 1889

On a cool, rainy Monday morning, Jennie Johnson, Samuel
Perry, and a New Jersey state assemblyman, Captain Shep-
herd Hudson, boarded a train at Mays Landing, bound for
Philadelphia. Once arrived, they were driven to the home of a
Philadelphia policeman, Officer Harry Shourds. Elizabeth
Rupp and Beatrice Ray Hamilton were waiting for them at
Shourds's modest, three-story brick home on Fifth Street in
the city center. Elizabeth Rupp registered her misgivings
about allowing Beatrice to leave her care, but after repeated

assurances that the baby would be well-looked-after, Jennie Johnson tucked Beatrice into a carriage and the three adults returned to Mays Landing that same afternoon with the Hamilton infant.

Word had passed among the townsfolk that Beatrice Hamilton was returning to Mays Landing that day—almost everyone in town was on hand to receive Jennie Johnson, Perry, and Hudson when the trio stepped off the train, and they formed a processional behind Mrs. Johnson and the baby for the short walk to the sheriff's house. Eva Hamilton, temporarily freed from her cell, was there to meet them. Sheriff Johnson allowed Eva to remain in his custody with Beatrice until the time arrived for her to be taken to Trenton.

The next day, several visitors called on Eva Hamilton. The first two to arrive at the sheriff's house were Elizabeth Rupp, and "a stout, plainly dressed woman" who accompanied her. The unidentified woman was either directed to, or chose to, remain anonymous—but the chatter in Mays Landing was that the unnamed matron was expected to take final charge of the baby in New York as soon as Mrs. Hamilton was transferred to Trenton. Elizabeth Rupp and the stout woman stayed with Eva and Beatrice for two hours, with Jennie Johnson never leaving their side.

Samuel Perry came to bid Mrs. Hamilton farewell and to inform her that as she was soon to depart for Trenton, he was formally relinquishing his role as her counsel. Perry stayed less than thirty minutes before returning to Atlantic City on a five o'clock train.

The stream of visitors to Mays Landing relieved Eva Hamilton of the tedium of waiting for her impending incarceration. Two potential visitors with whom Eva could have had an undoubtedly long conversation, Anna Swinton and Josh Mann, were still locked up in New York at The Tombs, un-

able to square their version of events with that of their
co-conspirator. And any feelings that Eva may have still har-
bored for Ray Hamilton were unreciprocated, their relationship irrevocably broken.

## October 3, 1889

Less than ten months after his wedding, and two weeks after
Eva's conviction, Ray Hamilton filed for divorce on the grounds
of fraud and the existence of a previous marriage. As Eva was
behind bars in New Jersey, Judge Edward Patterson of the
New York State Supreme Court ruled that service of the divorce summons to Mrs. Hamilton could be made by publication of a legal notice in two newspapers for six weeks, and that
a copy of the summons be mailed to her at both Mays Landing
and Trenton.

The conventional wisdom in the press was that "there
would be no defense, and that Eva would allow the marriage
to be annulled by default." The newspapers were convinced
that the lawsuit to annul the marriage was evidence that
"Robert Ray Hamilton is cured of his infatuation for Mrs. Swinton's protégé."

## October 5, 1889

Eva Hamilton's days in the comfort of Sheriff Johnson's home
had come to an end. In the early morning of October 5, news-
men who had been staked out in Mays Landing for nine con-
secutive days after Eva's conviction huddled to stay warm as
the temperature near the Jersey shore had dropped to forty
degrees. The intersection of Main Street and Railroad Avenue
was deserted at the predawn hour of 4:00 A.M. when two shad-
owy figures emerged from the sheriff's house, their breath visible in the brisk autumn air. From across the street, the
reporters could hear one of them sobbing.

Jennie Johnson held a shaken and reluctant Eva Hamilton

by the arm, tugging her toward the street as a carriage driven by Sheriff Johnson pulled up to the front of the courthouse for their journey to the state prison. Trenton was sixty miles directly north of Mays Landing—a train ride of just over an hour—but the sheriff took a roundabout and unusual route in hopes of throwing any reporters off their trail.

From Mays Landing, Sheriff Johnson's two spirited bays pulled the carriage fifteen miles west to Landisville, where he, his wife, and Eva waited thirty minutes to board a northbound New Jersey Southern train. They traveled almost a hundred miles north to Elizabeth, New Jersey, stopping for lunch near the train station before boarding a New Jersey Central to ride fifty miles south to Trenton. Once arrived in the state capital, they took a Reading Railroad shuttle for the short trip to the state prison, finally reaching their destination at 4:10 in the afternoon.

The sheriff's elaborate plan to evade the press failed, however; the threesome were tailed from Mays Landing until the doors of the state prison closed behind them. And Johnson's ploy did not sit particularly well with reporters. "The poor prisoner had been kept on the road twelve hours and dragged almost all over New Jersey because of the whim of a stupid official who wished to beat the newspapers."

Trenton State Prison was the third oldest state prison in the United States (after Walnut Street Jail in Philadelphia and Newgate in New York), opening in 1798. The Fortress, where Eva was to be housed, was an adjoining facility that opened in 1836. Massive, russet-colored sandstone blocks formed twenty-foot-high walls that were two city blocks long and had been set in place by prison labor. Guard towers shaped like truncated obelisks rose above the walls at regular intervals along the entire perimeter of the facility. The prison held nearly 1,000 convicts in total; men who made shoes, shirts, and horse whips and women who did the sewing and mending for the institution. The prison had a full library, night school, and chapel and "efforts were made to improve the convicts both mentally and morally."

Deputy Warden Thomas Manning stood outside of the Fortress awaiting the arrival of Mrs. Hamilton. When Eva stepped down from Sheriff Johnson's carriage at the prison entrance, she burst into tears, threw her arms around Jennie Johnson's neck, and clung to her for dear life.

"Come with me," Manning said firmly, but Eva continued to hold tightly to the sheriff's wife.

He managed to tear Eva away, "forcibly, but not roughly," and led her inside to the women's wing where she was processed into the facility by the prison matron, Margaret Patterson, wife of John Patterson, head keeper of the entire facility. Eva cried bitterly, despite the matron's repeated attempts to speak to her new prisoner softly and soothingly.

The greatest indignity that could befall the smartly dressed Mrs. Hamilton occurred when a girl dressed in prison garb removed Eva's silk wrap and Gainsborough hat. She helped Eva step out of her dress and into a shapeless, black-and-white-checked prison gown that fell limply to her ankles. The ever-fashionable Eva had been reduced in appearance to the commonality of every other inmate. She was led to her cell by a fellow prisoner who was posted outside of her door with instructions to not allow anyone to approach or speak to the infamous new prisoner, allowing time for Eva Hamilton to sit quietly and acclimate to her new surroundings.

### October 9, 1889

Eva Hamilton's silence and isolation in Trenton lasted three days. On Tuesday, October 8, a visitor from New York managed to talk her way into the prison to visit their newest inmate. The visitor was neither a friend nor acquaintance, nor a religious volunteer who had come to administer a dose of faith and redemption. The visitor was the most famous investigative reporter of the day—Nellie Bly of the *New York World*.

Nellie Bly was born Elizabeth Jane Cochran in 1864, near Pittsburgh, Pennsylvania. Her father died when she was seven, and her mother moved her family of five children into Pittsburgh-proper to run a boarding house. In 1885, at age twenty, Elizabeth read an article published in the *Pittsburgh Dispatch* titled "What Girls Are Good For," that described housekeeping and birthing children as a woman's principal contributions to society.

Angered by such a simplistic description of a woman's worth, Elizabeth wrote a scathing rebuttal, signed "Little Orphan Girl," that impressed *Dispatch* editor, George Madden, and led to an assignment to work up a feature article. Written under the pen name Nellie Bly, a character in a Stephen Foster song, "The Girl Puzzle" described how women were adversely affected by divorce and advocated for the reform of divorce laws.

Madden brought her on full-time and sent to her to Mexico when she was twenty-one years old to write travel articles. In her six months there, Nellie Bly turned from reporting on sunny beaches, food, and culture to what she saw as oppression of the Mexican people by the government of President Porfirio Díaz, including the imprisonment of a local journalist who wrote critically of the Díaz regime. Threatened with jail herself, Nellie Bly fled the country before the authorities closed in on her.

Safely back in the United States, Bly longed for a grander stage and moved to New York in 1887 without a job. She was offered an assignment from Joseph Pulitzer's *New York World*—to go undercover at an insane asylum to shine a light on the conditions and treatment of patients. Bly readily accepted, checked into Bellevue Hospital, and convinced doctors there that she was out of her mind. She was put on a boat to Blackwell's Island (now Roosevelt Island), the long, narrow strip of land in the East River between Manhattan and Queens and was admitted to the New York City Lunatic Asylum.

For ten days, Nellie Bly wrote of the deplorable conditions at the Asylum—the oily broth and spider-infested bread that patients were given to eat, the cold baths before bedtime, the thin, tattered blankets covering rock-hard bunks, and the hours made to sit upright in wooden chairs with nothing at all to do. And Bly wrote extensively of the indifference, at best—and cruelty, at its worst—of the doctors, nurses, and attendants charged with the care of the Asylum's patients.

Pulitzer's readers couldn't get enough of the agonizing, horrific tales that Nellie Bly told in dispatches headlined "Inside the Madhouse." She emerged from her stint at Blackwell's Island as the *New York World*'s star reporter, and in a period of less than two weeks, Nellie Bly effectively invented undercover, investigative reporting. She capitalized on her popularity and writing style to pen exposés about unfair labor practices in factories, huckster physicians, and political corruption.

Nellie Bly gravitated naturally to the stories left untold by others. She had followed the Hamilton story along with millions of others, but noted that while Ray Hamilton and his advocates had effectively gotten his side of the story out to the public, his wife Eva had yet to be heard from. Nellie Bly was determined to change that and used her star power to convince New Jersey prison officials to allow her access to their high-profile prisoner for a jailhouse interview.

On October 9, under the headline, "Mrs. Eva Hamilton's Story. She Talks Fully to 'Nellie Bly' in Trenton State Prison," the intrepid reporter began her article that ran a full column on page one and two additional columns on page two:

> I interviewed Mrs. Eva Hamilton late this afternoon in her prison cell in the Trenton jail. Everybody has heard Robert Ray Hamilton's side of the story. It seemed only fair that the woman be given a show. I have seen her. I have talked with her, and I write her story as she gave it. She has been judged in more ways than one. I smooth over nothing in the telling of what she told me.

What Eva told Nellie Bly stood in wild contradiction to anything that had come to light in six weeks of newspaper reporting, police investigations, and courtroom testimony. Anyone who had followed the Hamilton story from its beginning in late August would have been astonished to read Eva's own account of her life and present situation. Whether one believed any of it, all of it, or something in between, what could not be disputed was Eva Hamilton's ability to tell a story.

"To begin at the first, I am not the child of the Steeles, as has been said. I was only their adopted child. My mother died when I was born, and when I was three years old my father died of consumption. I was born in Tunkhannock, Pennsylvania. The Steeles adopted me and I never knew any other people but them. When I was fifteen years old, I moved to Towanda and there I met Walter Parsons, who was then superintendent of a railroad."

Eva continued, "We were married, my folks and his folks fought about it. It made a great deal of trouble. I had one child, a daughter to Walter Parsons, and then things went so badly by others interfering that we separated."

"What became of your daughter?" Bly asked.

"I don't like to bring her in this," Eva plaintively replied. "She is thirteen years old now. I have her at school and she does not know anything about this. I don't want her to, and it is not right to drag Walter Parsons up, for he is married again."

No evidence had come to light in any previous reporting that Eva had given birth—if she had, she would have almost certainly had the ability to lactate.

"Then tell me what you did next."

"In 1879, I think it was, Father Steele and the Parsons arranged to get a divorce to free Walter and myself. This was all done by them in Elmira. After the divorce was granted, I went to Elmira, where I lived for three months. Then I went to New York. I immediately got an engagement with a dramatic company and went on the road."

"Tell me what company?"

"Don't ask me," she said, "I do not wish to drag the names of people before the public who have so far escaped. While I was traveling with this company, I met Joshua Mann. The company was stopping at the West End Hotel, Philadelphia, and Josh Mann was there. One of the girls in the company knew him and she introduced him to me. I was two years with this company and then I was out for nine months with Billy Florence. Then I went to New York to stay."

An actress who played alongside an actor of Billy Florence's caliber—one of the leading theatrical talents of the day— would more than likely be publicly noted in some way. This did not occur in Eva's case. Oddly though, Billy Florence did appear, without explanation, at Anna Swinton and Josh Mann's arraignment. Whether or not Eva read that in the newspapers and wove him into her story, or if she was being truthful to Nellie Bly, remains a mystery.

"Of course, you know how I met Mr. Hamilton?"

"I do not," Bly answered. "Tell me the story."

"A friend of mine took me to a home one night. Mr. Hamilton and two friends of his were calling there at the time. We were all introduced and Mr. Hamilton and I became the most intimate friends from that time. That is five years ago this coming spring."

Mournfully, Eva added, "We cared for each other. I mean by that that he paid all my expenses and was with me all the time he was in New York, which was usually from Friday night until Monday morning, coming down from Albany. He was a member of the legislature then."

Eva's next statement was an absolute surprise to anyone following the story.

"Twice during that time I was going to be a mother. I told Mr. Hamilton and he was very angry. Both times he compelled me to consult a doctor and he gave me $300 each time to pay expenses. Once he gave me the money and the other time he sent the money in a registered letter to me at the Passaic Bridge Post Office in New Jersey."

Continuing, Eva added, "All this time I was friendly with the Swintons. 'Dot' as we called Joshua Mann, had introduced me to his mother Mrs. Swinton. Josh lost his position and they were hard pushed, so I began to lend them money. I like them; they treated me kindly, and I didn't miss what I gave them. After I met Mr. Hamilton, I tried to keep it from Grandmother (Swinton), but she found it out, little by little, and then my trouble began. Every time they wanted money they came to me. If I refused, they would threaten and then I would give up."

"What would they threaten?"

"They threatened to tell people and they threatened to separate me from Mr. Hamilton, so I gave them money to buy

their silence and my own happiness. Mr. Hamilton knew I
supported them, but he never made any objections."

"Why did you not get rid of them?"

"I couldn't. I was afraid of them. They followed me every-
where and they threatened until I was glad to get peace at
any price. They somehow found out everything I had ever
done in my life and they held my own deeds over me."

Eva's story became a bit more implausible when she explained that she never took money from Ray Hamilton—and
that it was he who took money from her.

She told Bly that "Ray and a friend of his went out on the
road. They stopped at a roadhouse with a female friend and
they all drank too much wine, and when Mr. Hamilton came
back, he told me all about it and what had happened, which
was something dreadful. I got angry and we had a quarrel,
and I threatened to go to the husband of the lady and tell him
the whole thing. Mr. Hamilton begged me not and said if I
promised never to tell he would give me $10,000."

She claimed that Ray soon asked for the money back and
that she "loaned" it back to him in small increments that he
was to repay. She told Bly that there were ledger books in an
Atlantic City bank to back up her claims, but those books, if
they existed, never saw the light of day. Bly was able to steer
Eva back to the subject of Anna Swinton and more specifically, Josh Mann.

"Mr. Hamilton, as I have told you, never raised any objections to my giving money to the Swintons. I kept Mrs. Swinton, Josh Mann, Mrs. Swinton's granddaughter, Carrie Collens.
I kept them all, because they threatened me. At last Kate Collens, Mrs. Swinton's daughter, found out about Mr. Hamilton
and she also made me pay her money. When I went to Jersey
they all went along and lived with me, and Mr. Hamilton
knew it and did not object. Josh Mann got knocked down with

my horse, which was very vicious, while in Jersey. He struck on the back of his head and lay insensible for almost twenty-four hours. When we returned to New York I took him to half a dozen doctors. He has never been right since that and should not be held responsible for what he says."

The only statement by Eva Hamilton thus far in her interview that would be met with universal agreement was that of Josh Mann's limited mental capacity. The subject then turned to Beatrice. Even though the baby-purchase plan had been well established by Tommy Byrnes and confessed to in detail by Anna Swinton, Eva held to her version of the story.

"I kept very quiet about the fact that I was going to become a mother. Mr. Hamilton knew it, and he knew I didn't want Mrs. Swinton to know it because it would be something more for her to threaten me about. I slipped off to Elmira, to my brother's. Mr. Hamilton gave me $200 to buy baby clothes, and $150 for myself before I left. He also sent me a check for $500. My brother knew what was wrong with me.

"I had not been at his house three days until Josh came. He followed me up. On Nov. 15 I slipped away and went to some good, honest people in the country. On the Nineteenth my baby was born. On December First, I returned to Elmira, and on the Twenty-fourth of December I returned to New York, leaving my baby at the house where it was born. On the morning of January Second, I had my baby brought home.

"At this time Mr. Hamilton and I quarreled. I found out about him being off on a spree and with women. We had a terrible quarrel and I said I was going to leave him. He begged me not to, but I was determined, so he said for me not to leave him and he would marry me. We had never thought or spoken of marriage before, and at this moment our child was not thought of.

"Mr. Hamilton had been wishing she would die from the

time he knew it was to be born. So we did not have much to say on the subject. This fight was on the night of the 8th of January.

"When Mr. Hamilton asked me to marry him I said I would not. I would not marry him to take his people's abuse afterwards for having lived with him before we were married. He said if I would only marry him we would keep it secret until after the legislature and then we would take a trip to Southern California and he would say he met and married me there. I loved him and with these promises I consented."

The fact that Ray and Eva were married on January 7, before their alleged fight on January 8, might be attributed to a simple confusion of dates on Eva's part, but the rest of her story careened wildly between truths, half-truths, and outright lies. Nellie Bly concluded her interview by asking Eva about the events surrounding the stabbing of Mary Ann Donnelly. Eva Hamilton's scorn for her former baby nurse was clearly evident.

"I had discharged the nurse several times, but Mr. Hamilton would always tell her not to go. Twice I found Mr. Hamilton in her room. That is the secret of the fuss. After the fight, when I had called for the police, someone came upstairs and said the nurse was cut. I said, 'Ray, go downstairs and see if it is true.' He went down and when he returned, he said, 'she was.' He said that (Mary) accused me and advised me to say 'I did it.'"

Eva explained that Ray said, "'There can be no trouble, and it will end sooner if you just say you did it.'

"So when the officers asked me," Eva recounted to Bly, "I said 'I did it.' The knife was never mine, I had never seen it before. After they took me to jail, Mr. Hamilton wrote me several notes, in which he said for me to 'bear up,' that he would have me 'freed' but that 'the innocent have to suffer with the guilty.' Whether she cut herself or Mr. Hamilton cut her I do not know, but I do know if I had a knife I surely would have known something about it. I did not even see a knife during the fight."

Eva's ability to weave fact and fiction together so flawlessly was an undeniable talent. For any reader of the *World* who may have thought that she had been unjustly punished, Eva's interview with Nellie Bly confirmed what they had felt all along. For the reader who had already determined that Eva Hamilton was manipulative, a schemer, and a liar, the contradictions riddled throughout the article only reinforced their established opinion.

### Late October 1889

As dumbstruck as Ray may have been about Nellie Bly's interview with Eva, he never publicly commented about it or used the press to rebut her claims. By the time the *World* article hit the newsstands, Ray was six hundred miles from Manhattan, sitting in a duck blind in Monroe, Michigan.

In early November, Ray's aunt Nathalie penned a letter to Ray from her home in Taunton, Massachusetts, inviting him to come north and "celebrate Thanksgiving in New England fashion" with her family. She acknowledged, though, that her invitation might go unanswered. "Schuyler wrote that you were over in Michigan shooting and I do not at all know when you will return eastward."

Even before Eva's trial ended, friends were encouraging Ray to get away from the maelstrom in Atlantic City and New York. One of his best friends, Casimir de Rham Moore (a grandson of Clement Clark Moore), wrote from Southampton inviting Ray to sail with him to England on the RMS *Umbria*.

"If you could manage to do so it would be a real kindness to me . . . I shall be gone six weeks and not more than two months. I am sure it would do you good to go over with me and we could review old times once more." Even though events were still unfolding with Eva in Atlantic City, Moore wrote to Ray on September 9, more concerned with arrangements for his trip than he was with Ray's predicament. "If you are still with Charlie (Peabody), would you ask him if he can enquire with the Cunard office about the prospects of getting a good stateroom . . . one on the outside and well forward."

Whatever accommodation Moore was able to secure on the *Umbria* is unknown, but Ray did not take his friend up on his offer to join the trip. An avid outdoorsman, Ray opted instead to take the train west to Monroe, a small town on the shores of Lake Erie between Toledo, Ohio, and Detroit, to meet up with fellow members of the Monroe Marsh Company.

Men of Ray's social stature were not only members of private clubs in Manhattan, some also joined the new "country clubs" that were forming just outside of the city and offered golf, tennis, and other outdoor activities to their members. The more adventurous of the elite joined sporting clubs— hunting and fishing as far north as the Adirondacks and points west that were accessible by the railroads.

In 1853, the schooner *West Wing* arrived in Buffalo after sailing across Lake Erie from Monroe with a cargo of corn. The barrels of corn didn't attract much attention when the ship docked, but admiring crowds along the piers gawked at the multitude of ducks festooned from the ship's riggings—the result of three days of shooting by the ship's charter, Henry Mixer. The following autumn, Mixer and his New York friends returned to Monroe for the fall hunting season and formed the Golo Club, the first sporting club in Monroe.

By 1870, the Golo Club's members (including General

George Armstrong Custer) had either died or moved to more far-flung environs beyond the Great Lakes. The legend of Monroe remained, however, and the marshes along the River Raisin that emptied into Lake Erie still drew numerous hunters each fall in search of canvasbacks, redheads, mallards, and teal.

On May 30, 1881, twenty-four sportsmen met at the Globe Hotel in Syracuse, New York, to form the Monroe Marsh Company and arranged for the purchase of two thousand acres of prime wetlands for the club's exclusive use. By the time Ray Hamilton acquired a share of ownership in the late 1880s, the club had eighteen members and a well-appointed clubhouse. The main lodge featured a sitting room on the main floor with "a fireplace capable of receiving logs four or five feet long, comfortable chairs and couches, cases of wall-mounted game birds, gun racks and other befitting furnishings making a most agreeable *tout-ensemble*." And each member had their own bedroom and an adjoining sitting room, both comfortably heated and tastefully furnished.

Not only were the accommodations first class, the banquets prepared by the chefs at the club were legendary—particularly their annual muskrat dinner. The club members sought protection for the muskrats that shared the marshes with the prized ducks and hosted a dinner for the entire Michigan State Legislature to press their case for the semiaquatic rodent to not be overhunted. The legislators had no clue that the entrée was muskrat until the meal was complete and the toastmaster informed the guests that the club desired to have a law passed giving protection to the excellent game they had just consumed. The law was passed without opposition and an invitation to the club's annual muskrat dinner became a coveted ticket in southeast Michigan.

Monroe Marsh Company members included brothers Frank-

lin and Ralph Brandreth, heirs to the Brandreth Pills fortune
and who managed a 24,000-acre preserve in the Adirondacks
inherited from their father, and Henry de Forest, a prominent
New York attorney who became president of the Metropolitan
Museum of Art.

Annual dues were $100, plus one additional dollar per day
for every day spent on the property, whether the member
hunted or not. It was noted by those connected to the club that
it might "appear to the casual observer that to gratify one's
taste for such a luxurious hunter's life involves something
rather more than time."

### November–December 1889

Given Ray's love of the outdoors and tarnished reputation at
home, it is easy to understand his desire to linger in Monroe
for as long as possible. By mid-November, though, he had returned to New York.

*Nov. 16, 1889*

*My dear son:*

*Mr. Vollmer informed me you are at No. 125 W. 42nd
Street. I would like as an affectionate father and sympa-
thizing friend to come to see you. Let me know if you
would like me to come—my wife and I have apartment
No. 614 Windsor Hotel. We will be most glad to see you if
you care to come.*

*Your Affect. Father,*
*Schuyler Hamilton*

The General's new residence, the Windsor Hotel in Manhattan, opened in 1873 at a cost of over a million dollars. In an

era of increasingly opulent displays of wealth, the hotel set a new standard in elegance and sophistication. Every detail was thoughtfully considered, down to the reported $10,000 spent fitting out the hotel's barbershop. The Windsor was described at its opening as "the most luxurious and aristocratic hostelry in New York."

Each of its five hundred rooms was fitted with a private bathroom and a fireplace, and "the grand entrance and rotunda are of such magnitude as to afford abundance of room for many hundreds to assemble. The same may be said of the large drawing-room, the two adjoining parlors, and the elegant octagon room." In addition to welcoming visiting heads of state, royalty, and industrialists, the Windsor catered to an upper-class clientele that took up permanent residency in finer hotels.

When John D. Rockefeller's business interests began keeping him in New York for increasingly longer periods of time, he moved his family into the Windsor for two years, beginning in 1875. Andrew Carnegie and his mother took up residence in adjoining suites in the exceedingly handsome hotel in 1880. Jay Gould, whose new mansion sat majestically one block north of the Windsor on Fifth Avenue, was regularly seen in the hotel in the evenings "plotting market strategy with other leading financiers."

The needs of the Carnegies, Rockefellers, Hamiltons, and other discerning guests of the Windsor were met under the watchful eyes of the hotel's proprietors, Samuel Hawk and Gardner Wetherbee, who took pride in their ability to "conduct one of the finest public houses in the metropolis in a proper manner."

While the General sat in his sixth-floor suite on November 16, penning the invitation to his eldest son, thorough readers of that morning's *New York Times* might have been amused by a one-paragraph story that ran on the bottom of page five, detailing Mary Ann Donnelly's ongoing love for a tipple. The story was headlined "An Echo of the Hamilton Scandal":

> Nurse Donnelly, whose recent stab wound became famous as the immediate cause of the exposure of the Robert Ray Hamilton scandal, was in the city yesterday. She had been toying with the rosy and went to the Tombs Prison as a visitor in a state of hilarious inebriation. She wanted to see Mrs. Swinton and "Josh" Mann but was not allowed to do so. She said she had just been visiting Mrs. Robert Ray Hamilton at Trenton jail and had important messages for "Josh." Finally she left, muttering weirdly as she tapped her bosom with her first finger: "Well, it's all there. It's all there."

The meeting of father and son for the first time since the stabbing in Atlantic City is unremarked upon, but Ray was undoubtedly relieved to find himself off the front pages after his return from Monroe. A titillating nugget like the Mary Ann Donnelly article would have run on page one in September—by mid-November, only the most ardent readers of the newspapers could find a story related to Robert Ray Hamilton. That changed shortly after Christmas of 1889.

Even though the newspapers were certain that Eva Hamilton would not contest the divorce proceedings initiated by Ray in October, she was legally entitled to a ninety-day period in which to do so. On December 28, with only one week to go before the expiration of her rebuttal period, attorney Charles W. Fuller filed an answer on behalf of Mrs. Hamilton. To the surprise of those parties aligned with Ray Hamilton, Eva asserted "a general denial to the complaint of Mr. Hamilton and a special denial of his allegation that she had contracted a marriage prior to her union with him." She added that "since June 1, 1885, he has lived with her at various places, always registering as Robert Ray Hamilton and wife."

As the festivities of the holiday season wound down and New Yorkers returned to their routines after celebrating the new year, the relative anonymity that Ray enjoyed after his return from Monroe came to an end. In the first months of 1890, the Hamilton name again graced the front pages of the newspapers—for all of the same reasons that Ray and his family had hoped were behind them.

## CHAPTER SEVEN

# MANN OR HAMILTON?

**January 1890**

As the last decade of the nineteenth century began, the Hamilton saga crept back into the press, somewhat innocuously, beginning on January 1, 1890. Many newspapers ran chronological "Year in Review" features on the front page of their New Year editions—in the long lists of the year's notable events, August 26, 1889, was marked by the vast majority as the day of the stabbing at Noll Cottage. These snippets, however, were only a prelude to the legal battle that publicly unfolded in the Hamiltons' divorce case shortly thereafter.

In 1890, divorce was a relatively rare occurrence in the United States; only three couples per 1,000 had their marriages legally dissolved in any given year. Divorce in the late nineteenth century was considered to be a moral stain, and the high cost of legal fees required to obtain a divorce was prohibitive to all but the upper classes of society—men like Ray Hamilton.

Upon being informed of Eva's surprise decision to fight the annulment in court, Ray's attorneys, Elihu Root and Samuel Clarke, immediately got to work. Using the list of names gathered by Bobby McNaught in Elmira the previous September, Root and Clarke obtained permission from the court to arrange for witness testimony to be taken in upstate New York.

By mid-January, only two weeks after Eva's contest to the divorce proceedings was filed, Root and Clarke retained George M. Diven, a prominent local attorney in Elmira, to interview twenty-four witnesses in the presence of a court-appointed referee, E. C. Van Duzer. Keenly interested in all matters regarding his pending divorce, Ray Hamilton took the trip to Elmira to join Diven. Charles Fuller was on hand to represent Mrs. Hamilton. The testimony was taken in private, but the Hamilton camp made sure that the press learned that "sufficient information was gained to show that the witnesses told long stories of what they knew of the bold adventuress."

Two women held in the Waverly, New York, jail, associates of Mrs. Hamilton when she was the terror of a brothel there, were escorted twenty miles to Elmira in police custody. They testified to the incident four years prior when Eva shot the ear off of the man with whom she had quarreled. Other women from notorious houses in Oswego, New York; Towanda, Pennsylvania; and Bernice, Pennsylvania, were also on hand to testify about Eva's character and nefarious activities before her move to New York.

The heart of the matter, though—the legal merit of Ray's allegation—was Eva's prior relationship with, and alleged marriage to, Joshua Mann. Neither Root and Clarke, nor Tommy Byrnes, was able to locate a marriage certificate acknowledging a lawful union of Josh and Eva—their case was built on the assertion of a common-law marriage between the two and their public representation as man and wife.

Diven called William Foyle, W. J. Young, Joseph Ochs, ex-Sheriff A. J. Layton—all of Towanda, Pennsylvania—to testify that Eva lived in that village with Joshua Mann, that they lived together as a married couple, and that they called them-

selves man and wife. But Ray Hamilton's allies were not the
only ones to leak the closed-door proceedings to the newspapers. Charles Fuller's cross-examination of each witness,
whispered to members of the press, was reported to be "scathing, his purpose being to discredit the witnesses, who, in several instances contradicted each other."

One of the most important witnesses for the Hamilton side
came from another Towanda resident, Alice Steele, the wife of
William Steele Jr. and Eva Hamilton's sister-in-law. She testified that in late fall, 1888, she was "about to become a mother
while Eva and Josh Mann were living in this city." Alice Steele
swore before the referee that "Mrs. Hamilton made a proposition to me to take the child when born and palm it off on
Hamilton as the offspring of the latter." Mrs. Steele added
that she "declined to accede to the proposition, and from that
moment lost all respect for my sister-in-law."

At the outset of the proceedings, Ray Hamilton appeared to
be "as chipper as a schoolboy"—by the conclusion of witness
testimony two days later, the parade of witnesses who consis-
tently told of Josh and Eva's appearance as husband and wife
had taken its toll on the beleaguered Hamilton. He was exhausted, worn down, and knew that Charles Fuller had effectively cross-examined Root and Clarke's witnesses—when the
case came before a judge, Fuller could mount a credible defense that Eva was indeed Hamilton's legal wife.

Ray also knew that the testimony was only taken in
Elmira to save witnesses the expense of attending a hearing
in Manhattan. Legally, the testimony could only be considered to be preliminary and was subject to being set aside by
a judge hearing the case in New York. What was certain was
that the effective release of witness testimony to the press
from Ray's side—particularly the statements made by Alice
Steele—further diminished Eva's reputation in the court of
public opinion.

## March 1890

Eva Hamilton's reputation may have been left in tatters by the events in Atlantic City and subsequent revelations of her past behavior, but to this point, any scorn directed at her had been based solely on her direct actions and personal history. In the spring of 1890, her name appeared in headlines once again, this time for a seemingly inexplicable reason—the shortage of bricks available to the building trade.

In the last half of the nineteenth century, the major manufacturing center for bricks used in building construction across the United States was based in the towns that lined both sides of the Hudson River, less than fifty miles north of New York City. At its peak, there were over 130 brickyards in the lower Hudson valley—the town of Haverstraw alone contained forty-three separate brick-making companies that produced over 300 million bricks in 1883.

In 1888, Ray Hamilton's brother, Schuyler Jr., opened his own brickyard in Croton Landing, the Anchor Brick Company. An architect by trade, Schuyler had an inherent understanding of the need for massive quantities of bricks required in building construction. He also lived in nearby Ossining, allowing him the opportunity to see firsthand just how well the brick makers in the area were doing financially.

A relatively mild winter in 1889 allowed construction across the country to proliferate in cold-weather regions throughout the year, creating a nationwide shortage of bricks by the spring of 1890. There were only 24 million bricks on hand along the Hudson River—less than one-third of 75 million bricks normally held at this time of year. In a roundabout way, brick manufacturers blamed Eva Hamilton.

The *Pittsburg Press* reported that "Eva's brother-in-law, Schuyler Hamilton, was largely engaged in the manufacture of brick in Croton, and failed last week for a large amount, and his failure has led to others, until the trade is in a very panicky position." Schuyler needed somewhere between $300,000 and $750,000 to pay his expenses, buy raw materials, and cover the labor costs required to ramp up production. Brick manufacturers explained to the press that "Robert Ray Hamilton was willing to help his brother financially, but could not raise the money on real estate because, being a married man, his wife's signature is necessary on mortgages and deeds, and in the existing legal complications it could not be obtained on terms worthy of being considered."

No mention was made in the press of reports of Schuyler's own responsibility for his mismanagement of the business— instead it was noted that "the measure of the fair but frail Eva seems to be considerable, if entirely unpremeditated on her part." However unfairly it was that Eva made her way into the papers in March, in April she returned to the news in a way that regular followers of the Hamilton saga were more accustomed.

### April 1890

Eva had been in the Trenton State Prison for six months when, on April 7, the news broke of her supposed "High Life Behind the Bars." The timing of the article was curious, to say the least. In mid-March, Eva's counsel, Charles Fuller, filed a petition with the New Jersey Court of Pardons asking for a pardon from her conviction in the stabbing of Mary Ann Donnelly. If a recommendation was made for a pardon by the three judges on the court, the case would be sent to Governor Leon Abbett for his signature and the prisoner's subsequent release.

It is likely that powerful figures aligned with Ray Hamilton— Elihu Root, Tommy Byrnes, Charlie Peabody—coordinated with New Jersey officials to get a story into the newspapers intended to reinforce a negative public perception of Eva

Hamilton and perhaps influence the judges sitting on the
Court of Pardons. Ray Hamilton had no interest in seeing his
wife sprung from behind bars and make an attempt to get
back into his life.

Two New Jersey state assemblymen, James Murphy and
Michael Mallone, led a delegation of officials to Trenton, ostensibly to investigate reports of the treatment of prisons at
the state prison. Murphy and Mallone both represented dis-
tricts in Hudson County, of which Jersey City was the county
seat. Jersey City was also the home of Ray's good friend, the
well-connected Charlie Peabody. On April 8, the story that
Murphy and Mallone had fed to the press appeared in newspapers that were only too eager to update their readers about
Eva Hamilton. One of those newspapers, the *Allentown Critic*,
ran the article about Eva under this headline:

## EVA'S PRISON CAREER.

A SENSATIONAL STORY OF
HER HIGH LIFE BEHIND THE BARS.

## WHISKEY AND ROAST DUCK.

*That is What it is Alleged She Enjoys,*
*As Well as Champagne, Cigarettes*
*And Morphine—the Assertions*
*Are to be Investigated.*

The two representatives charged that "she is enjoying all of
the luxuries that money can procure, even whisky, champagne,
cigarettes and roast duck." Based on their investigation, Mallone called for the appointment of a special committee to investigate the management of the prison. Other members of

the Hudson County delegation added that Eva Hamilton "was allowed all the liquor she wanted and to have a supply of cigarettes and morphine."

Eva's attorney, Charles Fuller, and ex-Judge William Hoffman, Fuller's co-counsel, strongly refuted the charges. "These stories about Mrs. Hamilton getting whisky sours and cigarettes are cut out of the whole cloth, and this investigation is only intended to besmirch Keeper Patterson." Hoffman explained that when a delegation from the State Assembly visited the prison, they became indignant when Eva "was not ordered out of her cell and put on exhibition," adding that the entire investigation is being conducted to "injure her standing with the Court of Pardons and affect her divorce case in New York."

Governor Abbett was reported to be "indignant that he is in favor of granting a pardon to Mrs. Hamilton," and denied that he had visited the prison and personally interviewed her concerning her situation. The governor explained that Eva's counsel had only made a petition and had not yet fully laid out her case before the Court of Pardons. He reiterated that he could "form no opinion as to the merit of her application for release until they had done so."

Head Keeper John Patterson made himself available to the press and stoutly defended both his own actions and those of his wife, who oversaw the women's ward of the prison. "Mrs. Patterson has been even more careful with Mrs. Hamilton than any other prisoner, because she knew that any extra attention shown her would cause dissatisfaction among the other women. I say positively that Mrs. Hamilton never had any cigarettes, liquor or fancy food since she has been here. All the charges made against the prison management will be found untrue."

Patterson emphasized that Eva "works every day at sewing buttonholes in prison garments and does a bigger day's work than any other woman," and closed with an unsolicited medical update about his famous prisoner. "She has been sick of late with neuralgia and has a troublesome carbuncle."

### May 1890

The first half of 1890 didn't see the same frenzy of Hamilton-related stories as in the fall of 1889, but Ray Hamilton, Eva, and Mary Ann Donnelly had all made appearances in the news, for one reason or another, in the winter and spring of the new year. The last mention of any of the principal actors in the stabbing drama came in the first week of May—the fact that the story didn't involve scandal, turmoil, or pending legal action made it unique in the coverage of the Hamilton affair.

The *New York Star* ran a lifestyle feature about "the various fads that Gotham's prominent citizens indulge in." It was headlined, "Some Men of New York," and the writer described the book-buying habits, at stores and art sales, of prominent collectors in the city.

"George Vanderbilt, probably the least talked about of anyone in that family, spends a great deal of time among the fine bookstores of the city. It is no uncommon thing for him to pay $3,000 or $4,000 for a dozen rare books, and as many thousands for their binding."

Robert Hoe II and his brothers were the pre-eminent manufacturers of printing presses in the United States. They took the business over from their father, Richard March Hoe, inventor of the web-perfecting-press. Robert was described as a "great deal of a dilettante in regards to books, bindings, etchings, engravings and the like. He can be found in those curious stores uptown whose sole stock in trade consists of valuable engravings and works of art of that class."

Paul Dana, who succeeded his father as editor of the *New York Sun* and "seems to inherit his father's taste, if not all of the latter's abilities," was also profiled. Dana and his wife were members of Ward McAllister's "Four Hundred," and he was "considered quite an expert in porcelain, ceramics, orchids, books and pictures."

George Gould, son of the legendary industrialist Jay Gould, was relatively new to the collection of rare books and *objets d'art*. "Before his marriage, he had little taste for anything outside of Wall Street. Since then, and probably owing to the influence of his wife, he has begun to develop a taste for handsome books, fine pictures and expensive bric-a-brac."

The *Star* wrote of Ray Hamilton that, "up to within a short time, he was a liberal purchaser of new books. There is no necessity for his buying old ones, as the Hamilton library has long been famous for both its quality and quantity. During his political career he brought together a very fine collection of works, bearing upon topics pertaining to New York state, which he is said to keep in the hope that he will some of these days be sent back to Albany to represent the people of this city."

The name Robert Ray Hamilton next appeared in the news at the end of August as a result of circumstances occurring more than 2,000 miles away from the fine bookstores, private clubs, and rarified social air of "Gotham's prominent citizens."

## CHAPTER EIGHT

# MR. HAMILTON'S FATE

**Summer 1890**

A s spring turned to summer in 1890, Ray Hamilton's whereabouts were unknown to most people, including his father. "I have known little of Ray's acts since he became involved with this woman Eva. I knew he went to Montana, but where he went, or what his intentions were, I do not know. Since the Atlantic City occurrence, he has kept to himself, his closest friends seeing little of him."

Other than the brief mention about his book collection in the *New York Star* article, nothing was written about Ray in the press (there were only tangential references to him in stories about Eva) and if he was out and about in New York, his comings and goings were left unremarked upon by reporters. What is known about the publicly embarrassed Ray Hamilton is that in June he arrived, unaccompanied, in Jackson Hole, Wyoming, not Montana.

It would be understandable if Ray chose to locate in Jackson Hole solely for its sheer natural beauty. In June, the valley floor is carpeted in the electric yellow blooms of arrow-leaf balsam root flowers, and the early summer sun shimmers on the mirror finish of Jackson Lake. The Teton Mountains rise abruptly from the west side of the water's edge to 13,000 feet—there are no foothills—to meet a sky that, on any given

day, changes from cerulean to indigo to violet and back depending on the weather.

For a hunter, Jackson Hole and the lower elevations of the
surrounding mountains offer an abundance of wildlife: elk,
mule deer, bighorn sheep, moose, and black bears. Geese and
ducks abound on the Snake River and lakes that run through
the valley—a fishing line dropped in a mountain stream is
met by cutthroat trout and mountain whitefish. For an avid
outdoorsman like Ray Hamilton, Jackson Hole was close to
heaven on earth.

Or perhaps Ray merely sought seclusion and relief from his
travails that could be found in such a sparsely populated area.
For six months out of the year it was difficult to get into and
out of Jackson Hole—the snow-choked mountain passes prohibited all but the heartiest of homesteaders and trappers to
live year-round in the valley. The nearest post office was a
hundred miles away in Kaintuck, Idaho, and there were no
railroad depots within fifty miles, no telegraph office, and
maybe most importantly to a man who needed a respite from
constantly seeing his name in boldface type—there were no
daily newspapers.

In addition to leaving his father and brother, Ray also sepa-
rated from his friends and colleagues in New York—men who
also made abundant sums of money and lived the high life in
Manhattan. They spent their days in their offices on lower
Broadway, followed by dinners at Delmonico's or the Hoffman
House, and took stock of their fortunes over a nightcap of
cigars and brandy at the University Club or the Union
League. Those heady evenings of good cheer and clinking
glasses, illuminated by soft, amber gaslight, gave way in
Wyoming to starry skies and the sound of the wind blowing
through stands of lodgepole pines.

It is conceivable to think of Ray Hamilton in transcendent
solitude in the Tetons, heeding the advice of the naturalist,

1. Robert Ray Hamilton

2. The woman born as Evangeline Steele. She used many surnames: Parsons, Brill, Mann, Hamilton, and Gaul.

3. Atlantic County Courthouse in Mays Landing, New Jersey, where Eva was convicted of Atrocious Assault. The jail where she was held while awaiting trial can be seen in the back right of this photo.

Court House May's Landing. N. J.
Photo by F. A. Austin

4. Noll Cottage. Rendering from a newspaper illustration of the site in Atlantic City where the stabbing of Mary Ann Donnelly occurred.

5. Robert Ray Hamilton's father, Major General Schuyler Hamilton, photographed here by Matthew Brady. A graduate of West Point in 1841, Gen. Hamilton served in both the Mexican-American and Civil Wars. The general's sword knot was handed down from his grandfather, Major General Alexander Hamilton.

6. Robert Ray Hamilton's younger brother, Schuyler Hamilton, Jr. An architect by profession, Schuyler, Jr. was the primary beneficiary of Ray Hamilton's estate.

7. L: Casimir de Rham Moore. 8. R: Gilbert M. Speir, Jr. Two of Ray Hamilton's best friends, they arrived in Jackson Hole, Wyoming, in September 1890 to join Hamilton on a hunting trip, only to learn that Ray had been buried at Marymere the previous day.

9. Elihu Root, lead attorney for the Hamilton family in the probate of Robert Ray Hamilton's will and with the legal issues with Eva after Ray's death.

10. Thomas F. Byrnes, Chief of Detectives for the New York Police Department. Byrnes led the investigation that uncovered the conspiracy concocted by Eva, Josh Mann, and Anna Swinton to swindle Ray Hamilton.

11. Newspaper depictions of Joshua Mann and his mother, Anna Swinton.

JOSH MANN.     MRS. SWINTON.

12. Reporter's Clubhouse, 301 Mulberry, directly across the street from the NYPD Central Office. *Photograph by Jacob Riis.*

13. The Globe Museum, 298 Bowery in lower Manhattan. Mary Ann Donnelly appeared at this "dime museum" after she recovered from being stabbed. She displayed the scar on her abdomen, as well as the whiskey bottle that Eva drank from on the morning of the incident.

14. Monroe Marsh Club, on the shore of the River Raisin, Monroe, Michigan. Robert Ray Hamilton was a member of the club and likely had the clubhouse in mind as a model for Marymere.

15. John Dudley Sargent. Originally from Machias, Maine, Sargent moved his family to Jackson Hole, WY in 1888 to claim land and build his family's home. Sargent formed a partnership with Ray Hamilton to develop a hunting lodge on his property to be called Marymere.

16. Marymere, Jackson Hole, WY, c.1890s, was located on present-day Colter Bay. Only two rooms were completed at the time of Ray Hamilton's death.

17. Robert Ray Hamilton's room at Marymere.
The room became a study and library after Hamilton's death.

18. Warren and Wetmore's design for the Hamilton Fountain,
accepted by the New York Art Commission, 1904.

19. Hamilton Fountain, 76th Street and Riverside Drive, New York City. Photographed here in 1909, three years after its completion.

John Muir, who had passed through the area fifteen years earlier and wrote, "Climb the mountains and get their good tid-
ings. Nature's peace will flow into you as sunshine flows into
trees. The winds will blow their own freshness into you and
the storms their energy, while cares will drop away like autumn leaves."

For all of the aesthetic wonderment offered in the Tetons,
though, and for all that Ray abandoned when he left New
York, he arrived in Jackson Hole with one desire that remained unshakable—his desire to develop real estate. By mid-
July, only one month after settling in Jackson Hole, Ray wrote
to his friend Gil Spier in New York, requesting that he send
out, among other things, "five hundred cards printed on good
cardboard and rather nice looking," adding that he thought
"blue ink would look well." Ray needed the business cards for
a new venture that he had begun with a new business partner,
a man he met for the first time in Jackson Hole—John Dudley
Sargent.

Ray Hamilton shared a similar background with his new
partner in that they were both progenies of prominent, establishment families in the northeast. The Sargent name was associated with the same wealth, propriety, and social standing
in Maine and Massachusetts as was the Hamilton name in
New York. John and the artist John Singer Sargent shared
the same great-grandfather, Epes Sargent, though different
great-grandmothers as the result of death and remarriage.

John Dudley Sargent was born December 16, 1861, in
Machias, Maine, a small coastal town near the Canadian bor-
der—the only child of Henry Sargent and Alice Hemenway
Sargent. The Sargents of Machias acquired their wealth
through controlling interests in nearby mills, factories, quar-
ries, and shipyards. The Hemenways had similar invest-
ments, as well as an extensive real estate portfolio.

Henry and Alice met as students at the Washington Academy, a college preparatory school in nearby East Machias, and were married on July 18, 1861. Five months later, John Dudley was born—the timing of his birth was left unremarked upon in the close-knit community. The newlyweds moved into Alice's father's house in the center of Machias, at the corner of Court Street and Broadway. Henry Sargent was absent from Machias for long periods of time, serving for a time with the Union Army in the Civil War, and then striking out for California alone upon his discharge.

Just before John Dudley began his schooling, his grandmother escorted a stranger—"tall, dark and slender" as Sargent later described him—into their house and introduced him to John as Mr. Edward J. Talbot, a classmate of Henry and Alice at Washington Academy. During the gentleman's visit, his mother Alice pulled young John aside and quietly explained that Mr. Talbot was, in fact, his real father. Father and son never had the opportunity to form a relationship, however, as the Talbot family was involved in the maritime trade and in 1866, when John was five years old, Edward Talbot was lost at sea and pronounced dead.

Alice Sargent divorced her absent husband in 1872 and moved to Boston. John remained in Machias and was moved to the home of his paternal "grandfather," Ignatius Sargent, and away from the only father figure he ever really had, his maternal grandfather William Hemenway. Both the elder Hemenway and John's mother Alice passed away when John was thirteen years old. As close as the grandfather and grandson may have been, John was cut out of the elder Hemenway's will entirely as a result of being considered a bastard child. "The bottom dropped out of everything," John later admitted when discussing his grandfather's death.

By 1880, nineteen-year-old John Dudley Sargent had set out for the West, working as a cowpuncher in Colorado and a stagecoach driver in Wyoming. He returned to Machias periodically from 1880 to 1885 to court Adelaide Crane, the daughter of Leander and Edwina Crane. The Cranes were another prominent Machias family with ties to the lumber and maritime industries.

The Cranes were bitterly opposed to John's courtship of their daughter, but eventually acquiesced to their marriage. John and Adelaide were wed on February 22, 1885, in a private ceremony in her parents' home—a far cry from the society wedding that Leander and Edwina might have dreamed of for their daughter. A terse, two-sentence announcement in the *Machias Union* was the only public recognition of the couple's nuptials.

Not long after their marriage, John again drifted west while Adelaide moved to New Haven, Connecticut, with her parents where her father had a business venture. Adelaide gave birth to the Sargent's first child, Charles, in December 1885 while John was away.

Sargent traveled in an out of Jackson Hole on several occasions over the next two years and in August 1887, the entire Sargent family—John, Adelaide, Charles, and a second child, newborn Mary—entered Jackson Hole from Cheyenne. John had claimed land on a point on Jackson Lake, and it was there that he intended to settle his family. The Sargents returned to Machias for the winter, but by the summer of 1889, while Ray Hamilton's life was coming undone in Atlantic City, the Sargent clan had started their new life in the idyllic Wyoming Territory.

### *July 1890*

From its beginnings in Yellowstone National Park, the Snake River takes a meandering, elaborate path south, and then west, for 1,078 miles until it joins the Columbia River and empties, eventually, into the Pacific Ocean. Within the first fifty miles of the Snake's journey to the sea, the river fills a

438-foot-deep depression at the base of the Teton Mountains to form Jackson Lake. It is nearly impossible for the glacial movements of 15,000 years ago to form a more perfect union than that of the majestic, granite peaks of the Tetons reflected in the lake's crystalline water.

There are more than a dozen small islands dotted throughout Jackson Lake as well as numerous coves and inlets that protrude and recede along its jagged shoreline. One of the most spectacular vistas across Jackson Lake to the mountains on the opposite shore is seen from a peninsular spot of land just north of present-day Colter Bay. Shaped liked the thumb of a mitten, the land is situated roughly at the mid-point north and south of the fifteen-mile-long lake. It was here that John Dudley Sargent filed his homestead claim and planned to build Marymere, a hunting lodge and home for his family.

As passenger train travel to the West increased in the late 1800s, and with Yellowstone designated as America's first national park in 1872, an increasing number of visitors began to arrive in the surrounding area. Many were like Ray Hamilton, wealthy easterners who were avid hunters and fishermen. Thanks to the railroads, these citified outdoorsmen who had previously formed sporting clubs in the Adirondacks, or places like the Monroe Marsh Company in Michigan, could now venture farther west to indulge their pastimes.

Hotels in Yellowstone were built in increasing numbers to accommodate the influx of visitors. The first, McCartney's Hotel, opened in 1871 and was joined in the 1880s by Marshalls, the Shack Hotel, the Norris, Canyon Hotel, and Yancey's Pleasant Valley Hotel. Some hotels were better equipped to serve their guests than others. One guest who stayed at "Uncle John" Yancey's hotel wrote:

> We asked to be shown to our rooms. A pink cheeked little
> maid leads the way up a stairway of creaking, rough boards

and when we reach the top announces that the lady and her husband, meaning me and my daughter, can take Room No. 1. The little hallway in which we are standing is formed by undressed boards and the doors leading from it have large numbers marked upon them in chalk from one to five. Inspection of the bedrooms prove them to be large enough for a single bedstead with a box on which are washbowl, pitcher and part of a crash towel. Of the four window lights, at least one was broken in each room. The cracks in the wall are pasted up with strips of newspaper. No. 1, being the bridal chamber, was distinguished from the others by a four by six looking glass. The beds showed they were changed at least twice, once in the spring and once in the fall of the year. A little bribe on the side and a promise to keep the act of criminality a secret from Uncle John induces the maid to provide us with clean sheets.

Thirty miles south of Yellowstone, in Jackson Hole, Yancey's would have been considered a five-star establishment. The only shelter for the homesteaders, trappers, rogues, and ne'er-do-wells who roamed the Teton Valley were tents, lean-tos, and ramshackle log cabins that dotted the landscape. But as an increasingly sophisticated class of travelers began to trickle into Jackson Hole, Sargent saw the need for a better class of lodging. And so did Ray Hamilton.

There is no record of the introduction of Ray Hamilton and John Sargent, but it is possible that members of their respective families knew each other back east. What is known is that by mid-July, Hamilton and Sargent had reached a verbal agreement to jointly develop Marymere as a ranch and hunting lodge. No documents were kept by either man that provide a written record or any details of their partnership.

After five years of moving in and out of Jackson Hole, Sargent held a deep knowledge of the surroundings, and as Ray could plainly see, he also held the most desirable piece of prop-

erty on Jackson Lake. Hamilton likely had the luxe surroundings of the Monroe Marsh Company clubhouse in mind when
he envisioned Marymere, and he had the financial resources
to see that vision realized. He also had a wealth of connections
that he could tap into to build a loyal and deep-pocketed clientele for the ranch.

But the actual construction of Marymere was a far different
proposition than building a four-story brownstone in Brooklyn
or Manhattan on a fifty-foot-wide lot. There were no readily
available materials with which to build—no large blocks of
stone that could be quarried, cut to size, and then floated down
the lake to the job site, no sawmills to cut the necessary joists
and beams to support the structure, and no terra cotta embel-
lishments that could be ordered to add an elegant finish over
window and door openings. There were no steam-powered
drills available to dig out a foundation, no hoists and pulleys
to aid in the placement of material, and most importantly,
there were no carpenters or laborers nearby to put Marymere
together.

By the beginning of July, Ray had hired Swedish log work-
ers from Idaho in anticipation of having the main cabin under
roof by August first. John Dodge, another man raised in a
wealthy family who had drifted into Jackson Hole, wrote to a
friend that "Hamilton got log men from Ashton who rip-sawed
the logs on three sides and laid them with pegged corners."
Felled trees were dragged by teams of oxen to the site and cut
and finished as needed. The stones required to build the fireplaces were hauled out of the river and set in place as the
frame of the lodge went up around the hearths.

The Swedes did all of their work from whip-saw stands they
set up at the job site. The stands consisted of two sets of trestle legs that stood eight feet tall and roughly twelve feet apart.
They were utilized by two-man teams of sawyers—one man
working on top of the trestle and one man working below—

each man holding one end of a six-foot-long ripsaw and rhythmically cutting their way through each timber. The logs were hewed flat on the inside surfaces, and the dovetail-coped end joints were sometimes supplemented with wooden pegs. The same whip-saw stands were used to cut two-inch planks that were used for flooring and boards for window, door casements, and ceilings.

In a valley where cabins that measured 12 feet by 12 feet were considered spacious, the plans for Marymere were decidedly ambitious. The main building was to be 70 feet long, 22 feet deep, with a 12-foot-high gabled roof. There were seven rooms planned—a huge main room with a stone hearth flanked by a bedroom on either side, two more bedrooms in the rear, a study at the north end of the building, and a kitchen at the south. The plans called for an outdoor summer kitchen and icehouse to be built adjacent to the main building. Six windows in the front of Marymere looked out over Jackson Lake to the Tetons beyond.

Even as the lodge was still in construction, Sargent and his family moved into two rooms at the rear of the building and Hamilton occupied the front corner room that would eventually become the study. The sawyers camped in tents dotted around the property. The most optimistic schedule called for Marymere to be fully built and ready to host hunting parties that began arriving in Jackson Hole each year by mid-August.

Sargent had been steadily collecting fine furniture and china back east for the lodge and arranged for the items to be brought to the site in its various stages of completion. He even had a baby grand piano slung between two mules and brought to Marymere over the Conant Pass trail from Idaho in anticipation of the lodge's opening. The legs of the piano had been removed for transport, and it was not as wide as a modern-day Steinway, but it was still considered by those in Jackson Hole to be a worthy feat.

On July 14, Ray excitedly wrote to Gil Spier in New York asking for items that were not of much use to an outdoorsman, but were definitely of interest to a hotelier. Ray Hamilton needed linens:

8 single sheets.
10 double sheets.
2 doz. towels.
1 doz. fine towels.
12 pillow cases.
3 table cloths for table 6 x 4.
2 doz. napkins, large size.
Felt for table.

He also requested a taxidermy manual so that he could learn to mount deer heads to adorn the walls of the lodge. Ray asked that everything be "expressed to me at Market Lake Station, Utah and Northern Railroad, Union Pacific, Idaho." He then extended an invitation to Gil to visit Jackson Hole between August 15 and September 1.

*I am delighted by the country . . . The scenery is beautiful and up by the lake the country is full of game. I have seen several deers and two or three hundred antelopes. I have seen some bear tracks. There are lots of trout, blue and willow grouse, and sage hens almost as large as turkey around the lakes and the climate is superb . . . You must be sure to come out. You will have a first rate time and be sure to kill an elk, and perhaps a bear . . . We will meet you at Market Lake with a four-horse wagon and drive you to the foot of the lake and then take the boat to the house . . . You want thick underclothes, your shooting suit, shot-gun . . . I will have rum, and ammunition for*

*10 and 12-shot gun . . . I wish you could get Cass Moore
or someone else to come out with you . . . Of course you
understand, you and anyone you can bring out are to be
my guests. I hope you manage to come out, for I am sure
you will have a good time.*

*Hoping to see you out here soon, I am*

*Yours truly,*
*R.R. Hamilton*

When Ray was not busy with the construction of Marymere,
he set out on long rides around Jackson Lake to better famil-
iarize himself with the territory. He had not engaged in any
hunting since his arrival as it was too early in the season, but
he did have time to fish and realized he lacked everything he
needed for the lakes and streams around Marymere. Two
weeks after his initial request of Gil Spier, Ray sent his friend
another letter on July 29.

*Will you send me by mail to Kaintuck P.O., Bingham
Co., Idaho:*
   *24-1-0 hooks on snells.*
   *12 larger weak fish hooks on snells.*
   *3 doz. Hooks, without snells, about the size or a little
      larger than the 1-0 hooks.*
   *6 double-gut short leaders.*
   *3 little tip pieces and half a dozen guide rings for a fly
      rod.*
   *12 small sinkers.*
   *If you can send it by mail, some varnish for rods and a
      brush.*

Ray also noted that "our log house is not up yet, but hope it
will be by the middle of the month. We are having some trou-

ble getting our things hauled in, as the mountain trail is pretty steep."

By mid-August, the construction of Marymere was close enough to completion that the urge to hunt that had tugged at Ray since his arrival in the valley could finally be satisfied. Hamilton and Sargent kept a storehouse near the southern tip of Jackson Lake, South Landing, where material for Marymere that had been hauled over the mountain passes from Idaho was stored until needed at the job site. On Friday morning, August 22, Ray informed the others at the site that he was taking the Sheridan Trail south to the area around the storehouse, six miles away, and that he would return to Marymere by sundown in two or three days.

John Sargent tried to talk Hamilton out of going out solo. He cautioned that Ray was still new to the area and that it was too easy to lose track of a known trail while off in the forest hunting. He also warned that as Ray was still a stranger to many of the inhabitants of Jackson Hole, some of them being decidedly unsavory characters, he was susceptible to falling prey to men of bad intentions. Finally, Sargent tried to reason, should Ray have any kind of accident while out alone, there would be no one to assist him.

Hamilton was having none of it. Sargent's wife, Adelaide, saw that her husband's words of caution fell on deaf ears and she joined in the attempt to dissuade Ray from going alone. When it became clear that Ray was adamant about leaving solo, Sargent insisted that Hamilton take the best mare in camp, Baby. And knowing that Ray had arrived in Jackson Hole with proper riding boots, but no spurs, Sargent lent his partner his own. By late Friday morning, Hamilton hit the trail, his hunting dog, Jocko, walking stride for stride with Baby. John Sargent departed Marymere shortly after Ray, telling his wife and the sawyers that he was riding over to

Kaintuck to pick up mail and that he would return himself in five days.

The two or three days that Hamilton planned to be away hunting had passed on Monday, August 25, and he had yet to return to Marymere. In the twilight of Wednesday evening, August 27, John Sargent was nearing home from his trip to Idaho. He stopped at the storehouse at South Landing before riding the last six miles to Marymere and found a note from Hamilton stating that he (Ray) was returning to the lodge on Tuesday evening, August 26, coincidentally, the one-year anniversary of the stabbing in Atlantic City.

As stars emerged overhead, John Sargent rode the last leg of his journey up the Sheridan Trail, reaching Marymere under an inky black sky at 9:00 P.M. He expected to find his partner at home, and to see what Hamilton had bagged on his first foray out of camp. Instead, Adelaide told him anxiously, "Hamilton has not returned from his hunt." Sargent grasped the urgency of the situation and sent messengers from Marymere at first light to turn out the best mountaineers in the lower valley to search for his partner. By Friday morning, August 29, one week after Ray had left Marymere, the search began in earnest.

John Holland, one of the original homesteaders to settle in Jackson Hole in 1884, led one group of men. Dr. James O. Green, a nonpracticing physician from back east who was a frequent visitor to the valley, joined up as well. A number of other small groups formed to fan out on either side of the Snake River and methodically make their way toward Ray Hamilton's last known location, South Landing. Just east of South Landing stood an unnamed mountain with an elevation of 7,700 feet. The search parties agreed that if anyone found Hamilton, they were to climb to its summit and set a fire to signal to everyone involved in the search that the wayward hunter had been found. The anonymous peak gained a name, Signal Mountain, as a result of its place in the search for Ray Hamilton—the name exists to this day.

For the next four days, no one saw any reason for a fire to be lit on the mountain, but a clue regarding the whereabouts of Ray Hamilton was finally found on Monday, September 1. That evening, Holland's party spotted the campfire of Dr. Green and rode to him, somberly explaining that earlier that day they had found Baby and Jocko, but there was still no sign of Hamilton.

Ray had apparently shot and field-dressed an antelope, as the hams and antlers were still tied to his horse. Baby's saddle had been twisted so hard that it cut into the horse's back and left open sores that were now festering, and the ends of the hams had been tugged at and gnawed off in bits by the hungry dog. The state of the two animals did not offer encouragement regarding the fate of Ray Hamilton.

The men planned to work in tandem the next morning, walking in parallel on either side of the Snake, with one man navigating the middle of the river in a small boat. Green rode on horseback just ahead of the men, acting as a lookout for possible signs of Hamilton's presence. At 9:30 in the morning, Green spotted two pine trees on the far shore that had fallen into the river, their roots still planted in the riverbank. They rested over a pool of still water near the shore, away from the rushing current of the main flow of the Snake—dead water as it was called. Green reckoned that if Hamilton had an accident trying to ford the river, his body was likely to have washed downstream into one of these pools and hung up in the detritus along the shore.

Green was unable to reach the trees from horseback and called out for Holland to go over and take a look. The old homesteader scooted down to the shore and spotted a bloated body, facedown, its arms and legs extended, caught in the branches of the fallen pines. He was able to turn the man's head and see that he had been in the water long enough for some fish to begin nibbling away at the soft tissue of his lips and ear lobes, but that the easily recognizable bushy mustache of the recently arrived man from New York was still intact. "Here he is," Holland somberly announced.

One year after suffering public humiliation as a result of the events in Atlantic City, and after traveling 2,000 miles from his home and family in New York to start life anew, the progeny of one of the most notable families in the history of the United States lay lifelessly bobbing in two feet of water in the Snake River. At age thirty-nine, Robert Ray Hamilton was dead.

### *September 2, 1890*

The mountaineers who found Ray Hamilton didn't stop to mourn the man caught in the pine trees—he wasn't the first hunter to be claimed by the wilderness, and he surely wouldn't be the last. Instead, they got to work. Dr. Green tossed a picket rope out to John Holland, who tied it under Hamilton's arms so that the other men could pull his body ashore. Once they had him on land, one of the searchers unfolded a canvas tarpaulin brought on the search expressly for this unfortunate situation.

Before the men wrapped Hamilton's body, Dr. Green, from force of habit, performed a physical examination to determine if anything untoward had led to Hamilton's death. He wrote in his journal that Ray's "clothing and other articles about the body were entirely undisturbed and there was no sign of violence nor wound of any kind to be seen." The only clue to a possible cause of the drowning were the clumps of sedge wrapped around the spurs of Hamilton's boots. The men surmised that Hamilton may have gotten tangled up in a cluster of the sedge that grew in the shallows of the river and was thrown from his horse when he tried to extricate himself. Curiously though, there were no signs of contusions or bleeding as there would have been if Hamilton had gotten dashed against a boulder in a fall.

For the moment, any theory of what may have happened was set aside so that the grim work of recovery could continue. Green and Holland compiled a list of the personal effects found on Hamilton's body: a penknife, a small canvas bag of wet tobacco, some soaked matches, a handkerchief, a pencil, a leather book of trout flies, three silver dollars, and one cent. They also noted a medium-size gold hunting case, stem-winding watch—the waterlogged timepiece had stopped at 9:32 P.M. It appeared to the men handling Hamilton's body that he foolishly tried to ford the river in darkness, something that even a more experienced mountaineer would not attempt without a companion.

Holland and Green both signed their names to the inventory of personal items taken off of Ray's body, and after he was wrapped in the tarpaulin, Holland's men hauled him into the boat to be taken upriver to South Landing. When John Sargent was notified of the situation, he rode the six miles down to the storehouse to make the official identification of his now-deceased partner. Before leaving Marymere, however, Sargent had the foresight to direct two of the Swedish sawyers, Gottlieb Bieri and Christian Aeschbacher, to stop their work on the lodge and to begin making a coffin.

### Notification

When the cortège from South Landing arrived at Marymere on September 2, John Sargent was faced with two immediate tasks: informing Ray's next of kin about his partner's sad demise and arranging a proper burial. Unbeknownst to Sargent, while Ray Hamilton was floating lifelessly in the Snake

River, Gil Spier had composed and posted a letter from New
York with what was intended as good news—he and Cass de
Moore were about to embark for Jackson Hole.

NEW YORK, *Aug. 26, 1890.*

*Dear Ray,*

*Cass and I leave here for your ranch on Friday morning,
the 29th inst., and expect us to be at Market Lake station
on the evening of the 1st or morning of the 2nd of
September.*

*I have never rec'd any word from you, whether you ever
rec'd any of my letters or things I sent out to you, but I
suppose you did, else I certainly would have heard the
growls from the West.*

*Cass' little girl has been sick, but I think she will be all
right by the time we leave.*
*Hoping to see you sound and well on the 1st of next
month, I am*

> *Yours truly,*
> *Gil*

When Ray didn't appear at the train station in Idaho to
meet his longtime friends, Gil and Cass arranged to get to
Jackson Hole on their own. "We left the railroad at Market
Lake Station, drove over to Kaintuck, then down by the basin
and through Teton Pass into Wyoming. We traveled part of
the way in a wagon and part of the way on horseback, and
then over the lake in a boat," Spier later recounted. They arrived at the storehouse at South Landing on Friday, September 5, three days after disembarking the train at Market
Lake.

While Spier and Moore were coming over the mountains from Idaho, Dr. Green made tracks north to Yellowstone, where he packed up his belongings and started farther north for the nearest telegraph office, three hundred miles away in Helena, Montana. While James Green didn't know Ray Hamilton personally, he understood the gravity of who he had found in the Snake River. Depending on the weather and availability of fresh horses along the route, Green could be expected to reach Helena in six to ten days.

Green had good reason to know the location of the telegraph station nearest to Jackson Hole—he was the eldest son of Norvin Green, chairman of the Western Union Telegraph Co., and a man of spectacular wealth. The elder Green often remarked that the Western Union's 800,000 miles of wire would make a quadruple line to the moon. Norvin Green lived primarily in Louisville, Kentucky, but as one of the board of directors of the New York Mercantile Exchange, he kept a residence in New York on Madison Avenue and socialized in some of the same circles as the Hamilton family. Upon James Green's arrival in Helena, he wired his father in an effort to see if Norvin Green could use his contacts in New York to determine who was the most appropriate member of the Hamilton family to inform about Ray's death.

While Green was in route to Helena, John Sargent composed a letter to mail to Schuyler Hamilton Jr., informing him of his brother's death. He stopped at the storehouse on his way to Kaintuck to post his letter and found Gil and Cass, freshly arrived and waiting for Ray to escort them on the last leg of their trip up to Marymere. John Sargent introduced himself to Hamilton's friends and informed them of the grim news that Ray had been found dead in the Snake River three days before. He explained that Hamilton had since been buried under a stand of pine trees at Marymere and then invited them up to the property to view their friend's final resting place and determine what they would like done with his personal effects.

Sargent drafted a letter to mail to Schuyler Jr. so that he could personally explain the unfortunate circumstances surrounding the death of his brother. Cass Moore drafted his own account of what he and Gil discovered upon reaching Jackson Hole and both letters were mailed to Schuyler Hamilton Jr. in Ossining, New York.

Sargent outlined the timeline of events in his letter to Schuyler and described the conditions in the section of the Snake River where Ray's body was found. He also explained his decision to bury Ray at Marymere and to not have his body prepared to be sent back east: "He is buried close to our house on a spot overlooking Marymere and the Teton Mountains. He once told me he would rather be buried here should anything happen. I know he was going to change his residence and make this his home."

Sargent closed with a heartfelt note to Schuyler:

*Although we have known him but a short time, we grieve for him from the bottom of our hearts. I have done everything I could do and will take care of his things until I hear from you. In sorrow and respect, I am faithfully yours . . .*

*John D. Sargent.*

While Schuyler may have been skeptical of such tragic news coming from a complete stranger, the letter from Cass de Moore, one of Ray's best friends, corroborating the tragic circumstances of Ray's death, stood as confirmation that the news indeed was true.

*Lake Mary Mere, Sept. 5, 1890*

DEAR SCHUYLER:

*Gillie and I have just arrived at the lake and met*
*Mr. Sargent, who was on the way out to mail the letter*
*telling you of poor Ray's sad death. You can imagine*
*that we feel dreadfully and have no desire to continue*
*our hunting expedition. But Sargent wants us to come to*
*the house, up the lake twelve miles and see Ray's grave.*

*If you will allow me a word of advice, I should*
*recommend you not to attempt to have Ray's body*
*removed now. It could not be done. If you write to*
*Mr. Sargent, he will choose the best time to remove the*
*body and notify you. But this I say, knowing that Ray*
*had expressed a wish to be buried here, I have tried to*
*let you have such information as might be of use to you,*
*and have kept the man waiting until I write. Will you*
*please send word to them at home, Hattie and mother,*
*that we are all well, and will probably stay here some*
*time, as Mr. Sargent seems to want us to. Please try and*
*do this if you can. In all your trouble, sincerely,*

CASIMIR DE R. MOORE

James Green's telegram to Schuyler arrived from Helena on
Saturday, September 13, beating the letters from Sargent and
de Moore to Ossining by a day. With the telegram and two letters in hand on Sunday, it was Schuyler's duty to travel to the
Windsor Hotel in Manhattan and inform the General about
the fate of his eldest son.

But before Schuyler could break the news about Ray to his
father, newspaper reporters were tipped—either by a telegraph operator who was in their pocket or by someone close to

Norvin Green—and had the details. Robert Ray Hamilton was back on the front pages, featured in a most unfortunate story.

## MR. HAMILTON'S SAD DEATH

### *No Doubt of the Unfortunate Man's Tragic Fate.*

THE STORY OF HIS DROWNING TOLD
BY THE KEEPER OF THE RANCH,
WHO RECOVERED THE BODY.

A reporter managed to locate the General at the Windsor Hotel and found a man in distress. "I have served in the war and have had my skull fractured and bullet wounds and sword thrusts, and am accustomed to shocks, but this is a hard one for me to bear. I am now waiting for the arrival of my son who lives in Sing Sing. When he arrives we shall determine what course to pursue. At present I am entirely at a loss what to do and too grieved to talk much about the matter."

The General fell silent, lost in his thoughts about his son. He resumed speaking by acknowledging that he found these first reports about his son's death to be curious, at best. "I have received absolutely no private information about the drowning, if drowning it was. Isn't it possible that there might have been foul play in Ray's death? Understand, I do not make such an assertion, but the accounts of his death which I have read in the papers are extremely mysterious and unsatisfactory."

The General wasn't the only person to ponder the death of Ray Hamilton with a raised eyebrow. Multiple rumors regarding the death of Robert Ray Hamilton, all of them based on the premise that his alleged drowning was no accident, began to echo throughout Jackson Hole not long after his tarpaulin-wrapped body was placed in the hastily made coffin and laid to rest at Marymere.

One held, simply, that Hamilton had committed suicide. But Edward Mitchell, U.S. attorney for the Southern District of New York and a friend of Ray's, told the press that "I knew Mr. Hamilton well, and consider that he was more sinned against than sinning. I do not believe he committed suicide. I am satisfied that when the details of his death are received they will show that he was accidentally drowned in the manner indicated by the newspaper reports."

The most preposterous of the rumors was that "the conspirators who had pursued Hamilton with such pernacity and malevolence as to palm off a child not his own, would be equal to having him followed on his western trip and dispatched with little evidence to show assassination." To believe this theory, one would have to accept that Eva Hamilton, clearly the brightest and most manipulative mind among her co-conspirators, Josh Mann and Anna Swinton, would have been responsible for the planning of her husband's death. The fact that she was behind bars and hardly in a position to organize a murder that was to take place 2,000 miles away did not lend credence to this rumor.

Another theory that was almost equally as senseless was that Hamilton faked his own death to avoid any possible financial liability in his bitter divorce from Eva. This theory required an unlikely alliance among multiple accomplices, including Dr. Green and John Holland, who didn't know Ray Hamilton, and had no outward interest in being involved in a complicated plot to allow a stranger to begin a new life under an assumed identity.

The most pervasive rumor regarding Hamilton's death was also considered by the habitués of Jackson Hole to be the most plausible—the central figure in this accusation of foul play was Ray's partner, John Sargent. Hamilton and Sargent did not have a written agreement to develop Marymere, but shortly after they formed their partnership, Hamilton took a lead role in the construction of the lodge, hiring the sawyers and directing their activity. Perhaps Sargent felt that Hamilton had assumed too prominent a role in the project that was also meant to serve as a home for the Sargent family.

Sargent's reputation as an eccentric, and possibly unstable, character fueled the suspicions. Dr. John Mitchell, accompanied by the western writer Owen Wister, traveled through the valley around the time of Hamilton's death and recorded in his journal that "all Jackson's Hole, a community of scalawags, renegades, discharged soldiers and predestined stinkers, unite in the belief that Sargent killed H."

Like the rumor of Hamilton's faked death, the accusations of nefarious circumstances surrounding the demise of Ray Hamilton never truly went away. Ralph Worthington, a wealthy merchant and banker from Cleveland, who had hunted in Jackson Hole with three of Andrew Carnegie's nephews, proclaimed that "Hamilton's death was due to foul play and not to accident." Worthington explained to the *New York Times* that when Hamilton's body was pulled from the river, "water grass was found entangled in his spurs," but that "the ford in the Snake River where the accident is said to have occurred is paved with white boulders, and that there is no sign of water grass in the river for some distance."

He added that "the depth of water in the ford is only fifteen inches on average, and a horse could easily wade on either side fifty feet away." Further, he related that he had spoken to guides and hunters in the area who agreed "that it would be folly to try to ride from the ford to Hamilton's lodge after nightfall and that Hamilton well knew the danger." Worthington closed by affirming that "members of the Mormon colony near Rexburg (home of the sawyers working at Marymere) had good reasons to believe that Hamilton met with foul play."

It was not lost on the men working at Marymere that John Sargent left the site on the same morning that Ray Hamilton departed for his hunt. What role any of the sawyers played in disseminating this nugget of information to the foul-play theorists is unknown, but the fact that there were no witnesses to the route that Sargent took to Kaintuck did nothing to stop the advance of the accusation.

## Eva

The General and Schuyler Jr. weren't the only people close to Ray Hamilton to be shocked by his death in Wyoming. When news of Hamilton's drowning reached Trenton State Prison, Keeper Patterson informed Eva of the drowning that claimed her husband's life. She stood in disbelief for a moment before collapsing onto the floor, completely prostrated. Once revived, Eva realized that their divorce had not been finalized at the time of Ray's death—she remained his lawful wife, and as such was entitled to a claim a portion of his estate, regardless of what his will may have stated.

Newspapers archly noted of Eva's reaction to Ray's death that "whether her grief was due to the sudden shock or real sorrow or fear she would lose her share in Robert Ray's estate is hard to tell." Lawyers and judges were interviewed for their legal opinions regarding the Hamilton divorce case and the prevailing opinion was that it could not legally go forward as a result of Ray's death. If that contention was indeed correct, one attorney opined that "Eva would be the lawful widow of Robert Ray Hamilton, with a dower right to his property unless his heirs should win a subsequent suit declaring that she was not a lawful widow."

The news of Hamilton's death hadn't been public for more than forty-eight hours and already the press appeared to be setting up a courtroom showdown between the Hamilton

family and Ray's incarcerated wife. The *New York Times* led
their front page on September 15 with the headline "Death
Has Divorced Them." The whereabouts of Hamilton's legal
team were breathlessly reported: Elihu Root was said to be
vacationing in Europe and Samuel Clarke in the Adirondacks. Those close to the Hamilton family telegraphed Ray's
legal associate, Edward Vollmer, himself on holiday in York-
ville, Wisconsin, and requested that he return to New York
immediately.

Ray Hamilton had revised his Last Will and Testament
after Eva's conviction the previous September and before
beginning divorce proceedings, leaving his estranged wife
entirely out of his estate. Ed Vollmer and D. W. Couch Jr., a
clerk who worked in their office, provided their signatures as
witnesses to the document. Couch told the *Times* that the will
"was in Mr. Vollmer's keeping, as well as Hamilton's business
affairs," including the deeds to properties in the city that were
in the deceased's name. It was in the best interest of Hamilton's family and heirs to have the will probated as expeditiously as possible while Eva was behind bars and unable to
insert herself into Ray's affairs.

Eva knew her rights, though, and stood ready to exercise
them whether she was in prison or not. She had also not lost
her ability to detect an opportunity for fraud and deception
while at Trenton. Sometime in September, around the time of
Ray's death, Eva learned that pardons in New Jersey weren't
granted merely based on time served in relation to the sever-
ity of the crime for which one was convicted. A cash payment
was highly suggested in order for the Court of Pardons to conduct a proper hearing of a prisoner's appeal. In Eva's case, the
payment was set at $1,000.

The cash-for-pardons scheme was only one piece of the
rampant corruption in the Democratic administration of Governor Leon Abbett. A later investigation showed that "from

the Executive Department to the janitor of the State House, the evidence is that thieving, thugism and blackmail were predominating characteristics. A premium was set upon ballot-box stuffing, and ruffianism, pardons by the score awaiting any who worked in Democracy's cause and for 'da gang.'"

Aware that Mrs. Hamilton had made several appearances before the Court of Pardons, all of them for naught, Head Keeper Patterson approached her with a suggestion as to how she may have a better chance of success. He explained that the court and Governor Abbett gave more credence to cases brought before them by certain attorneys and that her current counsel, ex-Judge William Hoffman and Charles Fuller, both Republicans, were not held in high regard by the Democrat governor. Patterson later admitted that he was requested to influence her to put up the right amount of money to the right person before she could secure her pardon.

The man that Abbett suggested to formally present Eva's case to the Court of Pardons was William C. Heppenheimer, an influential Democratic politician from Jersey City, and the Speaker of the New Jersey State Assembly at the time of her application. Eva managed to secure a check for $1,000 from a bank account in her own name, likely arranged through Charles Fuller—Patterson confirmed that he had seen the bank check that Heppenheimer received. And while it was later revealed that the Court of Pardons "was a mere political and money-making institution, run in the interest of the Democratic machine and a few chosen lawyers," it is doubtful that Eva Hamilton cared one whit.

On Tuesday afternoon, November 25, the Court of Pardons took up the petition of Mrs. Eva Hamilton and after only a brief consideration of her case, they granted the pardon by unanimous vote. Heppenheimer, accompanied by Eva's counsel, Charles Fuller, dashed from the courtroom to the secretary of state's office to secure the physical pardon document, and then climbed in a taxi to be taken directly to the state prison where they presented the pardon to Keeper Patterson. When Eva was called from her cell and informed of her immediate release, "Mrs. Hamilton was deeply affected, and, burying her face in her hands, wept bitterly for some time."

After serving a little more than one year of her two-year sentence, Eva Hamilton was a free woman, though she didn't remain in New Jersey for even one hour. She stepped outside of Trenton State Prison on the arm of Charles Fuller at 5:00 P.M., and the two of them boarded a 5:50 P.M. train back to New York.

# CHAPTER NINE
## EVA BEGINS HER FIGHT

*Autumn 1890*

While Eva was arranging for the kickback necessary to be granted a pardon in New Jersey, Robert Ray Hamilton's Last Will and Testament was filed for probate in New York. The co-executors of Ray's estate—his cousin, Edmund Baylies and his friend, Gil Spier—filed the document on Thursday, October 2, and Hamilton's will was made public and presented before Justice Rastus Seneca Ransom in New York County Surrogate Court on Monday, November 17. The beneficiaries named in the will were limited to close family, one friend, and a gift to the City of New York.

Ray owned a share of the prestigious Prescott House, located at the corner of Broadway and Spring Street. Prescott House was considered to be one of the finest hotels in New York and a destination for the cognoscenti. The highly ornamented entrance hall was befitting of the hotel's clientele, and a considerable collection of the furniture was made to order in Paris and London. Ray's ownership in Prescott House was bequeathed to his brother, Schuyler Jr.

Although it had been established that Beatrice Ray Hamilton was clearly not a blood relation, Ray felt some degree of empathy for the child swept up in the maelstrom of his relationship with Eva. His will specified that Beatrice was to receive an annuity of $1,200 per year, to be paid in monthly installments of $100 for the duration of her natural life. Ray's cousin, Edmund Baylies, was appointed as guardian of the person and estate of Beatrice Ray.

Ray Hamilton's aunt, Nathalie Baylies, was to retain all of his personal property with the exception of his books, silver, and jewelry, which were to be divided equally between three cousins: Edmund Baylies, Cornelia Lowell, and Walter Baylies.

Hamilton's hunting buddy and co-executor of his estate, Gil Spier, was bequeathed Ray's guns, rifles, boats, dogs, and his share of the Monroe Marsh Company, with the instruction to sell anything he did not desire to keep for his own use. The remainder of Ray's estate, with one exception, was to be divided equally between his brother's children: Violet, Schuyler III, and Gertrude Hamilton.

That one exception was for his executors, "as soon as possible, to expend the sum of ten thousand dollars in the purchase and erection of an ornamental fountain which I give and bequeath to the Mayor, Aldermen and Commonality of the City of New York, provided that such fountain may be erected in one of the streets, squares or public places in said City."

While this provision would prove to be contentious in the years following, it was not fraught with the same animus as the one noticeable omission in Ray's will—Evangeline L. Hamilton. And it didn't take long for Eva and her attorney, Charles Fuller, to recognize the slight. On November 19, less than forty-eight hours after Hamilton's will was made a matter of public record, Eva Hamilton, acting through her attorney, filed objections with the court.

Eva Hamilton contended that she was Ray's lawful widow, and as such, she legally held dower rights to a third of his property, regardless of whether or not she was actually named in his will. Her sights were set higher, though, than obtaining

a thirty-three percent share of property held in Ray's name—
her objections sought to invalidate Hamilton's will in its entirety in hopes of securing a greater portion of her husband's
estate. One might assume that Eva wasn't so interested in
Ray's guns, rifles, and boats, but a collection of silver and jewelry, not to mention real estate dotted through Manhattan
and Brooklyn, surely had her attention.

As Eva's release from Trenton State Prison had not oc-
curred when the will was filed, the objections were filed by
Charles Fuller with the acknowledgment that "Evangeline L.
Hamilton is absent from and not now within the County of
New York." Fuller raised, on Eva's behalf, four objections in
seeking to invalidate Ray's will:

   I.  That the alleged execution of the will was not his free
      and unconstrained or voluntary act.
  II.  He was not of sound mind, memory and understand-
      ing when the will was purported to be executed.
 III.  He was under the controlling will of one or more per-
      sons by whom he was unduly influenced . . . and
      deprived of free, unrestrained and independent action
      and will.
 IV.  That the paper propounded for probate is invalid as a
      last will and testament and is illegal and void.

Any of the named beneficiaries in Hamilton's will were free
to answer Eva's objections. On December 3, one week after
Eva Hamilton was released from jail, Henry Sprague, an attorney representing Schuyler Jr., stood before Judge Ransom
and filed "Answers to Objections" with the court. Sprague's
answer was brief: "that so-called Evangeline L. Hamilton was
never the lawful wife of Robert Ray Hamilton and is not one of
his heirs or next of kin therefore, she could not be his lawful
widow." That premise, asserted by the beneficiaries, "denies

the right of the person styling herself as Evangeline L. Hamilton to appear and contest the probate of the will of Robert Ray Hamilton."

Judge Ransom responded to Fuller's Objections and Sprague's Answers by directing his commentary to Eva's attorney, Mr. Fuller. "Her status is denied and her right to object to the probate of this paper is denied, and I think the burden is on you to show that she has status in this court."

By this time, Eva had secured her release from Trenton and had been a free woman for all of seven weeks before she found herself back in a familiar place—a courtroom. If she had any hope of receiving as much as a penny from Ray Hamilton's estate, she would need to prove to Judge Ransom that she was indeed Ray Hamilton's lawful wife. Given the investigative work conducted by Tommy Byrnes in advance of Eva's criminal trial, and the depositions taken in Elmira the previous January in anticipation of Ray's divorce proceeding, proof of a lawful union would require Eva and Charles Fuller to construct a believable account before Rastus Ransom.

### Monday, January 12, 1891
### Surrogate Court

The Hall of Records, a three-story Greek Revival building on Park Row at the foot of City Hall Park, had seen better days. Built in 1758, it was originally constructed as New York's Debtors Prison—a square, unadorned three-story stone edifice capped by an octagonal cupola. By the 1830s, the building had outlived its usefulness as a prison and was converted to a fireproof repository to house municipal documents. The exterior of the so-called new Hall of Records was tarted up with elements of the Greek style—portico, columns, and pediment—and the cupola was replaced by a fire-retardant flat roof.

The City Registrar, Street Commissioners, Office of the Comptroller, and the Surrogate Court all called the building

home at various points in the last half of the nineteenth century. While the exterior was refurbished in its entirety, the
city made exceedingly bad use of the interior—it was "patent
to the eyes and nose of whoever ventures within its dirty
precincts . . . within are recorded all of the bad smells which
have been known on this island from the earliest Dutch
times."

On January 12, a forty-degree, drizzly Monday morning, six
attorneys stood before Judge Ransom in the dank Surrogate
Court to determine Eva's legal standing in her contest of Ray
Hamilton's will. Charles Fuller and an associate, Lewis J.
Morrison, stood for the Contestant, Evangeline Hamilton. Fuller
was strikingly handsome, debonair, and presented himself to
all as a man of the world. It was said that "he presents a picture suggesting the fact that it is an easy matter for him to
gain victories in the courts if the appearance and powers of
counsel have anything to do with convincing judges."

The estimable Elihu Root represented the Proponents in
the case—the family and estate of his good friend, Ray Hamilton. The calm and self-confident Mr. Root may not have been
as dashing as Charles Fuller, but his reputation for possessing
one of the sharpest minds in the city was well known by everyone in New York legal circles. His practice was "characterized
by exhaustive work in the preparation of his cases and a keen
intellectuality which penetrates to the marrow of things." The
sheaf of depositions and list of witnesses with which Root entered the courtroom were testaments to his thorough preparation. John O'Conor, an associate at Root & Clarke, was there
to assist his firm's senior partner.

Henry Sprague, the attorney who filed the answers to the
objections raised by Fuller, was in the courtroom as counsel
for Schuyler Hamilton Jr. Sprague was not in attendance to
play an active role in the hearing, but rather to ensure that

the younger Hamilton was kept well apprised of the maneu-
verings in the proceedings.

The other attorney in the group of six, Sherman W. Knevals,
was a familiar face to Rastus Ransom. Knevals and Ransom
were former partners in a law firm that began its tenure as
Arthur, Phelps, Knevals and Ransom. Benjamin Phelps left
the firm in 1872 to become district attorney for New York
County. Chester A. Arthur remained in the firm until he was
sworn in as James A. Garfield's vice president in 1881.
Knevals and Ransom remained partners until Ransom's elec-
tion as Surrogate in 1887. For this case, Ransom named Knevals
as a Special Guardian to the Court, representing the legal interests of the infant, Beatrice Hamilton.

Nearly eighteen months after the stabbing in Atlantic City,
it was clear that the public's appetite for anything related to
the tawdry tale of Ray and Eva Hamilton had not diminished.
Every morning, the courtroom filled to capacity with spectators—the last of the curious to enter on any given day stood
against the back wall for the duration of the day's hearing.
The public was joined each day by one of the executors of his
will, Gil Spier (Edmund Baylies was ill and could not attend),
Ray's brother, Schuyler Jr. and his wife, Gertrude. Ray's father, General Hamilton, now nearing seventy years of age and
in ill health, attended only sporadically.

At the outset of the hearing, even such an accomplished attorney as Charles Fuller admitted to being flummoxed by the
judge's position. "I am not familiar with the procedure in a
case like this where the burden is on me to prove the fact of
widowhood." Judge Ransom held firm to his charge: "I think
the burden is on you to show that she has status in this
Court." Eva Hamilton, the "she" who Ransom referred to, was
conspicuous by her absence at the start of the hearing.

Fuller began by calling Reverend Edson Burr, the minister

in Paterson, New Jersey, who married Ray and Eva in January 1889. He recounted the circumstances of the wedding and stated that the Hamiltons' marriage certificate was properly submitted to the Bureau of Vital Statistics in Paterson. Burr reiterated that "I asked both of the contracting parties as to any prior marriage. Each of them said they had not been married before."

Elihu Root couldn't glean much additional substance from Reverend Burr in his cross-examination. He asked the reverend if he could identify Mrs. Hamilton from a photograph, to which Burr replied, "I would not be able to recognize her." Perhaps having a sense that Judge Ransom was unhappy with Eva's absence, Root used Burr's response to make a point to the judge that "there will be some testimony here which will depend, to some extent, upon identification of the person, and I think we are entitled to have her come to court."

Judge Ransom readily concurred. "I know of no manner in which she can be compelled to be present by any order that I can make in the present stage of the case. The fact that she is absent when her presence is necessary to enlighten the Court on this question of her status may be disadvantageous to her in considering the question."

The hearing was less than one hour old and Fuller was stymied. His client was nowhere to be found (an aide was sent out to locate her), he had no legal framework on which to build his case, and the only witness who could credibly attest to a legal marriage between the Hamiltons was on and off of the witness stand within a matter of minutes. When Burr concluded, Fuller, as if sheepishly turning his palms up in resignation, told Judge Ransom, "that is all the witnesses I have present. That is my *prima facie* case."

Conversely, Elihu Root had a surfeit of witnesses at the ready, all of them prepared to testify to the marital relationship of Eva and Josh Mann. Root's penchant for the exhaustive work in the preparation of his cases was on full display before Judge Ransom. The same witnesses who were deposed in Elmira the previous January for Ray Hamilton's annulment were now crowded into Surrogate Court, waiting to be called by the Proponent's counsel. He brought them forward, one after another, in a relentless barrage of testimony that caused severe damage to Eva's hopes of gaining a share of Ray Hamilton's estate.

William Steele, Eva's brother, began the parade of witnesses by stating that while the Steele family was living in New Albany Township, Pennsylvania, in 1885, Eva and Josh "lived there together, occupied the same room and were known by my father and mother, brothers and sister as man and wife." Alice Steele, William's wife, followed her husband and testified that in 1888, Evangeline "said she was married in Philadelphia and she was the wife of Joshua Mann."

William Foyle, a lawyer working in Dallas, Pennsylvania, testified that Josh Mann identified himself in a criminal court proceeding as being married to Eva for about seven years. John Mingos, proprietor of the Kennard House in Laceyville, stated that Josh and Eva registered at his hotel in 1888 as "J.J. Mann and wife, New York." Samuel Adams, father-in-law of Eva's brother Joseph Steele, testified that Josh and Eva "boarded and bedded there at my home as Mr. and Mrs. Mann." Adams's wife, Llewellyn, followed her husband to the witness stand and corroborated his testimony. It is doubtful that the attendees paid much attention to Mrs. Adams's account, though, for as she spoke, Eva Hamilton made a dramatic entrance into the courtroom.

Both the spectators and attorneys grew silent when Eva entered the Surrogate Court. Although her face was almost entirely concealed by a black widow's veil, her presence was felt by all in attendance. She walked in with a regal air, head held high as she made way to her counsel's side. Instead of immediately taking her chair, she turned and gazed around the courtroom, her skirts almost brushing those of Schuyler Jr.'s wife, Gertrude, as if scanning the crowd for a jury with whom to make eye contact. When she realized that there was no jury for this hearing, she smoothed her dress and sat next to Charles Fuller.

Earlier in the morning, Fuller had told the judge that Eva's absence was due to a bout of pneumonia, but she appeared to all to be fit and healthy. If anything, Eva appeared to be agitated, angrily whispering to Fuller as if it was his fault that she was not in court from the outset of the hearing.

Fuller maintained his focus and cross-examined each of Root's witnesses in hopes that they would contradict themselves, or each other, but he was unable to produce any cracks in their stories. Root probably could have rested his case after the testimony of the witnesses from Pennsylvania with a reasonable confidence that Ransom would deny Eva status to contest the will. However, the meticulous attorney was far from done. Root sought to make resoundingly clear, as a matter of public record, that Ray's marriage to Eva was a complete and total sham, and that she deserved absolutely nothing from the Hamilton family. Accordingly, the deluge of witnesses continued.

Francis Leake, a bookkeeper at the Union Dime Savings Institution in Manhattan, produced ledger books for accounts held in the name of Eva L. Mann. Below Eva's name on the registration form were three boxes that could be checked for marital status: Married, Single, or Widow. Eva had checked the Married box. Below the boxes, on the line to enter "the name of Wife or Husband," Eva entered Joshua. Assistant receiving teller, Charles Harriott of the Bank for Savings on Bleecker Street, also produced a ledger book in the name of Eva L. Mann. Both Leake and Harriott went through their books in detail, highlighting deposits in various amounts and checks paid to Joshua Mann.

Root wasn't finished. James Dixon, Anna Swinton's former next-door neighbor, testified that he knew Josh Mann and that he had known Eva as "Mrs. Mann. She was so called in my presence and the person who I understood to be her husband (Josh Mann)." He added that he and his wife had once joined Josh, Eva, and Anna Swinton for a day at Coney Island.

The day concluded with the testimony of Dr. William Kemp, who testified that he had treated Eva on several occasions and "was introduced to this person as Mrs. Mann by Mrs. Swinton." Dr. Kemp was also responsible for completing the death certificate of the first child that Eva intended to claim as the daughter of Ray Hamilton (Beatrice I). He stated that the last name on the death certificate was Mann and that Joshua and Eva Mann were listed as the parents. When asked who supplied the information to complete the paperwork, Kemp said, "I got it from Mrs. Mann. The same person I have seen here today."

Dr. Kemp was the last witness called on the first day of the probate hearing. Judge Ransom announced that witness testimony would resume on Wednesday and then adjourned court for the day. Eva practically bounced out of her chair, turned on her heels, and dashed out of the courtroom without saying a word to anyone. Charles Fuller look relieved to let her go.

### Wednesday, January 14, 1891

When the hearing resumed on Wednesday morning, the *New York Tribune* reported "an indiscriminate mob of court loungers pushed their way into the Surrogate's Court. The public interest in the proceedings was so great that the courtroom was crowded to the doors by a heterogeneous rabble." Eva entered the courtroom at 10:30 A.M., accompanied by

Charles Fuller. The court loungers didn't know whether to refer to Eva as Mrs. Hamilton or Mrs. Mann—nevertheless, they craned their necks and stood on tiptoes to get a glance of the notorious woman who was the subject of such public fascination.

Elihu Root and John O'Conor, counsel for the Proponents, were anxious to hammer their case shut. After Judge Ransom called the court to order, Root called William Little, an attorney from Tunkhannock, Pennsylvania. An old-timer with bushy eyebrows and an air of nonchalance, Little represented Eva in 1888 when she was charged with assaulting her brother, William, in a domestic dispute. He stated that he met Eva when he was first brought into the case and was introduced to Josh Mann, "as the husband of Mrs. Mann. They were introduced as husband and wife." When asked if he had seen the woman identified as Mrs. Mann in the courtroom, Little nodded at Eva and answered, "Yes sir; that's her, I believe."

The task of cross-examining William Little fell to Charles Fuller's associate, Lewis Morrison. The *New York World* described Morrison as "a little man and pugnacious, as most little men are." After Morrison failed to shake Little from his identification of Eva, he turned his attention to Little's identification of Joshua Mann. The cross-examination turned to near-farce when Morrison produced a photograph of a bearded Josh Mann and asked, "is that a picture of the man Mann?"

"Well—this has got a beard an' the man Mann didn't; but I should say that this was him from the upper half of his face."

"But you say the lower half wasn't that of the man Mann?"

"Well—if the man who posed for this picture had a beard on December 6, 1888, I should say this wasn't the picture of the man Mann. If he didn't—then I should say this was the man Mann."

Unable to have Little identify Mann with any certainty, Morrison changed his tack.

"You know there was no power in this Court to bring you here, don't you?"

"I come voluntarily," Little replied. "They told me I could have my testimony taken at Tunkhannock and I elected to come over here."

"Expect to be paid something, don't you?" Morrison asked, obliquely hinting that Little was in the pocket of the Hamilton family.

Little replied with a soft chuckle, "Well—yes, I do expect to get my expenses and per diem. Ain't any agreement, but I know what I'm going to charge."

The pugnacious attorney was irked by Little's folksy evasions. "You've got some feeling in this contest, haven't you?"

"No-o, not particularly," Little replied.

A frustrated Lewis Morrison gave up and Little was excused.

Root continued relentlessly through his witness list. Dr. Royal Ammidon, a physician once called to the Manns' residence; Charles Wright, a real estate agent who had let an apartment to Mr. and Mrs. Mann; Eva's former landlady, Julia Evers; Frank Mangin Jr., a New York City police sergeant; and John Lynherr, a Sixth Avenue jeweler, all testified that, in their own particular circumstances, they came to know Josh and Eva as husband and wife and each of them identified the woman in the widow's veil at the Contestant's table as Evangeline Mann.

Elihu Root caused a stir in the courtroom when, in an unorthodox move, he called Eva's attorney, Charles Fuller, as a witness. Fuller was taken aback to hear his name called and L. J. Morrison jumped up and offered numerous objections. Judge Ransom overruled all of them and Fuller took a seat on the witness stand.

Root's intention was to get Fuller to admit that documents signed by Evangeline L. Mann and Evangeline L. Hamilton

were, in fact, executed by the same person, in the same handwriting. After a great deal of legal quibbling, Mr. Fuller finally
admitted that he believed that the signatures had been written by the same person.

Satisfied that he had left Fuller no room to maneuver, Root
further astonished his opposing counsel by resting his case.
Fuller had no choice but to put Eva on the witness stand to re-
fute two days of testimony that tilted heavily against her assertion to be recognized as Ray Hamilton's lawful widow.
Given Eva's crumbling under the weight of the withering prosecution in Atlantic City eighteen months earlier, Fuller could
not have felt very confident about his ability to prevail before
Judge Ransom.

### Thursday, January 15, 1891

> As early as 10 o'clock this morning, well
> dressed women, attracted by curiosity,
> began to drift into the Surrogate's Court
> in twos and threes. Half of them looked as
> if they were afraid they would be recog-
> nized, and they blocked the doorway until
> Court Usher Mike Parker came gallantly
> to the rescue and escorted them to what
> might be called orchestra chairs. He showed
> them the chair where Mrs. Hamilton would
> be seated when she arrived and they all
> wanted to get as near that particular
> chair as possible.—*Philadelphia Inquirer*

Had Surrogate Ransom's court been three times as large as
it was it could not have held the crowd that attempted to gain
entry for the third day of the hearing. Schuyler Hamilton Jr.
and his wife, Gertrude, entered the courtroom and took their
customary seats behind Elihu Root. When Eva entered, the

smile disappeared from Gertrude Hamilton's face and her brown eyes, usually soft and delicate, took on a stony stare. She glared at Eva, her contempt for her alleged sister-in-law palpable. Schuyler Jr. and Gertrude were joined for the first time during the hearing by the General, who lowered his creaking body into a seat beside his son.

With Elihu Root resting his case the previous day, the onus of convincing the court to grant Eva status to contest Ray's will fell back to Charles Fuller. He opened the day's proceedings by arguing that at the outset of the hearing he had "established beyond a doubt that a legal marriage by a minister had been performed." It was Fuller's contention that it was "obligatory upon the other side to either disprove that marriage or render it null by proving a previous marriage."

Fuller asserted that the Proponents by no means disproved the marriage by Reverend Burr, but he admitted that Josh and Eva had "entertained a meretricious relationship for years." That relationship, Fuller concluded, had never "been regarded by either part as a contract of marriage . . . therefore, the only marriage that the court had to consider (was) the legal marriage with Hamilton." He then filed a motion to have the hearing dismissed and for Eva to be declared the lawful widow of Robert Ray Hamilton.

The normally staid Elihu Root rose to rebut Fuller's motion with fire and eloquence, launching a soliloquy of full-throated scorn directed at Eva Hamilton. "We have proved that Josh Mann and Eva Steele had lived together for years, holding themselves out to the world as man and wife. The evidence is that this woman took Joshua Mann to her own home and, standing before her father, her mother and her brothers, said 'this is my husband.' If that isn't evidence, what then is? It does not seem as if all of this was for the purpose of cloaking a meretricious relationship."

Root's rebuttal turned from a strictly legal argument to one of personal invective directed at the woman who had caused so much misery to his friend and the Hamilton family. "You are to weigh all of the conduct of this woman for years before. She was and is a creature of shame and infamy. She crept into and allied herself to one of the noblest families in this great Republic. She married herself to a (great) grandson of the first Secretary of the Treasury, and she took his money and gave it to her former paramour and acknowledged husband, Joshua Mann."

Root's speech had such an impact on Eva that she left her seat next to Fuller and sat in a corner of the courtroom reserved for the court stenographers, as far away from Elihu Root as possible, shielded from him by typewriters and stacks of papers.

After Elihu Root returned to his seat, Judge Ransom denied Fuller's motion and recessed for lunch before proceeding to any additional witnesses that Eva's counsel wished to call. As the attorneys and spectators all spilled out of the Hall of Records at midday, Eva Hamilton departed alone and climbed the stairs behind the courthouse to the Third Avenue elevated train. She rode uptown to Fourteenth Street, then walked east to a four-story rowhouse at 203 East Fourteenth Street. She was followed for the entirety of her twenty-minute journey by Louis Allen, a clerk in the law office of Howe & Hummel.

The corpulent William Howe and rail-thin Abraham Hummel were said to be nearly a law unto themselves, both high and low. Their offices were conveniently located across the street from The Tombs—ensuring a steady stream of clients—and while they kept a stable of professional witnesses at the ready, they purposefully kept no records. They were considered to be criminal lawyers in both senses: they were lawyers who defended criminals and they were criminals who practiced law. Their biographer, Richard H. Rovere, wrote that

"Howe and Hummel were as crooked as the horns of a Dorset ram."

Howe & Hummel had been retained by Anna Swinton to draw up divorce papers on behalf of her son, Joshua Mann, who wished to formally end his marriage to Eva. When Eva entered the vestibule of the rowhouse, Louis Allen called her name and thrust a packet of papers toward her. When she refused to accept them, he tucked them under her arm, scampered back down the stoop, and returned to the Howe & Hummel office.

Mann's affidavit stated that he and Eva met in 1881, "and after some preliminary acquaintance, we agreed to be man and wife and thereafter lived as such in the city of New York and in various places in Pennsylvania." He added that he believed that "when she informed him of her marriage to Hamilton, he thought she was playing a practical joke on him."

Mann's divorce action had no direct bearing on the hearing before Judge Ransom, but the timing was curious, to say the least. Outside of the courtroom, Fuller told reporters, "the divorce proceeding is simply indicative of the fact that our opponents are resorting to desperate means. Mann never brought that suit of his own accord. The truth is that Mann is an irresponsible idiot who is helpless in the hands of anybody who has a mind to direct him."

It is entirely plausible that the deep-pocketed Hamilton family offered a cash incentive to Anna Swinton to initiate the divorce proceeding on Josh Mann's behalf. Even if the motion to divorce might be later dismissed, Howe & Hummel's stunt was certain to play on page one for any interested reader of the newspapers, including, presumably, Rastus Ransom.

When the probate hearing resumed after lunch, Eva appeared to be both irritated and depressed after her encounter uptown with Louis Allen, fidgeting in her seat and speaking pointedly to Charles Fuller. The afternoon session began with Fuller trying, basically in vain, to crack the seemingly airtight case put on by Elihu Root on behalf of the Proponents. The testimony of Fuller's witnesses was vague and inconclusive, prompting an impatient Judge Ransom to state several times "that he could not see how the testimony had any bearing on the question of the law involved."

Esther Blake testified that she kept a lodging house on 65 West Ninth Street and that Eva rented rooms from her in 1885 and called herself, "Mrs. Brill." She further stated that Robert Ray Hamilton "came to the house frequently." Mary Ann Hagerty, who kept a lodging house at 115 West Eleventh Street, testified that Joshua Mann rented a room from her in 1885 and "lived there alone." Ray's friend and associate, Edward Vollmer, stated that he "could recollect almost nothing about meeting Eva," adding that he had always known her as Mrs. Mann. Fuller's case was going nowhere.

When Fuller called his last witness of the afternoon, Ray's father, General Schuyler Hamilton, the spectators partially rose from their seats and craned their necks to get a glimpse of the aging warrior. Fuller respectfully asked the General to identify letters that he had written to Eva to "welcome her warmly as his daughter-in-law." Eva insisted that they not be read aloud in court.

After verifying that, yes, he had authored the letters in question, the General was asked by Fuller if he could identify Eva in the courtroom. From her seat roughly ten feet from the witness stand, Eva raised her widow's veil.

"I am getting old and my sight is bad. Will the lady come here?"

Judge Ransom instructed Eva to do so. She and the General looked squarely at each other from close range before Ray's father asked, "Will you take off your veil altogether, so that I can be sure?"

The *New York Times* reported that "the old General partially stood up, looked steadfastly at her, and said in a tone that was the essence of sorrow: 'Yes, that is the woman I received as my son's wife.'"

On that somber note, court was adjourned for the day. The only witness left for Fuller to call was the star of the show, Evangeline.

### Friday, January 16, 1891

On Friday morning, as temperatures dipped below the freezing mark for the first time in the week, the court loungers who had packed Judge Ransom's courtroom all week lined up in the early morning cold to secure a seat for Eva's testimony. The hearing was scheduled to resume at 10:30 A.M., but such a large crowd had assembled that shortly after ten o'clock Surrogate Ransom found it necessary to order the doors of his courtroom to be closed.

The *New York Herald* dramatically framed the situation:

> Hundreds of people stood packed so closely that it was impossible for those inside the mass to draw a full breath or a handkerchief. The people swayed to and fro and endured torture to see the woman who had snared Alexander Hamilton's great-grandson, the Circe whose murderous assault on the nurse of her spurious child had driven young Hamilton to the remote Western river wherein he met his death.

The spectators respectfully cleared a path when the General, Schuyler Jr., and his wife entered the courtroom to take their usual seats behind Elihu Root. Eva and Charles Fuller were the last participants to enter the room before Judge Ransom gaveled the court to order. Eva wore her widow's veil, as she had all week, as well as her black mourning dress, partially concealed under a chocolate-brown sealskin coat. The *Herald* noted that "as a spectacle she was not disappointing. Above medium height, muscular but not stout beyond plumpness, her eyes are gray, large, defiant and not far apart."

In an effort to properly set the stage for his client to take her star turn, Fuller first called Dr. Frank H. Rice, a physician from Passaic, New Jersey, with thirty-five years of experience in the medical profession. Dr. Rice testified that he was called to the home of Joshua Mann in Passaic Bridge, New Jersey, two or three years prior after Mann had been pitched from a horse and suffered a severe blow to the head. He stated that he was introduced to Eva as Mrs. Mann at the time and that he understood Josh was her cousin. Rice testified that Mann was in a semi-comatose condition and that he had treated the patient for at least three weeks, possibly four.

Fuller's intent was to persuade the court that Eva was so often seen with Joshua Mann because of his inability to take care of himself, particularly after the accident. In order for that reasoning to seem plausible, Fuller needed the testimony of Dr. Rice to confirm Josh's physical incapacitation. After the doctor stepped down, Fuller got right to it.

Not averse to courtroom theatrics, Fuller rose and with an air of drama called "Mrs. Eva Hamilton." Eva walked determinedly to the witness chair, threw back her widow's veil with a flourish, and gazed intently at the spectators seated before her.

Eva's direct testimony was brief and in substance, and consisted of a denial that anything had ever existed between her and Joshua Mann that could be considered a contract of marriage. She was emphatic in her assertions about her relation-ship with Mann and began her side of the story at the same physical place that Elihu Root did with his witnesses—Penn-sylvania.

"I remember being in Pennsylvania some years ago at my uncle's place, where my brother, Joseph Steele and Joshua Mann met," Eva began. "I did not introduce Mr. Mann to my brother. I was not in the house at the time. I did not at that time say that Mr. Mann was my husband." She added for em-phasis, "I never at any time entered into a contract of mar-riage with Joshua J. Mann." Eva had an explanation for every bit of testimony given by the witnesses from Pennsylvania: ei-ther they heard conversations incorrectly, they were mistaken in their recollection of events, or Eva had no idea what they were talking about. She didn't give an inch.

She did, however, attempt to explain why she was so fre-quently found by others in Mann's company. "For the past three years, he has been incapable of caring for himself, prac-tically an idiot. He always drank to excess and the evil effects of his drinking, combined with the effect of the accident in Passaic have rendered him practically helpless. Someone had to be with him at all times and his guardians have been his mother and myself. It would not be safe to leave him alone for a moment." She added that Ray Hamilton had been with her when she had Mann under her care.

In an effort to blunt the news of Josh Mann's divorce filing the previous day, Fuller asked Eva if she could recognize Mann's handwriting. "I have seen him write very often and am familiar with his handwriting," she confirmed. He then produced a letter, allegedly written by Josh Mann and posted a week before Eva was released from prison. Fuller asked if she could verify that it was indeed written by Mann.

*New York, Nov. 19, 1890*

*My dear Eva—I see by the papers that your late husband
has ignored you entirely in his will on the grounds of a
previous marriage to me, this being entirely false, as no
marriage of any kind ever took place between us. I have
consulted with my lawyer and requested him to call upon
you at once, as you could affirm the same. Nothing of this
kind ever existed. By granting him an interview you will
oblige.*

*Yours respt.,*
*J.J. Mann*
*No. 8 St. Marks Place*

Eva acknowledged that, yes, the letter appeared to be in
Mann's handwriting. What was left unsaid was that if Josh
Mann was the drunken imbecile he was reported to be, the letter seemed to be a suspiciously cogent summation of his and
Eva's relationship. The letter may have been written by Mann,
but it stands to reason that the contents were dictated to him
by a third party. Just as Anna Swinton may have received a
tidy sum to convince Josh to file for divorce from Eva, perhaps
the hapless Josh had been coaxed into writing the letter by
means of his own cash incentive.

Elihu Root began his cross-examination with the same
thoughtful preparation he demonstrated in his direct questioning of the previous witnesses, but Eva was steadfast in her
denials. He questioned her about Dr. Kemp; Eva stated that
"Mr. Mann was never introduced to Dr. Kemp, in my presence,
as my husband." He questioned her about a house that had
been purchased in Passaic with the title holder as Evangeline
L. Mann; Eva stated, "I did not take title to that place in the
name of Brill because Mr. Hamilton did not wish me to."

When Root's attention turned to the copious documentation of the Union Dime bank account, Eva had a ready answer. "When I stated at the bank that I was the wife of J.J. Mann it was not true. I did not intend in that statement to admit that there had ever been any ceremony of marriage between Mann and myself. I was not asked the question either. I was not on good terms with my family at the time, and it had something to do with my assuming this name. I took the name and banked the money in that name in case anything had happened to me after. Mr. Mann would have got the money and not my people."

At the conclusion of testimony on Friday, the consensus among reporters was that "as a witness in her own behalf she was a success." Despite Root's relentless questioning intended to expose Eva's lies and contradictions, she remained calm and collected and bore Root's severe cross-examination admirably, answering his questions in a clear, confident voice.

### Monday, January 19, 1891

After court was adjourned on Friday, Elihu Root gave no interviews to the press or otherwise publicly shared his personal feelings about Eva's performance. But it is not hard to imagine his frustration with her seemingly impenetrable defense of her relationship with Josh Mann. When Root returned to the courtroom on Monday morning after a weekend's respite, he was, by all accounts, determined to expose Eva Mann (or Steele or Brill) for the scheming, manipulative fraud he believed her to be.

When court resumed at 10:30 at the beginning of a new week, Root wasted no time beginning a salvo of merciless, rapid-fire questions. The *New York Times* noted that "the questions were so direct that she could not evade them." Perhaps Eva sensed that the questions would be tougher, more pointed, than they had been on her first day on the stand. The confidence and defiance that she exhibited on the witness stand on Friday had been replaced by restlessness, her eyes darting from side to side and face nervously twitching as Root started his questioning.

He began by producing a guest book from the Delavan Hotel in Elmira, signed by "J.J. Mann and wife." Eva professed to know nothing about the registration, but when asked by Root if Mann was sober at the time, she replied that "he was never sober about that time." Root asked what her idea of an imbecile was—Eva replied that she had no ideas on the subject, but emphasized that Mann was not in his right mind.

Root quickly turned to the European trip that Eva took in the summer of 1888 (which Ray Hamilton financed). She in fact did not travel alone as she had told Ray, but was accompanied for the trip's entirety by Josh Mann. They sailed on the *City of Berlin*, stayed in the same stateroom, and both corresponded with Anna Swinton during their trip. In one letter, Eva addressed Anna Swinton as "grandma," spoke affectionately of "Dotty"—Swinton's pet nickname for her son—and signed it "Eva and Dotty."

"Do you mean to say that this is not a letter from a son's wife to a son's mother?" Root asked.

"It was not," Eva curtly replied.

Root continued reviewing letters written by Eva during the trip to both Anna Swinton and Josh's adopted sister, Kate. Eva continued to deny everything except her meretricious relationship with Josh Mann and peppered her answers with reminders of Mann's drunkenness and imbecility. But Root's relentless approach and litany of questions rattled Eva to the point that at noon she requested a break in the proceedings from Judge Ransom.

When Eva returned to the stand fifteen minutes later, Root struck at the heart of her deception. It was a letter dated December 18, 1888, from Josh Mann to his mother, Anna Swinton.

ELMIRA, *December 18*

*My dear mother:*

*We could not come to N.Y. on the 15th but will be down soon. Eva wants to know if you have the things done and not to disappoint her when she comes down. She will only stay one day. Will probably come next week. Now don't disappoint her. Hope you are well. Eva is not well and has not been. That is the reason we haven't been down. I have a bad cold.*

*Hoping to hear from you soon, I am,*

> *Your affectionate son,*
> DOTTY

Elihu Root pointedly ask Eva what Mann referred to as having the things done. Fuller rose to object, stating that the letter was irrelevant and immaterial. Judge Ransom had a different point of view. "I think it may be very material and I will take it," he replied. Ransom then turned to Eva and asked Eva directly, "What were the things that you heard that were mentioned in that letter?"

Eva hesitated and said that she didn't care to answer, but finally said that the "things" meant a wardrobe. Root pounced.

ROOT: What kind of a wardrobe?

EVA: An infant's wardrobe.

R: What infant's?

E: Mine.

R: Whose?

E: Mine.

R: Was this infant alive on the 18th of December, 1888?

Fuller rose and stoutly objected, claiming counsel had embarked on a fishing expedition. He forcefully stated that "the question before your honor is simply: Has she the right to come into this court to contest this will as the widow of Robert Ray Hamilton? This, I respectfully submit, is entirely outside." Ransom allowed the line of questioning, but Fuller continued to object to almost every query in an attempt to throw as many roadblocks into Root's path as possible.

When Root asked where the infant was born, Eva answered, "I refuse to answer the question because it tends to degrade me." Ransom leaned over the bench and spoke directly to her. "In refusing to obey the direction of the Court, you do so at the peril of being imprisoned in the common jail of the county until you comply with the Court's direction." After multiple objections by Fuller, and numerous sidebars between both attorneys and Judge Ransom, Eva finally answered Elihu Root's question, at least partially. She stated that the infant was born in "the State of Pennsylvania."

Root snidely responded, "Where were you at the time?"

It was now past midday and Eva had become so nervous that she appealed to the Surrogate for relief and an adjournment was taken until two o'clock. When court reconvened, it was clear that the break had done little to settle Eva's troubled mind. She was in an even worse condition than when the adjournment was taken, appearing to observers to be suffering a tremendous mental strain as she took the witness stand.

Fuller recognized the dire straits his client was in and rose to address the judge before Root could continue his questions.

He appealed to Judge Ransom that "the Contestant's examination, at least for the present, be suspended. She says she cannot remember now what she said this morning, and what she testified to. She is in a state of nervousness and excitement, and suffering from considerable physical pain."

Root reminded the judge that he still had witnesses to call and added, "if the Contestants choose to rest their case here, I can go on with my testimony." Fuller, of course, rejected Root's proposal and both attorneys turned their attention to Judge Ransom.

"I appreciate the situation of the witness," the judge began, "and my manly sympathies are very much aroused in her behalf, because of the situation she finds herself in at this time. I have no reason to doubt her statement to me that she is not physically able to sustain the strain of this examination at this time." With that, Judge Ransom adjourned the court until 9:30 A.M. Wednesday morning.

### Wednesday, January 21, 1891

> Sensational as have been the developments all through the now famous contest over the will of Robert Ray Hamilton carried on by Evangeline L. Steele, or Parsons, or Mann, or Brill, who wrecked the brilliant young Assemblyman's life and claims to be his widow, the proceedings today were so startling as fairly to dumbfound even those who have been listening to the case throughout. The interest in the day's doings was so intense that Surrogate Ransom had to use every effort to maintain order in the crowd, which literally forced itself into the courtroom.—*New York Times*

When Judge Ransom called the court to order at his customary 10:30 starting time, Charles Fuller immediately rose to read a dispatch that Eva received from her brother, sent from Kunkle Post Office, Luzerne County, Pennsylvania:

Mother is dead. Funeral Thursday at Kunkle.

WILLIAM STEELE

Fuller had approached Elihu Root before the beginning of the day's hearing to inform him of the development and to let his opposing number know that he would ask Ransom to allow Eva to be excused from testimony to attend her mother's funeral. She hoped to board a 1:00 P.M. train for Dallas, Pennsylvania—if Root was going to oppose the request, Fuller wished to know so that he could have his client make other arrangements.

Root sensed that Eva's believability, and her claim to a dower right, was close to complete collapse. He was concerned that if Eva was able to extend her time away from the witness chair, that she would be able to conjure up new answers to counter the testimony that was overwhelmingly against her. Root made a proposal: if Eva was willing to state under oath that Robert Ray Hamilton was not the father of the child christened as Beatrice Ray Hamilton, and if Fuller made an honest attempt at gaining clarity regarding the relationship of Eva and Josh Mann, Root would ensure she was off the witness stand in time for her train.

After Fuller read the dispatch, Judge Ransom reminded counsel that "while he felt sympathy for the witness, he could not grant her the privilege while she was under direct examination." As Eva took the witness stand, the judge reminded both Fuller and Root that "if questioning were begun at once it would be finished in time for her to leave town, as she desired."

"I have asked for a postponement," Fuller began, "and Mr. Root has assented provided that I will make an admission, which I now do make. The stenographer will please place this on the record: It is admitted by the contestant the child the contestant testifies was born in Pennsylvania on November 19, 1888, was not the child of Robert Ray Hamilton. It is admitted that the child known as Beatrice Ray, and christened as such in Atlantic City, New Jersey, and a respondent in these proceedings, is not the child of Robert Ray Hamilton."

Judge Ransom leaned toward Eva and asked, "Do you hear that? And is it so?"

Very faintly, she replied, "Yes."

Murmurs from the spectators ricocheted around the courtroom for several minutes before Judge Ransom was able to restore order. Eva raised her veil and prepared to answer any additional questions before departing the courthouse to catch her train. She clutched a small bottle of smelling salts and pulled the cork several times, inhaling deeply as she tried to gather herself to answer any remaining questions. When Fuller asked several more questions of his client, Eva's answers caused everyone in the courtroom, attorneys and spectators alike, to gasp in complete astonishment. She threw discretion, modesty, and any other qualities associated with a woman of propriety to the winds, and plainly asserted that she had been the mistress of Joshua L. Mann.

The crowd held its collective breath during this exchange between Eva and her own attorney:

FULLER: Where did you first meet Josh Mann?

EVA: In Philadelphia.

F: When?

E: In '81 or '82, I think.

F: Were your relations with him proper or improper?

E: Improper.

F: How long after your first meeting?

E: About a week.

Judge Ransom interjected. "Mr. Fuller, your examination is very direct and is a complete contradiction of all previous evidence. It no doubt surprises your adversaries very much and is likely to call out a very extended cross-examination. You may proceed."

FULLER: Did you ever agree with Mr. Mann to become his wife?

EVA: No. Not then nor at any other time. I never told anybody we were husband and wife.

F: Why did you say when you deposited money at the banks that you were the wife of Mann?

E: Simply because I wanted to bank money in that name.

Eva reiterated her rationale about keeping her money away from family members, and her teeth unclenched and the furrows left her brow as she appeared relieved to finally have everything out in the open. In a convoluted twist of logic, Eva then explained to the court that the reason she was known as Mrs. Mann was to conceal the improper nature of their relationship.

With head bowed, she told the court, "I was his mistress."

After Eva's admission, Fuller rested and Elihu Root, exasperated with Eva's lies and duplicity, jumped to his feet and walked quickly to the witness stand to confront Eva. Her latest ploy—to convince the court that she called herself Mrs. Mann only to conceal the fact that she was Mann's mistress—was too much for Root to take. Even though the odds of Eva prevailing in her fight to gain a share of Ray's estate were now infinitesimal, a lifetime of blending fact and fiction compelled her to make one more attempt to gain the wealth and stature she had long desired.

ROOT: What has caused you to change your testimony from that which you gave at first?

EVA: I have looked it over and found mistakes.

R: Were you not advised that you would have to change your testimony if you wanted to win this case?

E: I was not. I called Mr. Fuller's attention to the mistakes I had made and he said I would be allowed to correct them.

In rapid-fire succession, Root went back through every hotel Josh and Eva registered at, and every trip they made to her family in Pennsylvania, reminding her of her previous answers, and asking again whether Josh was truly an imbecile, or if his alleged mental state was merely a cover for their allegedly improper relationship. It was apparent to everyone that Eva was in a very deep hole and was hopelessly floundering.

Fuller objected to virtually every question that Root asked, if for no other reason than to give Eva time to provide a plausible answer. Judge Ransom overruled all of the objections.

"Why didn't you answer this way the other day?" Root asked again.

Eva sat back in the witness chair, resting her head on a stone pillar behind her. "I suppose I made a mistake, sir. Everybody is liable to mistakes and I may have made a great many in my testimony." She glared at Root for a moment before adding, "I don't know what to say; I cannot answer."

They had reached the end now. After eight hours of testimony over the course of three days, Elihu Root and Evangeline had gone toe-to-toe, their questions and answers exhaustingly circling back on each other.

"You appreciate that today you have radically changed your testimony as to the relations which existed between yourself and Mann?" Root asked.

Eva answered matter-of-factly. "No, I don't. I have simply said today plainly what I expected that you and everybody else would infer from what I previously testified."

"I guess we all got the proper inference," Root drily concluded.

Eva was excused from the witness chair, and after a few brief words with Charles Fuller, she was gone, off to Pennsylvania to mourn her mother.

### Thursday, January 22, 1891

As the temperature hovered near forty degrees and a steady rain fell on Manhattan, spectators again filed into Judge Ransom's courtroom—the crowd was as big as ever—to hear Fuller's and Root's closing arguments and await the Surrogate's decision regarding the right of Evangeline to contest the will of Robert Ray Hamilton. The General was the only member of the Hamilton family present.

Elihu Root was the first to rise and spoke deliberately, making no attempt to replicate his fiery oratory of the previous days. He acknowledged that nobody desired to deny the marriage ceremony performed by Reverend Burr on January 7, 1889, and that it was not surprising that Eva desired to ignore the marriage that existed between her and Joshua J. Mann.

The only point in his summation where Root injected a dose of drama into his argument was when he addressed the Surrogate directly: "I want your Honor to believe that Eva Mann and Joshua J. Mann were actually man and wife; not simply to think that it was a presumption from the evidence. To me it is clear as day. She nursed him when he was drunk and tried to cure him of his failing of drunkenness. She transferred money to him as his wife, and she told bank officers that she was his wife. The attitude of Eva's family goes conclusively to show that Eva was not living shamefully with Joshua J. Mann. Their relations were surely those of husband and wife and it was not until lately that the other monstrous assumption was put forth."

He concluded by stating that "the evidence implies a common-law marriage. It was the presumption of morality against immorality." He also noted, foreshadowing Fuller's likely appeal of a negative outcome for his client, that the Court of Appeals had held, "over and over again that it was the policy of the law to presume legitimacy over illegitimacy."

Charles Fuller, aware that he was playing a weak hand, nonetheless rose in defense of Eva. "A woman friendless and alone has been struggling for her right against an array of lawyers who have scoured the states for witnesses while she could not procure any. They have brought witnesses here and sometimes finding that their testimony not to be just what they wanted, have rejected them and we have been glad to take them up and call them as our witnesses."

He drew muffled laughter from the spectators when he wryly noted that if a man and woman registering at a hotel as husband and wife constituted proof of marriage, then "New York is not big enough to hold all of the married men."

Fuller only briefly mentioned Josh Mann. "That she did love Josh Mann, I am not here to dispute, but she loved Robert Ray Hamilton more, and for him she forsook Mann and went with Hamilton to New Jersey, where she took him to be her husband and he took her to be his wife in accordance with the law. The moment that the ceremony was concluded her right of dower in his estate was complete. The law does not even permit him to will it away from her. It is hers, absolutely."

He plaintively asked Judge Ransom, "Will this court say

that this woman should be thrown from her position as a lawful widow back into the slums from which she has been taken?" Fuller closed by stating that "the case was one of the most remarkable he had ever known, and one of the most pathetic."

As Fuller returned to his seat, it came as a surprise to everyone in the courtroom when the Surrogate indicated that he did not need to study the case in chambers—he was prepared to render a decision from the bench at the present time. The attorneys and spectators all leaned forward in their chairs and dared not make a sound in anticipation of the ruling from the bench.

Judge Ransom began by noting that "the trial has been one of great interest to the parties to the proceeding and its result to them is a matter of deep concern." He summed up the facts as presented before him and made special note that Eva's counsel, "has conducted the case from the beginning not only with great ability and fidelity to the interests of his client, but with candor, and whatever an honorable, industrious and skillful advocate could find to aid his client he has presented in a most attractive manner."

The Surrogate then lowered the boom on Evangeline:

I regret that duty compels me to say anything in the way of criticism of this contestant, and I shall content myself in the discharge of that duty by saying simply that substantially her evidence is unworthy of belief. I do not believe her. And I hold and decide in this case that on the 7th day of January, 1889, the date of the ceremony of marriage between herself and Robert Ray Hamilton, this contestant was the lawful wife of Joshua Mann and that her marriage to Robert Ray Hamilton was void, and that consequently, she has no standing in this court to contest the probate of the paper propounded as his last will and testament.

The *New York Herald* succinctly summarized Judge Ransom's decision. "Eva was dropped out of the contest over Robert Ray Hamilton's will like a sandbag from a balloon."

As everyone in the courtroom exhaled in unison and reporters positioned themselves near the doors to make a quick getaway, Rastus Ransom called a recess and announced that the case would proceed with the inquiry into the factum of the will.

Elihu Root had cleared a major hurdle in the probate of his friend's estate, but the case was not quite fully resolved. The factum of the will stipulated that proof of Ray Hamilton's death be entered into the record. Given the circumstances surrounding Hamilton's demise, Root still had to properly establish the factum of his friend's death.

### *January–March 1891*
### *The Factum*

The drama in Judge Ransom's Surrogate Court ebbed considerably after he ruled against Eva's dower right and she had departed for her mother's funeral. There was still work to be done, though, in order to properly probate Hamilton's estate. Edward Vollmer had signed as a witness to Ray's Last Will and Testament, as did another attorney, David W. Couch Jr. They both attested to the legitimacy of the document before Judge Ransom.

While there were no ambiguities with the will itself, one central issue remained: proof of Ray Hamilton's death. Neither a death certificate or a statement from a medical examiner certified the demise of Robert Ray Hamilton. Even though Gil Spier and Cass de Moore provided testimony regarding their arrival in Jackson Hole in August 1890, they never actually saw his body and could only verify what they were told by John Sargent to be the location of their friend's grave.

While Rastus Ransom had no reason to doubt the veracity of Spier's and de Moore's testimonies, he nonetheless had the legal obligation to ask, in essence: How do I know that Robert Ray Hamilton is really dead? In an attempt to answer that question, the judge issued a court order to have depositions taken from anyone involved in the removal of Hamilton's body from the Snake River or who may have assisted in the burial of the deceased. Ransom was particularly interested in hearing from James O. Green, the medical doctor who discovered the body, and John Dudley Sargent, who assumed responsibility for its burial.

On February 23, two Surrogate Court appointees, William Dye and Edwin Wright, arrived in Rexburg, Bingham County, Idaho, and took testimony from Gottlieb Bieri, Christian Aeschbacher, and Roman Sepert. The three men were the carpenters working at Marymere in the summer of 1890 who made the coffin and dug the grave in which Ray Hamilton was buried. Their testimony was entered into the record without issue.

Gathering testimony from the two witnesses that Judge Ransom most wanted to hear from, James Green and John Sargent, proved to be more problematic. Dr. Green was living in Pau, France, in the Pyrenees and had no immediate plans to return to the States. Judge Ransom authorized two American attorneys who were in France, J. Morris Post and William Thorne, to take Green's deposition under oath. Schuyler Hamilton Jr., who had the most to gain from the distribution of his brother's estate, sailed to France to ensure that Green's testimony was duly taken and sent back to the United States as expeditiously as possible. Dr. Green recounted his recollection of the physical condition of Ray's body and the personal effects that he and James Holland inventoried. But as Green had never actually met Ray Hamilton prior to discovering him in the Snake River, his testimony was not considered to be fully conclusive.

Green stated, "I had met searching parties looking about the country for a gentleman who was missing. Later I was told that the missing man was Robert Ray Hamilton."

He was specifically asked by Post and Thorne, "Whose body was it?"

Green replied, "I do not know."

Judge Ransom appointed David N. Carvalho as a Commissioner of the Court to travel to Jackson Hole to secure the testimony of John D. Sargent. However, timing was a problem. Sargent and his family had decided to remain in Jackson Hole for the winter of 1891—as it was now only March, the mountain passes into the valley were completely blocked by snow and ice. There was no way into or out of Jackson Hole for another four to six weeks. Sargent's bankers in Eagle Rock, Idaho (now Idaho Falls), confirmed to the court that he had not been seen in Eagle Rock during the winter and had not drawn any money from his account. Ransom explained to Elihu Root that he was reluctant to make a final determination regarding Ray Hamilton's death until he had Sargent's testimony in hand. Accordingly, the proceedings were held in abeyance until the spring thaw came to Jackson Hole.

While all of the interested parties waited for warmer weather to come to Wyoming, Elihu Root continued to swat down rumors that Ray was still alive. On Sunday, January 25, an editorial in the *New York Sun* titled, "Is Robert Ray Hamilton Alive?" began: "The story of Robert Ray Hamilton's downfall is a strange romance. It has not yet been proved that it is a tragedy. Perhaps it is not!"

The *Sun* editorial ran to almost two full columns of the broadsheet and was filled with speculation and innuendo. "The briefest possible announcement of his death was made, and it came from intimate friends of his family. The news, when borne to his venerable, affectionate father, sad as it was, did not fall, apparently, like an overwhelming blow. It seems almost as if it had been anticipated."

The newspaper found it odd that "Mr. Hamilton, who had only been in possession of his ranch for six weeks, should go out alone into the wilds of the West to hunt and shoot," and they found it perhaps more than a coincidence that his two friends arrived from New York just after his body had been found. Odder still, in the *Sun*'s view, was John Sargent's letter to Schuyler Jr. that stated Hamilton had told him that "he would rather be buried here *if anything should happen*" (emphasis, the *Sun*). They also noted that "neither Mr. Hamilton's father nor his brother hastened to the West to bring the body home, leaving it to be buried at the ranch."

In conclusion, they claimed that "there are those who knew Robert Ray Hamilton well who have never believed for a single moment the story of his death. Taciturn, secretive, self-assertive, adroit, skillful in expedients as they ever knew him to be, they believe he foresaw that his only and readiest way to escape from a most distressing situation was by hiding behind the shelter of an invented death." The editorial closed by noting the case "stands as one of the most sensational in these sensational times, and sadly recalls the philosophic poet's couplet":

> The open wayward life we see;
> The secret, hidden springs we may not know.

Three days later, a story out of Chicago alleged that Hamilton had maintained correspondence with two New York physicians who had an elegantly furnished, unoccupied apartment awaiting Hamilton in Chicago, in order that he may return there to reside in the near future. The anonymous source of the article stated that "Hamilton wrote to these friends requesting them to send by express certain articles, including several boxes of his private brand of cigars, a silver flask that he highly prized, jewelry and clothing." Allegedly, Hamilton directed that these items be sent to Elko, Nevada, where he supposedly remained in hiding seven months after the report of his death.

A separate, anonymous source in Boston stated with certainty that at least six of Ray's closest friends knew of his whereabouts and had exchanged correspondence with him. The Boston source also asserted that "there was a particular reason why certain of his relatives maintained that he was dead when they knew otherwise. The gentlemen mentioned were intimately associated with Hamilton and have sent him money."

Elihu Root told the *New York Times* that the reports coming in "are bosh. They probably found their inspiration in the editorial in last Sunday's *Sun*. The intimation that the family are conniving at false reports of his death is a figment of a diseased imagination." When Root was asked by the *Chicago Daily Tribune* about a report from Lewiston, Idaho, that a Frenchman there named Sanford reported that Ray Hamilton was alive and well, Root replied, "I believe there is no foundation for the statement. I think Robert Ray Hamilton is dead beyond doubt."

Eva's attorneys, Robert Fuller and Lewis Morrison, were not as quick to tamp down the rumors. Morrison told reporters, "I cannot give an opinion as to whether Hamilton is alive or not. The peculiar circumstances and place of his alleged death and the absence of satisfactory legal evidence would be circumstantial evidence that it is not impossible that he is still alive. If he is alive, we shall bring an action to obtain a dower for Eva."

The rumors regarding the possibility of Ray Hamilton still

being alive kept the ongoing scandal simmering in the newspapers. The story returned to a full boil in June when a visitor arrived in New York from Jackson Hole. At 9:30 P.M. on Tuesday, June 9, as the sun set behind the new, colossal Pennsylvania Railroad Depot that had recently opened in Jersey City, a solitary figure and his dog stepped off of an inbound train. After a nine-day journey, John Dudley Sargent had come back east to give testimony regarding the death of Ray Hamilton.

As was his habit, Sargent dressed in a mixture of eastern and western clothing. It wasn't unusual for him to pair a cowboy's flannel shirt and red handkerchief with eastern riding-trousers and puttees. On this warm evening, he walked through Penn Station garbed in corduroys and a sombrero, followed closely by Ray Hamilton's splendid setter, Jocko.

Reporters who had been tipped to Sargent's imminent arrival approached him as he made his way down the platform, then sauntered through the waiting room and out to the adjacent ferry slip for his trip across the river to New York. Initially, Sargent steadfastly denied his identity, but after repeated questioning by the reporters, he finally admitted that he was, indeed, John Sargent. He refused to talk about Mr. Hamilton and instead prodded the reporters for news about the case.

"Do some of the papers still say that Hamilton is alive?" Sargent asked.

The reporters turned the question right back on him. "Do *you* think there is any doubt of his death?" Sargent answered as if no further explanation was necessary. "I have brought all of Hamilton's effects with me."

Sargent also told the reporters at Penn Station that in addition to providing testimony regarding Ray Hamilton's death, he hoped to pay his respects to General Hamilton at the Windsor. With that, the eccentric stranger and his dog boarded a ferry for Manhattan, in route to the Park Avenue Hotel.

The Park Avenue Hotel occupied the entire block of Fourth Avenue between Thirty-Second and Thirty-Third Streets. Opened in 1878 as Stewart's Working-Women Hotel, the hotel's interior was praised for its modest collection of artwork, but the ornate, overwrought exterior was met with derision. The building was described as "a magnificent failure, a two-million-dollar example of what New York does not want if she is ever to show a decent architectural face along her principal thoroughfares."

When Sargent arrived in 1891, the hotel had been refurbished by new proprietors, William Earle and his son Arthur, and boasted of three new restaurants and five hundred newly furnished and re-decorated rooms—the U.S. census didn't record more than five hundred residents in Sargent's adopted home of Jackson, Wyoming, until 1930.

Reporters staked out Sargent's hotel and followed him whenever he left the premises. The day after he arrived in New York, he told reporters that he was anxious to return to his ranch and did not expect to stay in New York more than three or four days. Those three or four days turned into nearly two weeks, as Sargent had to wait for all of the attorneys involved to be available to take his testimony. While Sargent bided his time, he provided the press with more details concerning the death of Ray Hamilton.

"It was not until August 27 that we feared anything on account of Ray's absence. On that day I organized a search expedition. I offered five dollars to every man at a trappers' settlement who would meet at South Landing that night. I scattered them in every direction." Sargent said he was told that one of the searchers came upon Hamilton's horse and hunting dog. "The horse carried the haunches of an antelope, a heavy saddle and Ray's 45-90 Winchester rifle. A thirty-five-foot lariat was carelessly tied around them, as a tenderfoot would have done it. When I heard of this, I knew that the worst had happened."

After examining the area where Ray's body was found, Sargent drew his own conclusion as to what had happened. "He had come to the gap in the timber, which he had to cross, and rode up to the edge. There was sand for several feet and then he could see nothing but sedge. He saw it was shallow, but where the sand ended a ledge of shale slopes steeply down, and the water under the sedge was twelve feet deep. When Ray found it was deep, he left his horse, which returned to the shore and he started across."

Sargent then explained why Hamilton drowned. "He was a splendid swimmer, and the only thing that caused his drowning was a huge pair of California spurs, which he had borrowed of me. The huge rowels of the spurs were clogged with the sedgewood."

Sargent closed his conversation with reporters by stating unequivocally that the body was that of Robert Ray Hamilton. "That it was Ray's body I could have no doubt. There were a hundred things by which to identify him. It was a face which no one could see twice and not recognize again. The high, narrow forehead and peculiarly long teeth were unmistakable. He bore a strong resemblance to his ancestor, Alexander Hamilton."

Sargent was unable to connect with another of the Founding Father's descendants, Ray's father, in his first few days in New York. He did manage, however, to make contact with Gil Spier—the two men who had met under such unfortunate circumstances in Jackson Hole ten months before were seen out for a summer stroll one evening.

Finally, after nearly ten days in Manhattan, Sargent received word that all of the attorneys that were party to the probate of Ray Hamilton's will were available to hear his testimony. On Saturday, June 20, Sargent traveled downtown,

passing the landmarks on Broadway that were central in Ray
Hamilton's life: the Union League clubhouse near Union Square,
the Prescott House at Spring Street, and the former assemblyman's office in the Hamilton Building, across the street from
City Hall.

Not far past the Hall of Records and Surrogate Court, Sargent entered the tangle of narrow streets that held the offices
of stockbrokers, financiers, and attorneys working near the
New York Stock Exchange, finally arriving at the office of
Root & Clarke, four doors down from the Exchange on Broad
Street. Sargent was directed to a large armchair in a private
room of Root and Clarke's office and answered questions for
more than an hour.

Rastus Ransom had appointed ex-Surrogate Daniel G. Rollins as referee for Sargent's testimony. In addition to being the
predecessor of Judge Ransom, Rollins had served as assistant
U.S. attorney for the Southern District of New York and was,
like Elihu Root, a member of President Chester A. Arthur's
inner circle of friends and colleagues. Root was joined by his
partner, Samuel Clarke, and Edward Vollmer, appointed by
the Court as guardian *ad litem* for the children of Schuyler
Hamilton Jr.

John O'Conor, a local attorney, represented John Sargent.
Charles Fuller was on hand to represent Eva Mann. Eva was
invited to attend but declined the invitation.

It was in Fuller's (and Eva's) best interest to maintain the
proposition that Ray Hamilton may, in fact, still be alive. If
there was reasonable doubt about the proof of his demise, and
if the possibility of Hamilton still being alive was tenable,
there could be no cause to probate his will and Eva could live
to fight another day on a different legal front.

Accordingly, Fuller's cross-examination of Sargent was
pointed. Fuller hoped that Sargent would somehow—even in
the slightest measure—introduce a degree of doubt about the

certainty surrounding Hamilton's death. Barring that, perhaps Sargent would contradict himself or show that he was not one hundred percent certain about his testimony. In the end, Fuller was disappointed when Sargent remained resolute in his version of the story regarding Ray's death.

In his direct testimony, Sargent reiterated what he had already told the press off-the-record. Fuller began his cross-examination by contrasting Sargent's account with that of Dr. Green. "You say that the body identified by you as Mr. Hamilton's was not badly decomposed. If Dr. Green, who saw it before you did, swears that it must have been in the water for ten days; that it was so badly decomposed that recognition was impossible; that the upper lip and mustache were eaten away by fish and turtles; that the body was swollen as much as it could swell without bursting, and that the flesh had turned purple, would he be telling the truth?"

Sargent stood upright and shot back at Fuller, "Has he sworn to that?"

Fuller ignored Sargent's theatrics and repeated his question. "If he said that, is it the truth?"

"No," Sargent insisted. "The body was in good preservation and easy to be recognized by anyone who knew Mr. Hamilton."

"Can you explain the discrepancy between your statement and Dr. Green's?"

Sargent remained adamant in his response. "No; neither can Dr. Green. I stand by my statement. There were three men with me who can prove it. If Dr. Green testified to what you have just read he testified to a lie. There was no decomposition. The body was not more swollen than would be natural in the case of a drowned man. The face was not bitten away. There was a little something in the mouth that drew up his upper lip and showed his long white teeth. He was always very careful with his teeth. The face was not eaten away, I say. Dr. Green's imagination must have been working very strongly."

After some back and forth about the condition of one of Hamilton's legs, which may or may not have been previously broken, Fuller turned his attention to the detail surrounding the state of Hamilton's corpse when the recovery team returned with it to Marymere. Sargent turned in his chair and buried his face in his hands for several minutes before telling Fuller that "he wouldn't answer another question such as were being asked."

Fuller concluded by wondering aloud why Mr. Sargent took the trouble to travel for two weeks when he could have given this same testimony much closer to his own home. Obliquely referring to the deep pockets of the Hamilton family, Fuller asked, "had anyone invited you, or did you come merely for pleasure?"

Sargent replied with righteous indignation, "I came to stop the trash in the newspapers about Mr. Hamilton not being dead. He is dead. I saw him dead. I came here, without invitation, to put a stop to the ridiculous talk. It would be to my interest to find him alive, if I only could." With nothing left to add, the eccentric rancher signed his testimony, bid the gentlemen in attendance a good day, and began his return to the isolation and beauty of Marymere.

The testimony of Dr. Green and John Sargent provided sufficient evidence for the court to make a conclusive determination that Robert Ray Hamilton was in fact, dead. The probate of his will could proceed, pending Eva's appeal of Judge Ransom's decision before the New York State Supreme Court.

# CHAPTER TEN

# Eva at the Footlights

## May 1891

When Eva stepped off of the witness stand in Surrogate Court in January, she temporarily stepped out of the spotlight as well. Rastus Ransom had verbally denied her status as Ray's lawful widow in January, but he did not submit the formal written order of his decision until March 10. Charles Fuller immediately filed an appeal, but for Eva, there was no further testimony to provide and no more star-turns before a packed courtroom.

When Ray was alive, she attempted to take advantage of his wealth and privilege through fraud and subterfuge—after his death, Eva tried to use proper legal channels to gain access to his estate, to no avail. Although her appeal was pending, the prospects for Judge Ransom's ruling to be overturned were dim. With a dwindling bank account, no pronounced skills, and little education, Eva was forced to fend for herself using the one talent with which she truly excelled: storytelling.

Aware of the public's insatiable appetite for the Hamilton scandal and her limited ability to tell her side of the story, Eva devised a vehicle to capitalize on her notoriety and provide an opportunity for the public to fully appreciate her version of life with Robert Ray Hamilton. She wrote a play, titled *The Hab-*

*bertons*, with herself cast, naturally, in the lead role and supported by a company of players who were thinly veiled references to the actual characters in her real-life drama that began in Atlantic City.

The plot of *The Habbertons* centered around Nadine Brenn (Eva), a penniless orphan, surrounded by a cast of characters who sought to take advantage of her. Robert Ray Hamilton was cast as Roland Livingstone, a man of means. In a twist on the actual events of Eva's life, Josh Mann does not appear as her common-law husband, but as Ivan Vanteck, the best friend of Roland Livingstone. The script did not include a drunken baby nurse (Mary Ann Donnelly) but it did feature a drunken housekeeper, a Mrs. Preston.

While on a trip to the New Jersey countryside, Roland Livingstone and Ivan Vanteck meet Nadine Brenn, described as "a simple little miss of the milking stool." Ivan Vanteck is immediately smitten by the charms of Nadine Brenn, but to his dismay, Livingstone and Nadine fall hopelessly in love. Vanteck is not the only person upset by Roland and Nadine's burgeoning relationship—he is joined in his fury by Livingstone's longtime girlfriend, Miss Dean. Livingstone had grown weary of Miss Dean and her meddlesome mother and aunt.

After Livingstone and Nadine Brenn announce their plans to be wed, Ivan and Miss Dean conspire to hire a man to impersonate a priest and perform the marriage ceremony—Livingstone and Nadine think they are legally married, but they are not. The drunken housekeeper, Mrs. Preston, informs Nadine Brenn of the deception and a humiliated Nadine prepares to leave Roland, only to be convinced by him to stay and have a genuine marriage take place.

Roland and Nadine escape to the seashore for a much-needed vacation, but they are followed by Vanteck and Miss Dean. While ensconced at their oceanside hotel, Mrs. Pres-

ton, drunk as usual, attempts to stab Nadine. Roland inter-
venes and in the ensuing scuffle he accidentally stabs the
drunken housekeeper. To prove her undying love for her husband, Nadine takes the blame and Livingstone flees to parts
unknown.

After not hearing from Roland for some time, Nadine, believing him to be dead, prepares to marry Ivan Vanteck. She
feels that Roland would wish her to marry his best friend. But
just before Vanteck and Nadine are to exchange wedding
vows, Roland returns to reclaim his lawful wife and Vanteck
slinks away defeated. Miss Dean, overcome by the reunion of
the man she loved and Nadine, takes poison and kills herself.
In the end, Nadine gets everything she ever wanted: her
wealthy husband by her side, and her nemeses, Ivan Vanteck
and Miss Dean, vanquished.

Eva's announcement about the upcoming production to the
*New York World* in mid-May was picked up by the wire ser-
vices and published across the country. Newspapers had fresh
grist to feed a story for which the public never grew tired of—
after four months, the name "Hamilton" was again splashed
across their front pages. The story was published from coast to
coast with a mixture of enthusiasm, suspicion, and antipathy.
The *Topeka Daily Press* opined:

> The play will set forth with great power
> and effect the dramatic life story of the
> man who is supposed to have met his
> death among the tangled weeds of the
> Snake River. Again the skeleton which
> has disturbed the serenity of one of the
> most historic families in the history in
> this country is to be dragged forth from its
> charmed house and exposed to public
> view.

"I do not care to speak of the past," Eva told reporters. "It is too full of sadness. I have not only decided to go on the stage but have been in training for more than a month. I have signed a contract with a well-known and wealthy gentleman outside the theatrical business. It is our intention to have a strong supporting company and to play only in the best theaters. I shall open with a two-week's engagement at the Broadway Theater in November. I finally realized the necessity of doing something for a living and after careful study of the matter decided to go upon the stage."

As with almost everything to do with Eva, her announcement was a maddening entanglement of fact and fiction. She had secured financing from Charles W. Gardiner, an impresario of middling reputation, but a spokesman for the Broadway Theater, one of the pre-eminent houses in the emerging uptown theater district, confirmed that "no negotiations for an engagement with Eva Mann at any date have been made or suggested." And while Eva gave newspapers the impression that she had written the play herself, her attorney, Charles Fuller, casually told reporters, "She has been taking lessons and someone has written a play for her."

Edward Warren, a voice coach whom Eva had hired as her acting instructor, was effusive in his praise of her preparations. "She has been as extensively and ably advertised as any woman in America. Stories of her past life which have appeared in print will not easily be forgotten by the public. But even many of those who condemned her saw it was a struggle of a lone, friendless woman against power and wealth. No doubt every theatrical manager will be anxious to secure her as an attraction, for there can be no question about the drawing powers of Mrs. Robert Ray Hamilton's play, which is virtually the story of her life."

If Ray's family and friends were upset by the thought of Eva Mann making even one dollar off of the Hamilton name, they said nothing about it in the press, undoubtedly loathe to give Eva even a scintilla of publicity. When Ray's father was asked about the play by a reporter at the Windsor Hotel, he said that "he had given no thought to the story of the stage arrangements," of the woman he believed at one time to be his daughter-in-law. Immediately changing the subject, the General stated that he "was fully convinced that his son was drowned in the Snake River, just as had been represented."

### September 1891

In the last week in August, posters announcing Eva's stage debut began to appear in small towns in New Jersey.

THE SEASON'S SENSATION

## MRS. ROBERT RAY HAMILTON

UNDOUBTEDLY THE MOST FAMOUS WOMAN
IN THE LAND

**FOR ONE NIGHT ONLY**
*In Her Beautiful Realistic and Pretty Drama, entitled:*

## ALL A MISTAKE

Supported by a company of
Metropolitan Players

The title for Eva's drama, *The Habbertons*, was changed to *All a Mistake* by Charles Gardiner, who was financing the production and felt that *The Habbertons* didn't pack enough punch for a theatrical poster. Rehearsals had been frequent during July and August; when the calendar turned to September, Eva and her company were ready to raise the curtain on the curious interpretation of her life with Robert Ray Hamilton.

On Tuesday, September 1, *All a Mistake* opened decidedly off-Broadway, at the Opera House in Boonton, New Jersey, population 2,981. The three-story clapboard building on Main Street, next to City Hall, housed the finest stores in town on the ground floor and a six-hundred-seat auditorium on the double-height second and third floors. And unlike many performance venues in smaller towns in 1891, the Boonton Opera House could boast of being fully fitted with electric lights.

Gardiner had purposefully chosen Boonton to avoid the scrutiny of the New York press while the show found its footing, but as the town was only thirty miles from the city, at least one newsman from Manhattan made the journey to cover the opening. Writing for the *New York Sun*, the reporter located one of the actors in the company at his hotel, five hours before the curtain was due to go up on *All a Mistake*.

The actor, described as "a fat man, much soiled and bearing marks of personal contact with dusty things," freely offered his opinion about what was soon to transpire. "This is awful," he said. "Don't let her know. Don't. We sneaked away from New York yesterday morning and came down here because we thought no one would find us out. The woman just hasn't had any experience. We are doing these little towns to give her a chance to work off stage fright."

Eva sauntered through the hotel while the two men were talking, wearing a tight-fitting gray gown that flattered her appearance. She declined to speak to the reporter in detail, only stopping long enough to say that the night's production was merely an out-of-town tryout and that the actual premiere would be in Pittsburgh on September 4, followed by a run at the prestigious Chestnut Street Theater in Philadelphia.

As evening fell, 250 paying customers, less than half of the room's capacity, ascended the Opera House stairs to witness a dramatic departure from the facts of the Hamilton story that had been relentlessly reported for two years. The actors plodded through their lines, always ceding the spotlight to Eva, the heroine of the entire production.

The reviews for *All a Mistake* ranged from bemused to brutal, with newspapers focused primarily on the performance of Eva Mann. "Considering the fact that she never acted before on the stage, her poses and stage walk are quite good. Her form shows to advantage and her bare arms are round and white and tapering, but when it comes to reading the lines, Eva Mann is not there at all. (She) expressed tremendous passion in her gestures, while her voice had about as little excitement as a glass of rain water. The contrast was highly entertaining."

Another simply noted that "she failed to rise to the requirements of the emotional scenes and the play as a whole fell flat." By comparison, "The lady who played the cast-off mistress did very credibly, acting far better than the star."

While the show itself didn't garner any raves, the fact that some houses agreed to stage the play at all, and that it was patronized by a paying public, was met with indignation. The *Times* of Philadelphia offered, "It has long been the custom of unscrupulous theatrical managers to traffic in abandoned women. Let us understand this matter. The stage has always been and always will be a reflex of the manners, tastes and morality of its patrons. An adventuress on the stage is only possible because theatre-goers welcome adventuresses. Let us not blame these despicable creatures. The shame belongs to those who support them."

The *Times-Tribune* of Scranton agreed. "Both the woman and the play are an insult to the American stage and an added horror to a scandal that should be forgotten, and if by public patronage this adventuress is enabled to continue to exhibit herself it will be a disgrace to the American people."

After the debut in Boonton, *All a Mistake* played in Hackettstown, New Jersey, and Pottsville, Pennsylvania, before rolling into Shamokin, sixty miles northeast of Harrisburg, on Saturday, September 5. Upon the company's arrival, the show's manager, Arthur Cole, sent a telegram to Charles Gardiner in New York, explaining that the production required additional funding to continue. Gardiner, presumably having read the reviews, did not reply.

The only cash on hand was needed to cover the cost of printing posters. Two hours before the Shamokin performance, Cole gathered the actors for a meeting, explained the dire predicament, and took the decision to disband the troupe. This evening's production would be the last of *All a Mistake*. The spectacular failure of Eva's sure-fire vehicle to attain fame and fortune so troubled the star of the show that during the first act in Shamokin, she fainted.

The next morning, members of the company explained to the hotel manager that because they hadn't been paid for the prior evening's work, they were unable to pay their hotel bills. When the manager threatened to call the authorities, Eva produced a twenty-dollar bill from her pocketbook and handed it to a clerk, pointedly adding that she refused to pay any more for the rooms. At the train station, Eva paid $11.50 to cover the disconsolate cast's fare back to New York.

Shortly before boarding the train for Manhattan, Arthur Cole told reporters who had trailed the troupe to the station, "The great failure of the Mrs. Robert Ray Hamilton company is due to the city newspapers, which have been roasting Mrs. Hamilton since we made our first appearance in New Jersey."

The *Nebraska State Journal* in Lincoln, thirteen hundred miles away from the "city newspapers" referred to by Cole, summed up the production most succinctly: "'All A Mistake' is the name of the alleged play in which the notorious Eva Mann is now starring. The audiences generally agree that the piece is well named."

## CHAPTER ELEVEN

# Mrs. Gaul's Queer Goings-On

*July 1892*

After the lights had dimmed on *All a Mistake* and Eva had slinked out of Shamokin, there were no new headlines to be written about the bold adventuress for months. The spotlight in which she so clearly reveled, and the wealth and status she so desperately craved, proved to be elusive. Robert Fuller had appealed Rastus Ransom's decision against Eva to the New York State Supreme Court, but for readers who had dined on a full buffet of Ray-and-Eva stories for two years, a page-four, two-sentence notice about a legal maneuver was hardly the sustenance required to satisfy the public appetite for all things Hamilton.

With a lull in the seemingly perpetual news storm that had raged since Ray's death, the Hamilton family decided to bring home their son, cousin, and brother. As night fell on Monday, July 25, a New York Central train chugged into Grand Central Depot on Forty-Second Street, carrying a metallic casket. Ray's body had been exhumed from Marymere and was accompanied back to the city by General George E. P. Howard, a law colleague of Elihu Root's, who carried an affidavit signed by Henry Code, the Unitah County Coroner in Wyoming.

Howard was met at the depot by undertakers from Adair & Aldred of Fourth Avenue, who took possession of Ray Hamil-

ton's remains. (Coincidentally, it was Adair & Aldred who
made the burial arrangements for the first two babies that
Eva Mann had purchased at the end of 1889—Beatrice I and
II.) Although Ray's body was received in the City of New York,
it was planned for interment at Green-Wood Cemetery in the
City of Brooklyn and required a permit for transport to be issued by the New York Health Board.

The family desired the utmost secrecy in transferring Ray's
body from Marymere to Green-Wood. They were undoubtedly
averse to seeing the Hamilton name in the newspapers again,
but more importantly, they felt that if the transfer became
public knowledge, Eva might insist on seeing the remains and
create a spectacle of the situation. On Tuesday morning, July
26, Dr. John T. Nagle, registrar of Vital Statistics at the New
York Health Department, very quietly issued the permit au-
thorizing the transfer of Ray Hamilton's remains to Green-
Wood.

By early afternoon, a hearse containing the casket began
the six-mile journey from lower Manhattan over the Brooklyn
Bridge to the heights above Gowanus Bay, and then passed
through the ornate, gothic gates of Green-Wood Cemetery.
The hearse was followed by a coach carrying the two executors
of Ray's estate, Gil Spier and Edmund Baylies, as well as Dr.
Henry Satterlee, rector of the Calvary Episcopal Church near
Gramercy Park. Neither the General nor Ray's brother,
Schuyler Jr., attended the interment, in order to avoid bring-
ing undo attention to the proceedings. The General and his
wife had sailed for Europe several weeks before, and Schuyler
Jr. was at his country home on the Hudson River in Ossining.

Green-Wood Cemetery was an exquisite example of the
Rural Cemetery Movement that began in the United States in
the 1830s. Churchyards and small cemetery parcels in the
center of villages were filling up, and rapid urbanization made

it impossible to expand them. Mount Auburn Cemetery in Boston, Spring Grove Cemetery in Cincinnati, and others in large cities across the country became not only final resting places for the dead, but picturesque burial landscapes featuring lakes, fountains, and overshadowing trees that became ideal environments for an afternoon respite from the cramped quarters of the city. With nineteen miles of carriage roads, seventeen miles of footpaths, and a profusion of brilliant flowers, Green-Wood was known as a perfect wilderness of beauty.

It was said that "the ambition of the New Yorker is to live upon Fifth Avenue, to take his airings in Central Park, and to sleep with his fathers in Green-Wood." By the time Ray Hamilton's body arrived at the cemetery, more than 200,000 souls had been interred over Green-Wood's 478 acres. At the General's request, Ray was not buried in a Hamilton plot, but rather in the plot of his maternal grandfather (and namesake), Robert Ray. To help maintain the secrecy of the effort, no stone marked the grave, and no undertaker's name was recorded on the burial record.

Despite all of the effort on the part of the family to transfer Ray's body without the public being made aware, reporters who made a living lurking around courthouses and public records offices in hopes of gleaning a tip that might lead to a story found one at the Health Department, not long after the permit was issued to Adair & Aldred on Tuesday morning. When contacted, the undertakers refused to say anything about the matter and denied all knowledge of the transfer.

Before the dirt had fully settled on Ray Hamilton's grave, the press arrived at Green-Wood the next morning and tracked down Thomas Marchant, Superintendent of Interments at the cemetery. He returned the same answer to all questions: "I refuse to give any information whatsoever." As to a general inquiry about whether the Hamilton family even

possessed a plot in the cemetery, Marchant replied, "You had
better go see the family about the matter if you want any information."

Although the amount of detail regarding Ray's burial at
Green-Wood was scant, it didn't stop the papers from rehash-
ing the story that had created such an uproar in New York
(and beyond) two and a half years prior. And while the Hamilton family couldn't have been pleased about reading, once
more, about the man of high honors who became infatuated
with Eva Steele, who in turn "bled him like a leech," at least
the examination and affidavit that led to the interment at
Green-Wood established beyond doubt the fact that it really
was the body of Robert Ray Hamilton.

### February–November, 1893

While Eva Mann remained out of the headlines for most of
1892, she remained undaunted in her desire to obtain what
she deemed to be her rightful share of Ray Hamilton's estate.
While she waited to hear if the New York State Supreme
Court would hear her appeal regarding Judge Ransom's decision two years prior, she sought to rectify a different, but related, legal matter.

During the probate hearing in Surrogate Court in 1891,
Eva had been served by Howe & Hummel, acting on behalf of
Josh Mann, with divorce papers. Her attorney at the time,
Charles Fuller, dismissed the suit as a publicity stunt and
hinted that the Hamilton family had, through Howe & Hum-
mel, paid Josh Mann to bring the suit forward. Whether or not
that was the case, the possibility certainly fell within Howe &
Hummel's modus operandi.

A year later, in January 1892, Josh Mann requested that
the divorce suit be removed from the Supreme Court calendar
and marked "reserved generally." He was not prepared to
withdraw the suit—he only asked that the court not consider

moving forward with it at the present time. Eva was exasperated by the delay and wanted the matter resolved before her appeal of the Surrogate Court decision began.

Now, in February 1893—two years after being served divorce papers—Eva Mann stood before Justice George L. Ingraham in Supreme Court, flanked by a new attorney, Charles W. Brooke. Brooke was highly regarded at the New York Bar, described as "skillful, resourceful, and combative." Brooke told the judge that Eva "was ready to go with the trial previously and is ready now."

Further, Brooke alleged that "Joshua Mann has always prevented and evaded the trial, and that his client believes the suit was not brought in good faith or with any intention of ever trying it, but merely to harass and annoy her and to seek her from proceeding, or to affect her status in the proceedings to establish that she was the widow of Robert Ray Hamilton."

The diminutive Abraham Hummel, impeccably dressed as ever, appeared on behalf of Josh Mann. Feigning ignorance of a plan to harass and annoy, he told the judge matter-of-factly that they were ready to proceed as early as the first week of March.

### March 27, 1893

The Mann divorce hearing was scheduled for March 27, in the courtroom of the Honorable Edward Patterson. When the hearing began, Abraham Hummel rose and moved to strike the hearing from the calendar, bluntly explaining to the judge that "my client is crazy." Hummel submitted an affidavit from no less an authority on mental health than the noted alienist, Dr. Carlos MacDonald, who at that time was the chairman of the New York State Commission in Lunacy and professor of mental diseases at Bellevue Hospital Medical College.

The physician's affidavit stated he saw Mann several times between February 18 and 23 and noted the following: "He was below his usual weight, his flesh was flabby, color bleached, complexion muddy, and his digestive functions disturbed through want of exercise and outdoor air, which he refuses to take. Mann admitted that he was addicted to alcoholic and other excesses." MacDonald took care to note that he didn't consider Mann to be violent and saw no need for him to be committed to an asylum.

Charles Brooke stood and vigorously opposed the motion. He declared that "the suit had been brought as the result of a conspiracy on the part of the executors of Robert Ray Hamilton to injure his client" and asked that the motion be denied, because "like the suit, it was not brought in good faith." Brooke asserted that "a trial would expose the conduct of Mann and show that he was not the husband of the defendant. If the Court decided that there had been no marriage between plaintiff and defendant, then his client would be, in law, the widow of Robert Ray Hamilton." The suit was again delayed while Howe & Hummel prepared a rebuttal.

### September 1893

Six months passed with no improvement in Josh Mann's condition, or with any news about the resumption of the divorce trial between he and Eva. Unbeknownst to almost everyone, though, Eva had remarried around the same time as the hearing in March about Josh's mental state. Reporters who trolled the city courthouses noticed that a "petty lawsuit" involving a sum of $200, had been filed by attorney Charles W. Brooke on behalf of his client, Evangeline L. Hilton.

Eyebrows sufficiently raised, reporters reached out to Brooke, who confirmed that indeed, Eva's new marriage occurred in New York about six months prior. Her husband was identified as a young Englishman, Edward Hilton, who had only been in New York for a few months. He was described as about thirty years old, slight, pale and wiry, with dark eyes and a black mustache. Edward and Eva, the new Mrs. Hilton, were running a theatrical boarding house at 337 West Twenty-Ninth Street.

As expected, reporters descended on the Hiltons' address as soon as the link to Eva was confirmed. Hilton refused to talk about the marriage but denied that the Surrogate had decided that his wife was the wife of Josh Mann. When asked what he knew about his new wife's background, "He showed much familiarity with the remarkable story that closed its first chapter with the death of the young New York Assemblyman."

Eva was, if nothing else, a gift to the newspapermen who had followed the Hamilton saga for the past four years—just when it seemed that she had faded from sight, she became involved in something that warranted the retelling of the entire affair. Her marriage to Edward Hilton prompted at least one newspaper to write: "The question of interest is, how Eva freed herself of the matrimonial shackles to place herself in a position to be able to marry again. Still, Eva has always denied that she was Josh Mann's wife, and insisted right along that she was Mrs. Robert Ray Hamilton."

It was also reported that "according to those who are in a position to know what they are talking about, the somewhat checkered career of the woman is over and she is living a quiet life, thoroughly in love with the young Englishman who has taken her to be his wife." However, like almost everything, and everyone, connected to Eva, a seemingly straightforward marriage to a seemingly straightforward man wasn't nearly as straightforward as initially reported.

### December 1893

If in fact Eva did make an attempt at living a quiet life, she failed just three months after the public acknowledgment of her marriage to Edward Hilton. The assumed identities, ambiguities, and lies in which her life and loves were perpetually cloaked provided unlimited fodder for the newspapers. By December, Eva had found her way back onto the front page with a fresh cast of characters—her new husband and his in-laws.

In September, the press had been introduced to Eva's latest catch as Edward Hilton. In a succession of newspaper articles three months later, he was referred to as Frederick Hilton, and then Frederick Gaul. He was more familiarly known around New York simply as The Duke. It wasn't until his brother got involved in his own contretemps that The Duke's true identity was revealed; he was actually Mr. Archie Gaul. And while it was true that Archie Gaul was indeed an Englishman, he arrived in New York not three months before meeting Eva as was reported, but sometime between three and five years earlier.

For the first time since the stabbing in Atlantic City four years prior, Eva was cast in a supporting role in this new, emerging drama—the lead characters were her in-laws, Archie's brother, Robert and his wife, Alice. Robert, a short, slight man of thirty-seven, and his wife Alice, an attractive young woman of twenty-six, had been wed in Southsea, England, five years before, immigrated to New York, and were parents to two-year-old Madge Irene.

On the night of July 25, a card party was organized in the East Eighty-Seventh Street flat of Robert and Alice Gaul, attended by, among others, another Gaul brother, Richard, and a Gaul cousin, Harry Hayward. Alice Gaul was there, but her husband Robert was not. By late in the evening, as it became apparent that all of the guests would sleep in the Gaul apartment, Alice Gaul went to stay in a flat across the hall, on the pretense of making room for the others. Shortly thereafter, Harry Hayward left the Gaul apartment, ostensibly to go home. His suspicions aroused, Richard Gaul crept into the hall, put his ear to the door of the neighboring flat, and heard Alice Gaul and Harry talking.

The party was repeated the next evening, again without Robert Gaul in attendance, and with the same departure routine acted out by Alice Gaul and Harry Hayward. Like he did the previous night, Richard crept to the door across the hall, but after listening to Alice and Harry's conversation for some time, he could no longer contain himself. He shouted into the keyhole, "Alice, I know Hayward is in there with you!"

On Saturday, December 2, Robert Gaul realized the extent of the relationship between his wife and Harry Hayward when he found them in a compromising position. Alice immediately left their flat and went to live temporarily with Hayward's brother and his wife on Perry Street in Greenwich Village. She returned to East Ninety-Sixth Street three days later and took Madge away from her estranged husband.

Unable to properly care for her baby in temporary quarters, she made arrangements with the one woman who she felt could properly attend to her child. Inexplicably, that woman was her sister-in-law, Eva. Robert immediately contacted his attorney and a custody hearing was scheduled for the following Monday, December 11. An order to appear before the court was issued, instructing Eva to produce her niece, Madge Irene Gaul, at the hearing.

One could almost hear reporters sharpening their pencils and turning to a fresh page in their notebooks at the prospect of another court appearance by the never-boring, always-newsworthy Eva Mann . . . or Hamilton . . . or Gaul. But after four years in and out of courtrooms and headlines, this supporting role was not one that played to Eva's advantage—no money could be gained from the situation nor any chance to enhance her reputation.

After only one day of having Madge in her care, Eva turned the toddler over to Frederick Flowerden, Alice's father who was visiting from England. After Alice wrote a letter of contrition and promised to never see Hayward again, Flowerden returned Madge to her father until the courts could sort everything out.

As Eva was not directly named in the dispute between Robert Gaul and his wife, Alice, she had no legal prerogative to attend the court proceedings, much to the disappointment of the press. That did not, however, prevent the headline writers from including her name in their coverage of the Gaul story.

## MRS. GAUL'S QUEER GOINGS-ON.

*An Unsuccessful Attempt to Bring*
EVA RAY HAMILTON
*Into an Already Unsavory Case.*

## PERMITTED TO SEE HER CHILD.

A SCENE IN A NEW YORK COURT THIS MORNING.

*Eva Ray Hamilton Failed to Appear.*

## EVA RAY DID NOT APPEAR.

*Did Not Have Her Niece*
*When the Writ Was Issued.*

Eva had one more chance to play a leading role in the public eye. During the whirlwind of stories concerning Robert and Alice Gaul, newspapers across the country ran a brief announcement that "the case of Eva Mann Hamilton vs. the Estate of Robert Ray Hamilton has been placed on the New York Supreme Court calendar." Three years after Rastus Ransom's decision in Surrogate Court denying Eva's dower right as Ray Hamilton's widow, the woman who now called herself Lydia E. Gaul had one last chance to obtain the status and money she had long sought.

### February 1894

Eva's appeal was disposed of in short order by the State Supreme Court in February 1894. The case was reviewed by the four judges in the First Department: David L. Follett, Morgan J. O'Brien, Alton B. Parker, and the Presiding Judge, Charles H. Van Brunt.

Van Brunt penned the five-page decision, concluding:

> We not only see no reason to differ from the conclusions arrived at by the surrogate upon the questions of fact, but as already intimated, we do not see how, under the evidence, he could have reached any other result. The decree should be affirmed with costs.

O'BRIEN and PARKER, JJ, concur.

Four and a half years after Robert Ray Hamilton met his demise in the Snake River, it was now clear: Eva had no dower right and would receive nothing from his estate. The court's decision, however, didn't stop her from making one last desperate attempt to gain something—*anything*—from her relationship with Ray Hamilton.

Eva filed a separate lawsuit based on "a memorandum written on a leaf of a pocket pad which belonged to Mr. Hamilton." The undated, suspicious sheet of paper read simply:

*I intend to pay you, Eva, thirty-two hundred and fifty as soon as I can. R.R.H.*

Gilbert Spier and Edmund Baylies, co-executors of Ray's estate, countered that the paper was a forgery. They noted that "on close inspection, the letters are clear enough, though they seem to have been made with a light hand using a hard pencil." At the end of February, Eva's new lawsuit was postponed, dragging on without a fixed date for adjudication.

The Hamilton family had had enough. Root & Clarke were directed to negotiate a settlement with Charles Brooke—in exchange for an agreed-to sum, Eva would drop all legal action and agree to bring no new lawsuit against either the executors of the estate or the Hamilton family in perpetuity. In short, she was to cash her check and never darken their proverbial door again.

On July 5, a quit claim from Lydia E. Gaul to Edmund L. Baylies was filed with the New York City Registrar. Mrs. Gaul "relinquishes all claims to any interest in the estate of Robert Ray Hamilton, deceased, forevermore." In return, Edmund L. Baylies and Gilbert M. Spier "will agree to pay, and acknowledge that they have paid, Lydia E. Gaul $10,000 in full requital of her claims as widow or for any other reason, upon the Robert Ray Hamilton estate."

By the time the agreement was made public—two days after it had been signed—the *New York Sun* reported that "Mrs. Gaul had sailed, or intended sailing, for Europe." Whether Eva remained in New York, moved to New Jersey, or spent her days and money in Europe, it was of little consequence to the headline writers and reporters who had followed her for nearly five years.

It was almost with a sense of mourning that the newspapers published their articles about the end of the legal maneuvering between Eva and the Hamilton family. As the *Boston Post* somberly wrote, Eva's signature on the quit claim "closed the last chapter in the story of the ruin of Robert Ray

Hamilton by one of the most remarkable women that fin-de-siecle depravity has yet produced."

Whatever moral judgment one might have made about Eva's attempts to insinuate herself into one of the most prestigious families in nineteenth-century America, there was one undeniable fact about her actions and behavior over the course of nearly five years: she sold a hell of a lot of newspapers.

## CHAPTER TWELVE
# SEQUEL TO TRAGEDY

It is a testament to the public fascination with Ray and Eva that their story continued to be retold in the newspapers long after the bold adventuress had sailed for Europe and the fallen son had been laid to rest at Green-Wood Cemetery. Intrigue surrounding John Sargent and unfortunate circumstances involving Schuyler Hamilton Jr. gave license to newspaper writers to remind their readers, years after the fact, about Eva's bogus baby, the stabbing in Atlantic City, and Ray's unfortunate demise in Jackson Hole. The *St. Paul Globe* headlined a 1900 article about John Sargent:

**Sorry Story of**
**Robert Ray Hamilton**
**Again Called to Mind**

While the Hamiltons' and Eva's attorney negotiated a final settlement in 1894, John Sargent's family continued to grow. A fifth child, Adelaide, was born at Marymere in May 1894, joining older brother Charles and sisters Mary, Martha, and Catherine on the Wyoming frontier. Marymere was completed in 1891, one year after the death of Ray Hamilton. In addition to making their home in the ten-room cabin on Jackson Lake,

Sargent and his wife, Adelaide, struggled to operate Mary-mere as a dude ranch, supplying their guests with fine wines and cigars as part of their room and board while the family survived on basic necessities.

At the same time, more than 2,000 miles away, in Newport, Rhode Island, Schuyler Jr.'s family was coming undone. Like Ray, Schuyler was an alumnus of Columbia University, earning a degree in architecture from Columbia's School of Mines in 1876. As an architect, Schuyler had a reputation as a skilled practitioner, though his record of completed works was less than prodigious. He invested heavily in his Anchor Brick Company in Ossining, a venture that bore little financial success before he was forced to liquidate. And like his brother Ray, he held a share of title in various holdings in the Hamilton family real estate portfolio.

What Schuyler truly excelled at, though, was being a Hamilton. The dashing, younger son of the General was an extremely popular clubman whose name was included on guest lists to the finest parties in Manhattan. Schuyler was a member of the University Club, as many men of means were, and naturally, the Sons of the Revolution. Though it was at St. Anthony Hall, a successor of Columbia's Delta Psi fraternity, on East Twenty-Eighth Street, where Schuyler could be found holding court with regularity. At the Murray Hill clubhouse, Schuyler passed the time in the company of contemporaries with family names equal in stature to his own: James W. Roosevelt, Edward de Peyster Livingston, Stuyvesant Fish, and scores of others.

Schuyler Hamilton Jr. closely resembled his older brother Ray, with the same jet-black hair and handsome features, sans the bushy sideburns that connected Ray's mustache across his upper lip. But while Ray held a serious countenance befitting an attorney and legislator, Schuyler possessed a more rakish charm, with a hint of mischief emanating from his deep-set eyes. His good looks, social pedigree, and professional standing were sufficient to woo Gertrude Van Cortlandt Wells, who Schuyler took as his wife in 1877. Gertrude's grandparents, aunts, and uncles all hailed from the extremely wealthy, ancestral families at the very top of New York's social pyramid: Van Cortlandt, Van Rensselaer, Van Wyck, and Gardiner.

Schuyler and Gertrude were married at St. Paul's Episcopal Church in Ossining on April 11, 1877. They made their primary home in Ossining and Schuyler kept a suite at the Plaza Hotel when business and social engagements kept him in the city. They had three children, Violet, Schuyler III, and Gertrude, all beneficiaries in their uncle Ray's will. Two other daughters, Helena and Lillian, died just after childbirth. Violet was born in Ossining, but both Schuyler III and Gertrude were born in the Hamiltons' seasonal home in Newport.

The material excesses of the Gilded Age were nowhere more evident than on the crescent-shaped end of the narrow peninsula that separates Narragansett Bay from the Atlantic Ocean. New multi-millionaires who had amassed their fortunes after the end of the Civil War flocked to Newport, bought land, and built stately mansions, hiring the finest artisans and craftsmen available in an effort to showcase their wealth and taste. From June through September, days were filled with tennis, polo, croquet, and yacht races, followed by evenings of lavish dinner parties, costume balls, and debutante debuts.

Every June, newspapers breathlessly announced the start of the season:

> A visit now to this millionaires' paradise, decked as it is in its freshest and most co-

quettish robes, is provocative of mingled emotions of envy and delight. To a lover of the beautiful, unprovided with a golden pass key to the charmed circle of exclusiveness that walls in the "Summer City," it seems unjust that so much exquisite loveliness should be the property of a select few.

Schuyler and Gertrude were such fixtures during the season in Newport that they acquired a multi-acre plot at the intersection of Harrison and Halidon Avenues to build their own cottage, which they christened The Moorings. A vine-covered, arched pergola framed the drive that led in a long, graceful arc to the four-story house with six fireplaces and twenty rooms, all contained under soaring gable roofs.

The Moorings was regularly mentioned in the roster of fashionable Newport cottages and became a destination on the season's party circuit. The paint had barely dried in the new ballroom when Gertrude Hamilton hosted a notable party:

> One of most exquisite entertainments given at Newport was the pink dinner-dance recently given by Mrs. Schuyler Hamilton at "The Moorings." The floral decorations were entirely of pink roses, and wherever color could be introduced it was ever of this delicate hue.

Schuyler and Gertrude didn't occupy The Moorings for long as husband and wife, though. In September 1894, the papers reported that tongues would be wagging in Newport social circles, announcing that Gertrude Van Cortlandt Wells Hamilton had filed for divorce from her husband of seventeen years.

In filing suit, Gertrude alleged that "her husband had deserted her and neglected her for nearly four years during which time she had to support herself." She also requested full custody of their three children.

Schuyler answered by asserting that Gertrude left him voluntarily and that he was both able and willing to provide for her wants and those of his children. The General arrived in Newport upon hearing the news from his son, "for purpose of standing by the young man when the suit comes to trial." Despite being described as a young man, Schuyler Jr. was forty-two years old at the time. But unlike the court proceedings involving Ray and Eva, Schuyler and Gertrude's divorce was quick and headline-free. On September 27, two weeks after Gertrude filed suit, her divorce was granted on the basis of non-support by her husband.

A one-line newspaper mention that didn't garner much attention, but foretold the future for Schuyler Hamilton, was printed off-season in the *New York Times*, in April 1895. "Schuyler Hamilton Jr., of New York, is here visiting A.L. Mason." Schuyler's visit to Arthur Livingston Mason almost certainly had as much to do with seeing the Masons' governess, Jane Byrd Mercer, as it did with catching up with A.L. (as he was known) and his wife Edith.

Jane was described as a handsome woman and accomplished. Petite, with long dark hair that she kept closely pulled back, she was fourteen years younger than Schuyler and had never been married. Whether or not Schuyler and Jane Mercer had begun a relationship before his divorce, or if their dalliance may have spurred Gertrude to action, is unknown.

The Mercer family of Maryland, while not possessing quite the same name recognition as the Hamiltons, played their own significant role in the formation of the American Republic. Jane's great-grandfather, John F. Mercer, fought in the Revolutionary War, was a delegate to the Constitutional Convention in Philadelphia in 1787, served one term in the U.S. House of Representatives, and was then elected as the tenth governor of Maryland from 1801 to 1803.

Her grandfather was Colonel John Mercer, an aide-de-camp to General Winfield Scott in the Civil War. Jane's parents, Richard Sprigg Mercer and his wife, Elizabeth, were well known for hosting Baltimore society gatherings at the Mercer family home, Cedar Park, in Anne Arundel County.

Jane and Schuyler Hamilton were married in a ceremony attended only by immediate family and several close friends on the morning of August 13, 1895, in the East Biddle Street town house of Jane's sister, Ella. The *Baltimore Sun* noted that the drawing room "was profusely decorated with roses and adorned with palms and other exotics." Jane's wedding dress was made of a light blue summer silk, and Schuyler wore a dark cutaway coat, striped trousers, and a white vest. The newspaper made a point of noting in the headline that "The Groom Is a Brother of the Late Robert Ray Hamilton."

Just after their wedding, the newlyweds sailed for Dinard, France, a resort town on the Côte d'Émeraude in Brittany, across the Baie du Prieuré from St. Malo. In the twentieth century, the Côte d'Azur would supplant the Emerald Coast as a preferred destination for the rich and famous, but during the summer months at the close of the nineteenth century, titled Europeans and the affluent from America and Great Britain flocked to the seaside resorts on the French side of the English Channel. Schuyler and Jane Hamilton were so taken with Dinard that they bought a villa and over the next three years, spent the majority of their time there.

The fair climate and refined living that Schuyler and Jane enjoyed in France stood in marked contrast to the conditions faced by the Sargents in Wyoming. Their decision to live year-round at Marymere despite the brutal conditions proved to meet with disastrous consequences. In March of 1897, a soldier checking on homesteaders who had remained in Jackson Hole through the harsh winter stopped at Marymere and was refused entry by John Sargent. After insisting that it was his duty to check on the well-being of the occupants, the soldier entered and found Adelaide Sargent laid out on a sofa with a broken leg that had been left untreated. She had either fallen off a horse or had some other kind of accident and was withering away in the cabin.

Whether John was incapable of tending to her or refused to do so was a matter of debate; regardless, Adelaide was emaciated and incapable of moving. Mrs. Laura Nowlin and a nurse, Hattie Osborne, were summoned from the Nowlin Ranch, fifty miles south of Marymere and were pulled through the snow-choked trails up to Marymere on a toboggan by six men fitted with snowshoes. Upon their arrival, John Sargent ordered them off of the premises, but they refused to leave. When they finally gained entrance to the cabin, they found Sargent's wife near death, wasted and worn by disease and suffering.

Adelaide was strapped to the toboggan and brought down to the Nowlin Ranch. A Dr. Woodburn was summoned from Rexburg, Idaho, ninety miles west of the ranch. Upon examining Adelaide Sargent, Dr. Woodburn concluded that "Mrs. Sargent [was] beyond hope," and that "medical science could not save her." Adelaide Sargent died on April 11, 1897, and was buried at the Nowlin Ranch.

This was now the second death under mysterious circumstances in which the eccentric, erratic John Sargent was involved. When Ray Hamilton was found dead in 1890, Sargent remained at Marymere—when Adelaide was pronounced dead seven years later, Sargent fled Jackson Hole. His children were put into temporary custody with several families in the valley and then taken back to Machias, Maine, to be raised by Adelaide's family. Ostracized, isolated, and with very little money, Sargent left Marymere for New York City, where he could easily be lost in a crowd, and found work at the Swift and Company meatpacking plant on Barclay Street in lower Manhattan.

At the same time that Sargent was butchering hogs and cattle at the meatpacker, Schuyler and Jane Hamilton returned to New York and took up residence in the Florence Apartments on East Eighteenth Street, two miles from Sargent's place of employ.

They had previously traveled to Paris in 1897, where Jane gave birth to their daughter, Alexandra Schuyler Hamilton. Jane required surgery after the delivery and was prescribed morphine to ease her pain. While convalescing, she developed a nervous condition; she began taking morphine tablets regularly to allay both her physical pain and mental stress.

In addition to her growing morphine addiction while in Dinard, Jane also suffered from astraphobia—a fear of thunder and lightning. When the sky darkened in advance of an impending storm and the initial rumbles of thunder could be heard on the horizon, she became panicked. At the first sight of lightning touching down, Jane would shut herself in a dark closet so that she could not see the flashes of light bounce off of her villa walls. As thunderstorms regularly rolled across the English Channel to the French coastline and Jane's phobia became more pronounced, her morphine consumption accelerated, to the point that Schuyler thought it best to return to the United States and seek medical help to wean his wife from the narcotic.

After Schuyler, Jane, and eighteen-month-old Alexandra returned to New York, Schuyler Hamilton contacted a physician, George V. Foster, who began treating Jane in an effort to dissuade her from resorting to so powerful a narcotic. For a brief time, he succeeded in urging her to use less harmful sedatives, and in lesser amounts.

Unbeknownst to both Schuyler and Dr. Foster, however, Jane continued to discreetly obtain her preferred morphine tablets. Dr. Foster would later complain to reporters that "it is an outrage that such little restriction should be placed upon the sale of morphine in this city. It is supposed to be hard to get a glass of beer during prohibited hours, but morphine can be bought with greater facility. Such indiscriminate sale of poisons ought not to be allowed."

On Tuesday evening, May 3, a particularly bad thunderstorm that broke over the city threw Jane Hamilton into a state of hysteria—as was her habit, she hid in a dark closet for the duration of the downpour. By 10:00 P.M., the storm had passed and Schuyler made every effort to calm her until she fell asleep. Neither Schuyler, nor their maid, who slept with Alexandra in an adjoining room, heard Jane stir during the night.

At eight o'clock on Wednesday morning, Schuyler was awakened by Jane's heavy breathing and made multiple attempts to rouse her, but she had lapsed into unconsciousness. He immediately summoned Dr. Foster, who lived only four doors away, and when Foster failed to bring her to, he called in another doctor from the neighborhood. Despite both of the physicians' efforts, they were unable to improve her condition and at 1:30 in the afternoon, she passed away. A partially emptied box of morphine tablets was found near her bed—the doctors surmised that at some point in the night, she awoke and swallowed a number of them without waking either her husband or the maid.

Coroner Jacob Bausch and the coroner's physician, Dr. P. F.

O'Hanlon, arrived at the Hamilton apartment later in the afternoon and completed a permit for the interment. They determined that Jane's death was inadvertently caused and that there were no grounds whatever to justify any belief of foul play, concluding that it was unnecessary to perform an autopsy. Jane Byrd Mercer Hamilton, age thirty-two, was buried in Green-Wood Cemetery, and Schuyler Hamilton Jr., in addition to being once-divorced, was now, at age forty-six, a widower.

Schuyler's financial state compounded his situation. He was no longer working as a practicing architect, the refined tastes of his ex-wife cost a premium, and he now had four children to support. The utter failure of his brick business years before and the lavish home he built in Newport all compounded to put stress on his real estate holdings in New York.

When Ray bequeathed a $1,200 a year annuity to Beatrice in his will, the disbursement was planned to come from income generated from a property in Brooklyn that Schuyler now co-owned with his aunt Nathalie. The property was underperforming—at the same time as Schuyler's wife Jane was descending into her morphine habit, Nathalie Baylies went to court to release Beatrice's annuity from the Brooklyn property only and have it tied to the overall holdings of Ray's estate. The court agreed and the annuity was slated to be paid, in part, from the income generated by the Prescott House—Schuyler's principal holding from his brother's estate.

For Schuyler Jr., this was unacceptable. He filed an appeal to untie the annuity from any specific property and at the same time, petitioned the court for his daughter with Jane Mercer Hamilton (Alexandra) to be included in the distribution of the estate. The court ruled that only those persons who were living at the time of Ray's death—Schuyler's three children with Gertrude—were entitled to share in the estate as outlined in Ray's will, but released the burden of the annuity payments from Schuyler's holdings.

That ruling prompted Nathalie Baylies to petition the court, claiming that due to litigation and other circumstances arising from Ray Hamilton's untimely death, there were insufficient funds available to continue the annuity payments to Beatrice Ray Hamilton. The court agreed, ruling that "(Hamilton's) personal estate has been very materially diminished so that it is not sufficient for the production of this annuity."

With that, the child christened as Beatrice Ray Hamilton, abandoned at birth by her natural parents, illegally sold as part of a blackmail scheme, and shuttled from guardian to guardian for the first ten years of her life, was cast out, no longer the recipient of any financial benefit from her association with one of the most prestigious families in America.

John Sargent, cast out from his own family (albeit for different reasons), had saved enough money from working at Swift and Co. to return to Marymere in the fall of 1899. At the same time that Sargent prepared to trade the cacophony of New York for the solitude of the Tetons, the woman who originally claimed to be Beatrice's mother, the notorious Eva Mann, returned to the city after spending five years in Europe. Naturally, it wasn't long before she once again found herself generating headlines:

## IN A TENDERLOIN CELL

### *The Woman Who Posed*
### *As Mrs. Robert Ray Hamilton*
### *Arrested for High Kicking*

On August 24, two intoxicated women of an uncertain age delighted hundreds of onlookers in the red-light Tenderloin

District, at the corner of Twenty-Sixth Street and Broadway, by performing a can-can dance, "highly seasoned with high kicking." Timothy Sullivan, a police officer patrolling the area, promptly hauled them into the West Twentieth Street station.

They were sent to the Jefferson Market Police Court in Greenwich Village where the presiding judge asked them their names. Eva's companion answered, "Mrs. Victoria Cararet."

Eva replied, with a hint of a smirk, "Mrs. Robert Ray Hamilton. I guess you have heard of me, Judge."

"What is your age?"

"Well, Judge, put down 25 years . . . 35, 45, 55 or any old thing. I ain't as good looking as I once was, Judge, but good enough, eh? I have not got as much money as I once had, but I've got enough to get full." Eva punctuated her statement by executing a vigorous kick toward the ceiling of the courtroom.

The judge dismissed the case against Eva and Mrs. Cararet, admonishing them only as common drunks. One account of the incident noted that Eva possessed "a sorrowful history, but one of daily occurrence in this second Sodom where sin and crime of every degree grow rank in the Tenderloin." It would be another five years before Eva's name again appeared in the newspapers.

John Sargent would have undoubtedly been pleased with only a simple admonishment from a judge, for upon his return to Marymere, he was arrested on December 8 and charged with second-degree murder in the death of his wife. The *New York Times* reported at the time that he was incurably insane, and that the confinement in jail caused him to become a physical wreck and lose his mind.

In reality, Sargent petitioned the court to be released on his own recognizance because while in New York, he had reconnected with two of his daughters, Mary and Catherine, and they had returned to Marymere with him. Mary was now thirteen years old and Catherine was eight—Sargent intended to place them both in boarding school at the Sacred Heart Academy in Ogden, Utah, almost three hundred miles south of Marymere. He explained to the judge that he needed to care for his girls before they could travel to Ogden in the spring, and that he needed to get his ranch in order after it stood empty for two years. Justice Cunningham agreed to release him without bail—four months later, in April 1900, the case was dismissed entirely, due to conflicting testimony among the witnesses and an inability to obtain sufficient evidence to bring Sargent to trial. As a new century began, John Sargent once again started life anew on the Wyoming frontier.

## CHAPTER THIRTEEN
# Let Him Be Forgotten

Early in the evening of December 31, 1899, the elevated trains and surface cars in Manhattan began to bring New Yorkers by the thousands to Trinity Church on lower Broadway. "The numerous progeny of Father Knickerbocker had not forgotten the time-honored custom which takes the reverent and irreverent alike down into the old city where Trinity rears its stately pile and graceful spire." The present Trinity Church was consecrated in 1846 and featured something that the two earlier Trinity Churches did not have: a full octave of bells chiming in the belfry.

By 1885, the traditional pealing of Trinity's bells at midnight was joined by an earsplitting din of tin horns. The horns made such a racket that even a stranger unfamiliar with the maze of streets in lower Manhattan would have no problem finding the crowd's gathering place. As this night marked the end of the nineteenth century and the start of a new millennium, tens of thousands of New Yorkers in high spirits packed into Lower Broadway around Trinity Church. The revelers overflowed from Broadway into the side streets, filling the sidewalks, stoops, and porticos of the increasingly ornate office buildings that had been built during the Gilded Age.

In the Trinity churchyard, surrounded by the New Year's

Eve crowd, the body of Ray Hamilton's great-grandfather, Alexander Hamilton, lay under a stately granite chamber, topped by an obelisk with finials on each of its corners. Only four years after the beginning of the nineteenth century, a young nation was shocked by the death of one of the prime architects responsible for the formation of America, his life taken by a bullet fired from Aaron Burr's pistol.

As the century drew to a close, the sensational accounts of the death and ensuing courtroom dramas surrounding his great-grandson, Robert Ray Hamilton, had largely receded from the front pages of the newspapers and the public's consciousness. Ray Hamilton's memorial in his own name remained unbuilt in 1900, as the City of New York had yet to find a suitable location to build Hamilton's ornamental fountain.

The fact that the city fathers had yet to choose a location for Ray Hamilton's bequest ten years after his death was undoubtedly not lost on the Hamilton family—in all likelihood, the family used their considerable influence to encourage city officials to take their time in deciding where to erect Ray's fountain, as it was no secret that the Hamilton family had no desire to see it built at all.

In 1891, two months after Eva's dower right was denied by Rastus Ransom, and eight months after Ray's death, a petition filed by the Hamilton and Schuyler families to the Mayor and Board of Aldermen found its way into the *New York Times*. Titled, "Let Him Be Forgotten," the three-paragraph story related the family's unambiguous opposition to the provision in Ray's will that set aside $10,000 from his estate for creation of the fountain.

For the Hamiltons and Schuylers, Ray's bequest wasn't about money—they weren't looking for ten cents from the $10,000 bequest. Rather, the newspaper explained, "their objection is based on family pride." They were "very sensitive for

the good name of the families to which Alexander Hamilton
and Philip Schuyler brought distinguished honor. Such a
memorial as the will designates would perpetuate a name that
brought dishonor to the family." The petition was set aside
and the search for a suitable location for the Hamilton Fountain proceeded, but almost certainly by tacit agreement with
the family, the search proceeded very slowly.

It was Eva, the bane of the Hamilton family, who was responsible for the delay of the fountain moving forward. Due to
her various lawsuits and appeals, the money could not be dis-
bursed from the estate until the appeal of her claim of dower
right was ruled upon.

When the settlement between Eva and the Hamilton estate was agreed to in July 1894, that impediment to the site
selection and eventual placement of Ray's fountain was removed. Reporters asked Gil Spier "what steps, if any, had
been taken to carry out the wishes so long ago expressed in
the clause in the will providing for the erection of the memorial fountain?"

Befitting an experienced attorney, Spier answered in a way
that made clear, without stating specifically, that the estate
was in no rush to move forward.

*I am aware of the clause in Mr. Hamilton's will to which
you refer but owing to the protracted litigation growing
out of the claims set up by Eva Mann, we have not given
the matter much, if any, consideration. Nothing will be
done toward carrying the bequest into effect until the return of Mr. Baylies, my co-executor, from Europe. Then
we will address a communication to the Mayor and
Aldermen, inviting their attention to the matter, and suggesting that, if they wish to accept the gift, they designate
a suitable site within the city limits whereupon to erect
the fountain.*

In other words, nothing was happening anytime soon. And nothing was to happen for the rest of the decade. At midnight on December 31, 1899, as the bells at Trinity Church pealed to ring in the new century, Ray Hamilton's fountain was no closer to becoming a reality than it was when he penned his will ten years before, and it would be another three years before the project moved forward.

## March 1903

On the morning of March 20, 1903, the temperature hovered near sixty degrees on an unseasonably warm morning as a crowd of mourners stepped out of the sunshine on Fourth Avenue and took their seats in Calvary Church, around the corner from Gramercy Park. Long home to congregants from some of the wealthiest families in New York—Astors, Roosevelts, and Vanderbilts—on this morning the Gothic Revival brownstone was the funeral setting for a member of another prominent New York family.

Two days earlier, on March 18, Major General Schuyler Hamilton, grandson of Alexander Hamilton, passed away at his home on Central Park South at age eighty-three. For several years prior to his death, the General was housebound, the victim of colitis and the cumulative effects of old age.

General James G. Wilson, an old friend, recalled visiting his Civil War colleague in the General's last years. "To the last, the General enjoyed his cigar and book, living over his army experiences with a friend. He was certainly the most cheerful man for one suffering so much from painful body infirmities that I have ever met."

Philip Hone, a former mayor of New York and prodigious diarist, noted of Schuyler Hamilton, "With such blood in his veins, and such a name, he could not fail to acquit himself with honour. Nobly has he sustained them."

For all of the wealth and prestige that the General had been

blessed with in life, he sought to call as little attention to himself as possible in his funeral request. "It is my desire that my
funeral be of the simplest kind, my casket not to exceed in cost
$100, and but three or four carriages to follow it to Green-
Wood Cemetery. Bury me beside my deceased wife, Cornelia,
the daughter of Robert Ray and Cornelia Prime."

Schuyler Hamilton, who entered West Point at age fifteen
and graduated four years later in the Class of 1841, took
great pride in his military career and sought to ensure that
his service record and artifacts were properly accounted for.
"I give and bequeath my sword of honor, to which the sword
knot of my grandfather, Major General Alexander Hamilton is attached, together with my sword knot, my military
badges, commission and military papers to my son, Schuyler
Hamilton Jr."

Only two months after the burial of General Schuyler
Hamilton, the three-man Board of Commissioners for the New
York Department of Parks approved the selection of both a
site and an architect for Ray Hamilton's ornamental fountain.
While the Hamilton family was less than thrilled with the
idea of the memorial, it is likely that they had asked, in defer-
ence to the General, for the city to at least delay any announcement until after his passing. At a meeting of the Board
on May 28, Commissioners John E. Eustis and Richard Young
voted "Aye" on the proposal put forth by the Department of
Parks landscape architect, Samuel Parsons Jr., and the
Hamilton Fountain project began in earnest.

The site selected for the Hamilton Fountain wasn't in one of
the heavily trafficked public squares in lower Manhattan fre-
quented by the Hamilton family—City Hall Park, Madison
Square Park, or Union Square—but rather, in a location on
the Upper West Side that was not as visible to the general
public: Riverside Drive, at the end of West Seventy-Sixth
Street. The chance of Ray's aunts, uncles, or cousins passing

by on a day-to-day basis was remote. The plan called for the
fountain to sit within a gently curved brownstone retaining
wall that sat twenty feet above a riding path in Riverside
Park.

Riverside Park was less than thirty years old in 1903, an
idyllic respite from an increasingly crowded neighborhood.
Until the mid-1880s, much of the Upper West Side was virtually open countryside with only a few frame farmhouses, some
aging colonial mansions, and squatters' shacks dotting the
landscape. The opening of the Ninth Avenue El, the first elevated railway in the city, brought thousands of new residents
to this previously ignored enclave and builders began buying
up land on the grid of avenues and cross streets to erect four-
story brownstones for businessmen and other professionals.

Clarence True, a prolific architect and developer, began to
buy as many lots as possible on Riverside Drive and declared
with no small measure of hyperbole, "to-day, Riverside Drive,
with its branching side streets, is the most ideal home-site in
the western hemisphere—the Acropolis of the world's second
city." It is against this backdrop that the site for Ray Hamilton's statue was selected.

Plans for the fountain integrated the capability to provide
water for both man and horses that was in vogue in the city at
the time. An essay in the *New York Times* noted that "the
need for more fountains in this city, both drinking and ornamental structures, has only been partially supplied by generous and public-spirited men and women. There are a few
memorial fountains, but a very few when it is considered what
an exceedingly appropriate and useful thing a public fountain
really is."

The architectural firm selected to design the Hamilton
Fountain, Warren and Wetmore, was in existence for only five
years when they began work on the project. Though the firm
was still in its early period as a professional practice, Whitney

Warren and Charles Wetmore had formed what was to become one of the most prolific and successful architectural
practices in the history of America. Their design for Grand
Central Terminal on Forty-Second Street, in association with
Reed and Stern, and the surrounding Terminal City, is considered by some to be the twentieth century's first great building venture in America.

In all likelihood, Warren and Wetmore were chosen to design the Hamilton Fountain because of Charles Wetmore, a
practicing attorney before he entered into partnership with
Whitney Warren. When Wetmore began his career working in
the law office of Carter & Ledyard, he met a young attorney
who dabbled in real estate—Edmund L. Baylies, Ray Hamilton's cousin and co-executor of his estate. In addition to their
work at the law office, Wetmore and Baylies formed their own
company, City Real Property Investing Co., to buy and sell
property in New York. The company remained active for
years after the formation of Warren and Wetmore, affording
the opportunity for Wetmore and Baylies to continue their relationship well into Wetmore's tenure as a principal in the architectural firm.

Warren and Wetmore's proposal for the Hamilton Fountain
required approval by the New York Art Commission (today,
the New York Public Design Commission), which had the authority "to review and approve all designs for public works in
the city, including lamp post designs, signage, water fountains
and fire hydrants." The Art Commission comprised ten pro-
bono members: the mayor of New York City; the presidents of
the Metropolitan Museum of Art, the New York Public Library, and the Brooklyn Institute of Arts and Sciences; a
painter, a sculptor, an architect; and three laymen.

The three-man committee charged with reviewing the submission for the Hamilton Fountain were the sculptor Alexander Phimister Proctor, noted for his expertise as an animalier;

Henry Rutgers Marshall, the architect and psychologist who gained fame as the author of *Pain, Pleasure and Aesthetics* in 1894; and Loyall Farragut, writer and son of famed admiral David Farragut.

Warren and Wetmore's first submission left the committee underwhelmed. Their proposal called for a five-foot-tall granite stile to be centered in front of the two-foot-high brownstone retaining wall that bowed out from Riverside Drive. An inset panel, framed in egg-and-dart molding, contained symmetrical scrolled shields on either side with space for a chiseled inscription in the center. Below the inscription, the carved face of a bearded, mythical man spouted water from his mouth into a semi-circular basin below. In the basin, water burbled out of the mouths of four fish that were splayed out on the bottom of an unadorned, semi-circular six-inch deep pool.

It was a pedestrian solution. The proportions were simple, the forms basic, and the decorative elements were of the stock, generic type that an architect of far lesser imagination might order straight out of a catalog. Proctor, Marshall, and Farragut received the proposal from the Parks Board on June 9 and returned their decision on July 6. Written on the engraved stationery of the Century Club, the West Forty-Third Street private enclave for members of distinction in the arts and letters, their recommendation was brief and to the point:

*Your committee on the fountain, Riverside Drive & 76th st. recommend that the designs be disapproved.*

*A. Phimister Proctor*
*Henry Rutgers Marshall*
*Loyall Farragut*

Apprised of the Art Commission's decision, Warren and Wetmore returned to the drawing board and spent the next four months developing a memorial to Robert Ray Hamilton that better reflected both the principles they espoused and the immense talent of Whitney Warren.

Warren and Wetmore formally submitted their new proposal to the Art Commission on February 1, 1905. A. Phimister Proctor remained as chairman of the three-man committee, but the terms of Henry Marshall and Loyall Farragut on the Art Commission expired at the end of 1904—they were replaced by the architect, Walter Cook and John Bigelow, president of the New York Public Library.

Gone were the banalities and simplistic forms that comprised the emotionless first submittal; all of it was replaced by elegant proportions and a deft use of symbolic, decorative flourishes that lent a dignified magnificence to the fountain. On February 14, just shy of two weeks after receiving the proposal, the three men approved it. Nearly fifteen years after Robert Ray Hamilton's untimely death in the Snake River, the fountain in his name would finally be built.

The plain, semi-circular base was replaced by a gracefully bowed basin finished with an ornately carved edge. The simple, four-foot-tall rectangular stile that formed the backdrop of the fountain was now an eleven-foot-tall, elaborately carved amalgamation of pictorial references symbolizing water, land, and sky. These elements combined to symbolically tell the story of Ray Hamilton's sad passing.

The "river" was depicted by the head of a fish that spouted water into a scalloped seashell and then emptied into the basin below. Just above the fish head, centered within the entire tableau (on "land"), was a crest used by the ancient Hamilton clans in Scotland and Ireland. There were several variations of this crest used over the ages, all of them in the form of a shield, with two common elements utilized in each version: a lion standing on its hind legs, a symbol of determination and courage, and the cinquefoil, a five-petal flower of the rose family. The cinquefoil had several meanings in heraldry, but was often used as a symbol of plenty, or prosperity.

Sedge, reeds, and cattails, all commonly found at a river's edge, provided one of the most intriguing references that Warren employed in his revised proposal. Carved in high relief on either side of the crest, their wispy tendrils enveloped the shield and visually pulled it toward the water. Given the circumstances surrounding Ray's demise—his spurs getting tangled in sedge that led to his drowning—the stonework made a stark, almost literal, reference to Hamilton's cause of death.

The land and water were set into a rising, scrolled backdrop that echoed the curve of the basin at street level and featured clusters of snail shells and seaweed at its ends, framed by five-foot-tall columns that were topped with globe finials. The scrolls rose to a graceful plateau at the midpoint of the architectural sculpture and provided a mantle for the crowning element of the memorial—a five-foot-tall eagle that sat atop the lower half of the fountain, its wings fully and majestically spread, its talons nestled into a bed of carved oak leaves and acorns. The eagle provided not only a crowning visual denouement to the entire arrangement, but it also captured an ambiguity inherent in the life and death of Robert Ray Hamilton. One could view the eagle, the very symbol of America, as a metaphor for the history and prestige of the Hamilton family, either coming to rest within the bounds of earth or preparing to take flight toward the heavens.

The nuanced combination of architectural and sculptural elements, the deft use of pictorial and allegorical references, and the balance achieved by Whitney Warren between artistry and functionality—it was, after all, a fountain intended for use by "man and beast"—was sublime. In a thoughtful gesture, an additional, unadorned trough, twenty feet below the back of the fountain at the base of the retaining wall, allowed horses riding the trails through Riverside Park to drink from the same water that burbled through the fountain above.

The memorial, and all of the elements contained within its composition, could only have been about one man, Robert Ray Hamilton, yet the only direct reference to him in the entire arrangement was simple. Shallowly chiseled into the upward face of the basin perimeter were three-inch-high letters that read:

## BEQUEATHED TO THE PEOPLE OF NEW YORK BY ROBERT RAY HAMILTON.

The Hamilton Fountain was completed in 1906; there were no mentions of a dedication ceremony in the New York newspapers. Given the Hamilton family's long-standing opposition to the fountain in Ray's name, they likely prevailed upon the city to not make a formal announcement of its completion. By all indications, when the masons finished setting all of the intricately carved Tennessee marble pieces in place, they simply packed up their spirit levels, rinsed the mortar off of their trowels, and left the fountain for the horses clopping up and down on Riverside Drive.

By the time that the Hamilton Fountain was completed, sixteen years after Ray Hamilton's death, the front-page headlines, rumors, and detailed reporting of the machinations of his wife, Eva, had receded in the memories of those who so voraciously devoured every account of the Hamilton saga. There were no more stories for attorneys aligned with either Ray or Eva to feed to reporters in hopes of attaining favorable coverage for their respective clients. The only character from the dramatic end of Ray Hamilton's life to continue to generate provocative headlines was John Sargent—not so much for his own activities, but for those of his second wife, Edith Drake.

Born in 1866, Edith was the youngest of four children born
to James and Mary Drake of New York. Drake was a spectac-
ularly wealthy banker and cofounder of the prestigious Wall
Street firm, Drake Mastin & Co. The family lived in the Hotel
Beresford at Eighty-First Street and Central Park West from
September to June and whiled away their summers in New-
port at the Drake family cottage, Red Cross, on Old Beach
Road, less than two miles from Schuyler Hamilton's home,
The Moorings.

Tall and slender with a perfect complexion and very expressive features, Edith received the proper upbringing of a young
woman of privilege. She studied the violin, was educated in
the arts, and was poised to attract a man of her same class for
a suitable marriage. At age sixteen, though, her parents noticed her behavior becoming more erratic—Edith developed
compulsions that increasingly turned into infatuations with
men of fame, or infamy.

While staying in Paris with her mother in 1887, twenty-
one-year-old Edith made the acquaintance of Henri Panzini, a
man "unprepossessing in appearance, but possessed of some
unknown and potent attraction for women." Panzini became
front-page news when he was guillotined later that year for
the brutal, triple murder of a wealthy Parisienne, Mme. Marie
Regnault; her maid, Annette Gremeret; and Mme. Gremeret's
twelve-year-old daughter, Marie.

The day after the murders, Panzini cabled a young woman
to whom he claimed to be engaged: "Completely cured. I leave
for Nice with mother." It was signed "Dr. Foster," the name by
which Edith knew the killer. Her parents steadfastly denied
any involvement by their daughter with Panzini, but after his
beheading, a parcel of letters was found in his possessions, all
signed by "Miss E." of New York.

Upon Edith's return to New York, she became infatuated
with the comedian and actor, Francis Wilson, one of the most

celebrated entertainers of his time. She filled her room with his pictures, practiced his dance routines, and memorized all of his songs and jokes, reciting them for anyone within earshot. Whenever Wilson appeared on stage in Manhattan, Edith attended every performance, waited for him each night outside of the stage door, and walked behind him as he made his way into the New York night. Her parents were convinced she had become "a victim of strange exhilarations."

Edith also became obsessed with horse racing. She regularly hosted parties at the racetracks in Coney Island and Gravesend in Brooklyn, or Morris Park in the Bronx, providing ample funds for all of her bohemian friends who wished to place a bet. Whenever Edith won, bottles of wine were ordered all around to celebrate her winnings. She became enthralled with an Irish stage carpenter, Sam McGibney, who became a regular attendee of Edith's outings. Handsome, well-poised, and deferential, McGibney had a feel for the ponies and won his bets much more so than Edith or her other friends. Completely captivated, Edith decided in 1893 that McGibney would be the man she would marry.

When Edith informed her father of her plans, he refused to entertain the thought, as McGibney was "hardly the sort of husband that a banker's daughter would select, appearing to be, as he is, a mechanic." Edith promised her father that if he would allow her to marry McGibney and provide her a dowry of $5,000, she would never ask anything of him again. When Drake refused his daughter on both requests, Edith and McGibney went missing and James Drake went to the police.

Edith and McGibney surfaced five days later as husband and wife, married in the parsonage of the German Presbyterian Church, Brooklyn, by the Reverend John G. Hehr. They lived together as a married couple for only three years before separating. After Edith and McGibney split, James Drake had his daughter committed to an insane asylum in Middletown,

New York. She left there of her own accord only to be recommitted by her father two years later to a sanitarium in Goshen, New York.

Edith was next heard from in 1904:

## BANKER'S DAUGHTER LIVES IN SLUMS

### *Edith Drake McGibney Refuses Refined Home for Cheap Boarding House*

Edith was not exactly living in a slum as the newspapers breathlessly reported, but she did live in a one-room flat above a butcher shop in the Newport commercial district. She spent her days haunting the telegraph offices, claiming to be a newspaper correspondent and endeavoring to send dispatches. Her father wearily told reporters, "It was my daughter's wish that she live that way. Her mind was affected long before she married against my wishes. I have had her in various sanitariums, but she has never been absolutely sane."

While the circumstances regarding how John Sargent and Edith Drake met are unclear, what is known is that two years after generating headlines in Newport, Edith was living in Jackson Hole as Sargent's second wife. The rumor in Jackson Hole was that Sargent had been paid by Edith's family to care for her.

Edith quickly gained a reputation among the nearby homesteaders for being at least as eccentric, and possibly as unstable, as her new husband. She became known for aimlessly wandering the meadows around Marymere playing her violin or by simply sitting under a tree for hours, naked, enjoying the sun.

Like most relationships in both of John's and Edith's lives, their marriage didn't last. By 1912, Edith was living in California with hopes of opening a hotel—Sargent remained at Marymere and became increasingly depressed over the years. Sometime around July 1, 1913, he put a record, "Ye Who Have Yearned Alone," onto his beloved Victrola, placed the barrel of a rifle in his mouth, tied a string to the trigger, then to his big toe, and pulled it, ending his own life. He was buried with a small headstone just south of Marymere.

While most of the individuals connected to the saga of Eva and Ray Hamilton managed to live full and productive lives, John Sargent was not the only person whose life ended prematurely.

With the death of the General in 1903, Schuyler Hamilton Jr. assumed the mantle of patriarch of this particular line of Hamilton descendants. After the unfortunate death of his second wife, Jane, in 1899, Schuyler Jr. married again in 1902. His third wife, Emma Gray Hebbard, was the widow of an Episcopal clergyman who had the misfortune to fall from a Pennsylvania Railroad train and was killed. Schuyler and his new wife lived in Norwalk, Connecticut, where Schuyler acquired several acres on a bluff overlooking the Long Island Sound and built a new home, Highwood.

On February 13, 1907, not even a year after the completion of the Hamilton Fountain, Schuyler was struck with an acute case of Bright's disease (an inflammation of the kidneys) and passed away at age fifty-four. Schuyler never publicly commented about the fountain erected in memory of his older brother; he may have never even seen it.

In 1899, Elihu Root, Ray's erstwhile friend and attorney, was appointed secretary of war under President William McKinley. In 1901, McKinley was assassinated by Leon Czolgosz, a second-generation Polish-American steelworker and anarchist, in Buffalo, New York. Dr. Carlos MacDonald, who had testified that Joshua Mann was mentally unbalanced in 1893, certified that Czolgosz was sane and aware of his actions. After Czolgosz's conviction, he was executed while strapped to an electric chair—a device developed by Thomas Edison and others, including Dr. MacDonald.

After McKinley's assassination, Root continued to serve under his successor, Theodore Roosevelt, first as secretary of war and then, beginning in 1905, as secretary of state. He represented American interests abroad until 1909 when he was elected to the U.S. Senate from the State of New York. Root was awarded the Nobel Peace Prize in 1912 and served as chairman of the Carnegie Endowment for International Peace. He remained an influential voice in Washington policy circles until his death in 1937.

The man that Root, Clarke, and Peabody called when they heard of the stabbing in Atlantic City, the legendary Tommy Byrnes, also had his fate entwined with Teddy Roosevelt. In 1894, William L. Strong, a Republican reformer, was elected mayor of New York with a mandate to clean up a city government that had been plagued by corruption since the heyday of Tammany Hall. He appointed Roosevelt as a no-nonsense police commissioner, to not only weed out the bad actors on the force, but to impose a new discipline and sense of order to the day-to-day activities of the department. Thomas F. Byrnes became an immediate target for the new commissioner—Roosevelt wanted him out.

Byrnes, whose extensive network of contacts exposed the nefarious deeds of Eva, Josh Mann, and Anna Swinton only days after the stabbing in Atlantic City, was given a choice by Roosevelt and the Board of Commissioners. Byrnes could voluntarily retire from the force and retain his $3,000-per-year pension or stay on and face a formal inquiry into his activities as chief of detectives. On Saturday, May 28, 1895, Tommy Byrnes retired from the New York Police Department after thirty-two years on the force.

As Byrnes left police headquarters for the last time, reporters who had covered Byrnes for years wrote that "grown men who had wielded nightsticks and muscled thugs had to wipe away tears. Even the newspapermen at Headquarters showed more emotion than they usually do on hearing of a first-class murder or fire and begged for a well-used club or some other little souvenir of his hard-working days."

Famed reporter and photographer, Jacob Riis, long acquainted with Tommy Byrnes, noted his departure, writing, "we shall not soon have another like him, and that may be both good and bad." In comparing Byrnes to Teddy Roosevelt, who Riis also knew well, he said, "He was the very opposite of Roosevelt—quite without moral purpose or the comprehension of it, yet with a streak of kindness in him that sometimes put preaching to shame. Mulberry Street swears by him today, even as it does, under its breath, by Roosevelt." Byrnes spent his days in retirement taking on assignments as a private detective and insurance investigator for his Wall Street acquaintances.

All of Ray's attorney friends and fellow clubmen, Gil Spier, Charles Peabody, Casimir de Rham Moore, and Edward Vollmer continued in their law careers and served as directors and trustees of various cultural institutions and charitable organizations in New York. For the most part, they stayed out of the news, save for the occasional mention in a real estate transaction, society column, or in conjunction with a philanthropic initiative.

The one exception to these mentions involved Ray's old law associate, Edward Vollmer. He appeared in an article that ran in the *Brooklyn Daily Eagle* on June 28, 1901, under the headline, "Dakota Farmer Disappears." Edsell Waldron, a prosperous farmer from Clark County, North Dakota, who was visiting Vollmer at his home in Brooklyn, had left two days prior with the intention of visiting Grant's Tomb. Forty-eight hours later, he remained unheard from. The *Eagle* de-

scribed Waldron as "a man correct in all of his habits. He is in
no sense a 'hayseed' for he has traveled extensively and he has
an excellent sense of locality." The newspaper also noted that
"a general alarm has been sent out by the police for him."
When (or if) Waldron was found, it did not warrant a follow-up
in the *Eagle*.

Ray's cousin, Edmund L. Baylies, continued to practice law
as a partner at Carter, Ledyard & Milburn. He sat on numerous corporate boards, was a trustee of both St. Luke's and the
Lying in Hospitals, and a director of the Metropolitan Opera.
He was also a driving force in the creation of the Cathedral of
St. John the Divine in Morningside Heights. Baylies and his
wife, Louisa, remained prominent members of New York society until his death in 1932.

Three of the principal players in the scandal that began in
Atlantic City, stabbing victim Mary Ann Donnelly and co-
conspirators, Anna Swinton and Josh Mann, receded into the
shadows, their whereabouts unknown and their actions no
longer warranting the headlines they garnered years before.

The leading lady in the entire Hamilton drama, however,
the woman who sought her fortune by whatever means necessary, who craved respectability and reveled in the spotlight,
Eva Steele-Brill-Parsons-Mann-Hamilton-Gaul, could not
leave the stage without creating one last headline.

On December 7, 1904, as Whitney Warren was finalizing
his design for the Hamilton Fountain, Joseph Pulitzer's *New
York World*, the newspaper that lapped up the Hamilton story
in sensational, breathless gulps fifteen years before, ran a
boldface headline:

## EVA HAMILTON DIES A PAUPER

Eva continued to recklessly spend the $10,000 she received
from the Hamilton family, primarily on alcohol. On November

23, at age forty-four, Eva died of heart disease in the charity ward of St. Vincent's Hospital in Greenwich Village, her health compromised by years of excessive drinking.

In one last bit of the mystery and deception that perpetually surrounded Eva, the *World* reported that "there was one mourner present, a 'Mr. Hamilton' who acknowledged that was not his name and who said he had known her intimately for eight years." It is only fitting that the death of the woman born as Evangeline Steele would be punctuated not with a period, but with one last question mark. She was buried in a common grave at Mt. Olivet Cemetery in Queens, New York, ten miles from Robert Ray Hamilton at Green-Wood Cemetery in Brooklyn.

For all of the notoriety they attained as the result of their five tumultuous years together, and for all of the headlines generated by both of their actions, Ray and Eva were laid to rest separately in unmarked graves, their infamous affair ignominiously consigned to history.

Without doubt, the most vexing question of the entire Hamilton story is this: Whatever happened to baby Beatrice? After the incident in Atlantic City, scores of complete strangers begged Robert Ray Hamilton to place Beatrice in their home, promising to care for her as if she were their own. One letter noted, presciently, that "Beatrice will be followed all of her life by her past history."

It is a near certainty that Beatrice's name was changed before she was a teenager, either to shield her from publicity and make it more difficult for anyone connected to Eva to try to locate her, or by the Hamiltons seeking to uncouple her completely from the family name. In the five years that Eva remained in the public eye because of her involvement with Ray Hamilton, she only saw Beatrice once—at their brief meeting in the Mays Landing jail in the fall of 1889. After initially insisting that Beatrice was in fact her daughter, once it became apparent that she had lied about the entire situation, Eva disassociated herself from the baby girl.

It is also a near certainty that the child who never knew her birth parents, was abandoned in an illegal baby farm and unwittingly thrust into a front-page scandal as an infant, lived a full life into the middle of the twentieth century. The woman baptized as Beatrice Ray Hamilton moved to California with a new name, got married, had children of her own, and lived a life far removed from her cruel beginnings.

A woman close to her descendants has the impression that "Beatrice had a very sad childhood and didn't speak of it much." It is with respect for the anonymity that Beatrice so desired as an adult that this author chooses to leave the details about her later life in the memories of her loved ones.

# EPILOGUE

The etched inscription around the base of the Hamilton Fountain bearing Robert Ray Hamilton's name has worn away over time, a victim of 105 years of rain and snow that has fallen onto Riverside Drive. The outlines of the letters are barely visible to even those who know to look for them.

The fountain has been compromised by man as well. In a period of neglect during the 1970s, the beak of the majestic eagle was broken off (since replaced by the New York City Parks Department) and the lower trough at the bottom of the retaining wall has long been buried under shrubbery. More than a century after the fountain was erected, it stands in anonymity, save for a small sign put in place by the Parks Department, providing a brief synopsis of Ray's untimely demise and explaining that the Hamilton Fountain "is one of the finest and last surviving examples of the decorative horse troughs that once dotted the landscape."

In 1906, though, the Hamilton Fountain was more than a decorative horse trough. It was, despite the resistance of the Hamilton family, an unintended chance for an heir to the legacy of Alexander Hamilton to clear his name. In August 1890, when Robert Ray Hamilton's spurs got tangled up in the sedge of the Snake River, the entire Hamilton family got tangled up with him as well. His reputation, muddied by the circumstances surrounding his sad death, remained in a state of uncertainty until Whitney Warren's jewel of a memorial was erected. Sixteen years after Robert Ray Hamilton's death, the cool water that trickled into the basin of the Hamilton Fountain ran clear, as if to finally absolve the fallen son of an American legend.

# NOTES

## INTRODUCTION

**1 appetite for news:** *N.W. Ayer & Son's American Newspaper Annual* (Philadelphia: N.W. Ayer & Son, 1889), 17.

**1 recently arrived immigrants:** "New York City's long list of defunct newspapers," http://ephemeralnewyork.com, July 28, 2009.

**1 daily readers:** *N.W. Ayer*, 17.

**1 Brooklyn, 806,000:** John S. Billings, "Vital Statistics of New York City and Brooklyn." Washington DC: Bureau of the Census, Dept. of the Interior, 1894, 2.

**4 "financial holdings,"** New York City Parks Department signage, 2010.

## CHAPTER ONE: IN THE WOMAN'S POWER

**7 power:** "In the Woman's Power," *Washington Post*, September 7, 1889, 1.

**8 Wesleyan University:** C. B. Todd, *A General History of the Burr Family: With a Genealogical Record from 1193 to 1902*, 1891, 356.

**9 "thoroughbred dude":** "Mrs. Hamilton in Prison," *New York Times*, August 28, 1889, 1.

**9 Cornelia Ray:** "Supreme Court, General Term—First Department" (New York: The Evening Post Job Printing House, 1893), Contestant's Exhibit 1, 267.

**9 for women:** "Estimated Median Age at First Marriage: 1890 to present." U.S. Census Bureau, Current Population Survey, March and Annual Social and Economic Supplements.

**9 both answered no:** "Supreme Court, General Term—First Department," 16.

**9 to the marriage:** "Supreme Court, General Term—First Department," Contestant's Exhibit 1, 267.

**11 to be bright:** "From Hovel to Wealth," *New York World*, September 22, 1889, 1.

**12 arrived in 1885:** "San Diego History Center Timeline," sandiegohistory.org.

**12 thirty thousand residents:** Ibid.

**12 of Manhattan:** "Very Costly Infatuation," *New York Times*, August 30, 1889, 8.

**13 new housing:** "Ray Hamilton. A Large Lot of His Real Estate in Brooklyn Sold To-Day." *Standard Union* (Brooklyn). December 11, 1895, 1.

**13 vacant lots:** Ibid.

**14 desperate circumstances.:** Jacqueline H. Wolf, "Mercenary Hirelings" or "A Great Blessing"?: Doctors' and Mothers' Conflicted Perceptions of Wet Nurses and the Ramifications for Infant Feeding in Chicago, 1871–1961." *Journal of Social History*, Autumn, 1999, Vol. 33, No. 1, 97.

**14 unruly and ignorant:** Ibid.

**14 babies' lives.:** Ibid.

**15 good looking:** Ray Family Papers, 1794–1889. New York Historical Society.

CHAPTER TWO: A WOMAN'S READY DAGGER

**16 dagger:** "A Woman's Ready Dagger," *New York Times*, August 27, 1889, 1.

**16 for the day:** "Record of Climatological Observations," NOAA, Atlantic City, NJ, 1889.

**16 sixty-five thousand visitors:** A. M. Heston, *Handbook of Atlantic City, New Jersey* (Philadelphia, PA: Franklin Printing House, 1887), 48.

**17 ordinary life:** Ibid.

**17 boardwalk as well:** Marc Berman, "Atlantic City's Famous Rolling Chairs Celebrate 125th Anniversary Today." NJ.Com True Jersey, June 11, 2012.

**18 receive nothing:** "Mrs. Hamilton in Prison." *New York Times*, August 28, 1889, 1.

**18 of her mother:** "From Hovel to Wealth." *New York World*, September 22, 1889, 1.

**19 sex trade:** Ibid.

**19 right ear:** Ibid.

**19 as possible:** Ibid.

**19 in the city:** Richard Zacks, "Teddy Roosevelt's Battle With the Deeply Depraved New York of Yore." thirteen.org, March 5, 2012.

**20 and groceries:** Timothy J. Gilfoyle, *City of Eros: New York City, Prostitution and the Commercialization of Sex, 1790-1920* (New York and London: W.W. Norton & Company, 1992), 248.

**20 instinct of sex:** Ibid, 249.

**23 above them:** "A Woman's Ready Dagger."

**23 the Hamiltons:** Ibid.

**24 Tennessee Avenue:** Ibid.

**24 "hang for this.":** Ibid.

**24 "finish her.":** Ibid.

**25 "the exciting affair":** "Mr. Hamilton's Plight," *Philadelphia Inquirer*, August 28, 1889, 1.

**26 "know about it":** "Eva Makes a Confession," *New York Times*, January 22, 1891, 8.

**27 "for the present":** Ibid.

**28 "in jail long.":** Ibid.

**29 Hess, Murray, Hastings:** Telegrams, Ray Family Papers, 1794–1889.

**30 the prison floor:** "Mr. Hamilton's Plight," 1.

**30 "for my son":** "Eva Makes a Confession."

CHAPTER THREE: A VILLAINOUS CONSPIRACY

**32 conspiracy:** "A Villainous Conspiracy," *The New York Times*, September 4, 1889, 8.

**32 In Court:** "Mrs. Hamilton in Jail," *New York Tribune*, August 28, 1889, 2.

**32 Shocked:** "Murray Hill Shocked," *Rochester Daily Chronicle*, August 28, 1889, 1.

**32 Scrape:** "A Sensation Stirs Up the Town of Atlantic City," *Austin Statesman,* August 28, 1889, 1.

**32 Dagger:** "Killed Her With a Dagger," *Daily Chronicle* (Aspen, CO), August 28, 1889, 1.

**33 Dirk:** "Mrs. Hamilton's Dirk," *Los Angeles Times*, August 28, 1889, 1.

**33 "to stand by":** Letter from Hamilton Fish to Robert Ray Hamilton, August 29, 1889. Ray Family Papers.

**35 on deposit:** Luc Sante, *Low Life. Lures and Snares of Old New York* (New York: Farrar, Straus, Giroux, 1991), 248.

**38 Tommy's pocket:** Richard Zacks, *Island of Vice* (New York: Anchor Books, 2012), 33.

**39 single room**: "A Villainous Conspiracy."

**39 the slip:** Ibid.

**39 in sight:** "Record of Climatological Observations," NOAA, Atlantic City, NJ, 1889.

**40 "for many years":** "Solitary and Gloomy," *New York Times*, September 2, 1889, 1.

**40 to recover:** "Mrs. Hamilton Still in Jail," *New York Tribune*, August 31, 1889, 7.

**40 Atrocious Assault:** Ibid.

**41 "I want you":** "In the Toils," *New York Evening World*, September 4, 1889, 1.

**41 "are locked up":** "A Villainous Conspiracy."

**42 "in a melodrama?":** Charles Dickens, *American Notes for General Circulation* (Boston: Estes & Lauriat, 1890), 119.

**42 "in the world!":** Ibid, 131.

**42 "dime novel recital":** "300 Mulberry St. Passes into History," *New York Times*, November 28, 1909, 18.

**43 Eva didn't say:** "A Villainous Conspiracy."

**45 door or shutters:** Sherri Broder, "Child Care or Child Neglect?: Baby Farming in Late-Nineteenth-Century Philadelphia." *Gender and Society* 2, no. 2 (June 1988), 128.

**45 send for Kemp:** "A Villainous Conspiracy."

**45 third baby:** "A Bogus Baby." *Brooklyn Daily Eagle*, September 4, 1889, 1.

**46 "Dutch baby":** "A Villainous Conspiracy."

**46 "kiss it":** Ibid.

**46 "it had died":** Ibid.

**46 "its own course":** "To Annul the Marriage," *New York Times*, September 5, 1889, 1.


CHAPTER FOUR: MR. HAMILTON'S PLIGHT

**48 plight:** "Mr. Hamilton's Plight," *Philadelphia Inquirer*, August 28, 1889, 1.

**48 Duped:** "Ray Hamilton Duped," *Baltimore Sun*, September 4, 1889, 1.

**48 Fellow's:** "Ray's Baby. It was Some Other Fellow's," *Cincinnati Enquirer*, September 4, 1889, 1.

**48 Bought:** "Eva's Babe Was Bought," *Boston Daily Globe*, September 4, 1889, 1.

**48 Blackmailers:** "His Eyes Opened," *Atlanta Constitution*, September 4, 1889, 1.

**49 Woman:** "A Conspiracy. Scheme of a Designing Woman," *San Francisco Chronicle*, September 4, 1889, 1.

**49 a father:** "Hamilton's Story Is Told," *New York Times*, September 7, 1889, 1.

**51 "well darkened":** "A Villainous Conspiracy."

**52 "right angles,":** "Murder Intimated," *Philadelphia Inquirer*, September 6, 1889, 1.

**52 "bought it":** Ibid.

**52 "flat-faced thing":** Ibid.

**53 "this woman":** "Eva Asked for Morphine," *New York Times*, September 6, 1889, 5.

**53 in the county:** Ibid.

**53 "ten dollars":** Ibid.

**54 Hamilton:** Ibid.

**54 "than himself":** Ibid.

**55 attempts by Eva:** Ibid.

**56 Special Sessions:** "Hamilton's Story Is Told."

**56 into the eighties:** "Record of Climatological Observations." New York City, NOAA, 1889.

**56 "unattractive audience":** "Hamilton's Story Is Told."

**57 "she would be":** Ibid.

**58 "in Albany":** Ibid.

**58 "child was born":** Ibid.

**59 "gift of $500?":** Ibid.

**59 "hot for him":** "Mr. Hamilton Testifies," *New York Tribune*, September 7, 1889, 1.

**60 of his voice:** "Hamilton's Story Is Told."

**60 "that sum":** Ibid.

**60 smoked cigarettes:** "Held for the Grand Jury," *New York Times*, September 8, 1889, 9.

**61 "from afar.":** Ibid.

**61 "connection with it":** Ibid.

**61 "life itself.":** Ibid.

**62 set aside:** Ibid.

**62 "heart and soul.":** Ibid.


CHAPTER FIVE: MRS. HAMILTON WEEPS

**63 Weeps:** "Mrs. Hamilton Weeps," *Philadelphia Inquirer*, September 19, 1889, 1.

**64 direct you there:** Ray Family Papers.

**64 or another:** Ibid.

**64 "Ballroom":** Ibid.

**65 "Hamilton Heiress,":** "A Bogus Baby."

**65 "Robbed":** "In the Woman's Power."

**65 "Hamilton":** "Hamilton at Mays Landing," *New York Times*, September 13, 1889, 5.

**66 "fit to ask":** Ibid.

**66 approaching trial:** Ibid.

**67 "improbable fiction":** "Eva Hamilton at Bay," *New York World*, September 19, 1889, 1.

**68 was in session,:** Ibid.

**68 Directoire coat:** "Mrs. Hamilton on Trial," *New York Times*, September 19, 1889, 1.

**68 ostrich plumes:** "Eva Hamilton at Bay."

**68 "traces of tears":** Ibid.

68 **at his wife:** "Mrs. Hamilton on Trial."

69 **before the jurors:** "Eva Hamilton at Bay."

69 **witness chair:** Ibid.

69 **trunk at once:** "Mrs. Hamilton Weeps."

70 **husband's heart:** Ibid.

71 **"I had packed":** Ibid.

71 **"over a year":** Ibid.

72 **"over the bay":** Ibid.

72 **"getting drunk?":** Ibid.

73 **she repeated:** Ibid.

73 **"influence of liquor":** "Mrs. Hamilton on Trial."

73 **"her actions":** "Mrs. Hamilton Weeps."

74 **his demeanor:** Ibid.

74 **unfaltering voice,:** Ibid.

74 **his testimony,:** "Mrs. Hamilton on Trial."

74 **bodily harm:** "Mrs. Hamilton Weeps."

74 **leave together:** Ibid.

75 **her parasol:** Ibid.

75 **"kill her!":** "Mrs. Hamilton on Trial."

75 **"then cut Mary":** "Mrs. Hamilton Weeps."

75 **witness stand:** Ibid.

76 **"show it to me":** "Eva Hamilton at Bay."

77 **"policeman came":** Ibid.

77 **on the jury:** "Mrs. Hamilton Weeps."

77 **brightened considerably:** "Eva Hamilton at Bay."

79 **"on that ground":** "Mrs. Hamilton Weeps."

80 **about Beatrice:** "Eva Hamilton at Bay."

80 **near-collapse:** "Mrs. Hamilton Weeps."

80 **went unnoticed:** Ibid.

80 **"West Jersey":** "Put Away for a Time," *New York World*, September 20, 1889, 1.

81 **"the defendant":** "Two Years in Prison," *Baltimore Sun*, September 20, 1889, 1.

81 **"serious illness,":** Ibid.

81 **the aggressor:** Ibid.

81 **"she is held":** Ibid.

82 **"have been taken"**: Ibid.

82 **"charge of murder"**: Ibid.

82 **"Hamilton"**: "Sentenced to Prison," *Philadelphia Inquirer*, September 20, 1889, 1.

82 **"of the evidence"**: "Put Away for a Time."

82 **"to the cutting,"**: "Mrs. Hamilton Convicted," *New York Times*, September 20, 1889, 1.

82 **her own life**: Ibid.

82 **"the indictment"**: Ibid.

83 **"going to charge"**: "Put Away for a Time."

83 **"face met hers"**: "Sentenced to Prison."

83 **"a verdict?"**: "Put Away for a Time."

83 **to her chest**: "Sentenced to Prison."

83 **an ancient stoic**: Ibid.

84 **"shall be paid"**: "Mrs. Hamilton Convicted."

84 **"cared for."** "Sentenced to Prison."

84 **Atlantic City**: Ibid.

85 **"from his memory"**: "Mrs. Hamilton Convicted."


CHAPTER SIX: MRS. EVA HAMILTON'S STORY

86 **Story**: Nellie Bly, "Mrs. Eva Hamilton's Story." *New York World*, October 10, 1889, 1.

86 **on that day**: Ray Family Papers.

88 **"$75 per week"**: "Still Bleeding Hamilton," *New York Times*, September 27, 1889, 5.

88 **ADMISSION 10c**: "Globe Museum," *New York Evening World*, October 4, 1889, 8.

89 **to ignore**: "Nurse Donnelly Exhibits," *Philadelphia Inquirer*, October 1, 1889, 3.

89 **"Visits His Wife"**: "Mr. Hamilton Visits His Wife," *New York Times*, September 28, 1889, 1.

89 **"charges against her"**: Ibid.

90 **"Eva Steele's spell**: "Caught Again," *Buffalo Evening News*, September 30, 1889, 4.

90 **rainy Monday morning**: "Record of Climatological Observations," NOAA, 1889.

**90 leave her care,:** "Baby Beatrice in Atlantic City," *New York Times*, October 1, 1889, 1.

**91 sheriff's house:** Ibid.

**91 who accompanied her:** Ibid.

**91 transferred to Trenton:** Ibid.

**91 as her counsel:** Ibid.

**92 "annulled by default":** "He Asks a Divorce," *Philadelphia Inquirer*, October 4, 1889, 1.

**92 "Mrs. Swinton's protégé":** "Wants a Divorce," *New York Times*, October 4, 1889, 8.

**92 one of them sobbing:** "To Trenton Via Elizabeth," *New York Times*, October 6, 1889, 1.

**93 "closed behind them":** Ibid.

**93 "beat the newspapers":** Ibid.

**94 for the institution:** *The Industries and Advantages of the City of Trenton, N.J. 1889* (Trenton, NJ: The John L. Murphy Publishing Co., 1889), 74.

**94 mentally and morally:** Ibid.

**94 softly and soothingly:** "To Trenton Via Elizabeth."

**94 new surroundings:** Ibid.

**97 she told me:** Nellie Bly, "Mrs. Eva Hamilton's Story." *New York World*, October 10, 1889, 1.

**103 "during the fight":** Ibid.

**103 "New England fashion":** Letter from Nathalie Baylies to Robert Ray Hamilton, November 7, 1889. Ray Family Papers.

**103 "return eastward.":** Ibid.

**104 "well forward":** Letter from Casimir de Rham Moore to Robert Ray Hamilton, September 9, 1889. Ray Family Papers.

**104 in Monroe:** *Kathy Warnes*, "William Clark Sterling Sr., and Sterling State Park." *Monroe Memories and More.* Monroemichigan.wordpress.com.

**105 mallards and teal:** John McClellan Bulkley, *History of Monroe County Michigan.* Vol. 1 (Chicago, IL: The Lewis Publishing Co., 1913), 463.

**105 exclusive use:** Ibid.

**105 tastefully furnished:** Ibid, 464.

**105 southeast Michigan:** David E. Lantz, *The Muskrat* (Washington, DC: U.S. Dept. of Agriculture, 1910), 22.

**106 Metropolitan Museum of Art:** Talcott E. Wing, *History of Monroe County, Michigan* (New York: Munsell & Company, 1890), 409.

**106 "more than time":** Bulkley, *History of Monroe County Michigan*, 466.

**106 Schuyler Hamilton:** Ray Family Papers.

**106 a million dollars:** Tom Miller, "The Lost Windsor Hotel," *Daytonian in Manhattan*, November 19, 2012.

**107 "in New York":** Ibid.

**107 "octagon room":** Ibid.

**107 beginning in 1875:** Raymond B. Fosdick, *John D. Rockefeller, Jr. A Portrait* (Lexington, MA: Plunkett Lake Press, 2019), 238.

**107 handsome hotel:** Henry Hall, ed. *America's Successful Men of Affairs*. Vol. 1 (New York: The New York Tribune, 1895), 719.

**107 "leading financiers":** Fosdick, *John D. Rockefeller, Jr. A Portrait*, 238.

**107 "proper manner":** Hall, *America's Successful Men of Affairs*, 719.

**108 "It's all there":** "An Echo of the Hamilton Scandal," *New York Times*, November 16, 1889, 5.

**109 "and wife":** "Eva Hamilton Makes Answer," *New York Times*, December 28, 1889, 2.


CHAPTER SEVEN: MANN OR HAMILTON?

**110 HAMILTON?:** "Mann or Hamilton?" *Rochester Democrat and Chronicle*, January 16, 1891, 7.

**110 any given year:** Jone Johnson Lewis, "1848: Married Women Win Property Rights." ThoughtCo.com.

**111 Van Duzer:** "He Wants a Divorce," *New York Times*, January 14, 1890, 3.

**111 "bold adventuress":** Ibid.

**111 of a brothel:** "Home and Other Matters," *Wyoming Demo-crat*, January 17, 1890, 3.

**111 to New York:** Ibid.

**111 man and wife:** "He Wants a Divorce."

**112 "contradicted each other":** "Home and Other Matters."

**112 "in this city":** "He Wants a Divorce."

**112 "of the latter.":** Ibid.

**112 "sister-in-law":** "Home and Other Matters."

**112 credible defense:** "He Wants a Divorce."

**112 in New York:** Ibid.

**113 lower Hudson valley:** "The Extent of the Industry," brick-collecting.com.

**113 bricks in 1883:** ibid.

**113 spring of 1890:** "Eva Ray Hamilton," *The Pittsburg Press*, March 23, 1890, 1.

**114 "very panicky position":** Ibid.

**114 "of being considered":** Ibid.

**114 "on her part":** Ibid.

**115 in Hudson County,:** *Minutes of Votes and Proceedings of the One Hundred and Fourteenth General Assembly of the State of New Jersey* (Trenton, NJ: MacCrellish & Quigley), 1890, 141.

**115 Investigated:** "Eva's Prison Career," *Allentown Critic*, April 8, 1890, 4.

**115 "roast duck":** Ibid.

**116 "cigarettes and morphine":** Ibid.

**116 "in New York":** Ibid.

**116 her situation:** "Gov. Abbett Indignant," *New York Times*, March 27, 1890, 1.

**116 "had done so":** Ibid.

**116 "be found untrue":** "Eva's Prison Career."

**117 "troublesome carbuncle":** Ibid.

**118 "of this city":** "Some Men of New York," *Pittsburg Press*, May 12, 1890, 5.

CHAPTER EIGHT: MR. HAMILTON'S FATE

**119 Fate:** "Mr. Hamilton's Fate," *Philadelphia Inquirer*, September 16, 1890, 1.

**119 "little of him":** "Hamilton's Fate," *Northumberland County Democrat*, September 19, 1890, 1.

**121 "like autumn leaves":** John Muir, *Our National Parks* (Boston and New York: Houghton, Mifflin and Company, 1901), 56.

**121 "would look well":** "Supreme Court, General Term—First Department," 317.

**122 July 18, 1861:** Kenneth L. Diem, Lenore L. Diem, and William C. Lawrence, *A Tale of Dough Gods, Bear Grease, Cantaloupe and Sucker Oil* (Moran, WY: University of Wyoming—National Park Service Research Center, 1986), 2.

**122 pronounced dead:** Ibid.

**123 Wyoming Territory:** Ibid, 3.

**124 Pleasant Valley Hotel:** Mary Shivers Culpin, "A History of Concession Development in Yellowstone National Park, 1872 – 1966," National Park Service, Yellowstone Center for Resources, Yellowstone National Park, WY, 2003, 2-3.

**125 with clean sheets:** Carl E. Schmide, *A Western Trip* (Detroit, MI: Herold Press, 1910), 59-60.

**126 "with pegged corners":** Fern K. Nelson, *This Was Jackson's Hole* (Glendo, WY: High Plains Press, 1994), 84.

**127 casements and ceilings:** Kenneth L. Diem, Lenore L. Diem, and William C. Lawrence, *A Tale of Dough Gods, Bear Grease, Cantaloupe and Sucker Oil*, 7.

**127 between two mules:** Nelson, *This Was Jackson's Hole*, 84.

**127 a worthy feat:** Ibid.

**128 Felt for table:** "Supreme Court, General Term—First Department," 316.

**129 R.R. Hamilton:** "Supreme Court, General Term—First Department," 316–318.

**129 and a brush:** "Supreme Court, General Term—First Department," 318.

**130 "is pretty steep":** Ibid.

**130 or three days:** "Mr. Hamilton's Sad Death," *New York Times*, September 16, 1890, 1.

**131 in five days:** Ibid.

**131 August 26,:** Ibid.

**131 "from his hunt":** Ibid.

**131 for his partner:** Ibid.

**132 the hungry dog:** "Finding Ray Hamilton's Body," *New York Tribune*, September 17, 1890, 5.

**133 somberly announced:** "Supreme Court, General Term—First Department," 264.

**133 Hamilton's death:** Ibid.

**133 "to be seen":** Ibid.

**134 at 9:32 P.M:** Ibid, 265.

**134 making a coffin:** Ibid, 250.

**135 Gil:** Ibid, 320.

**135 later recounted:** Ibid, 247.

**136 to the moon:** "Dr. Norvin Green's Death," *New York Times*, February 13, 1893, 1.

**137 "this his home":** "Mr. Hamilton's Sad Death."

**137 John D. Sargent:** Ibid.

**138 MOORE:** Ibid.

**139 the Body:** Ibid.

**139 "about the matter":** "Divorce by Drowning," *Evening Leader*, September 15, 1890, 1.

**139 "mysterious and unsatisfactory":** Ibid.

**140 "the newspaper reports":** "Mr. Hamilton's Fate."

**140 "show assassination":** Ibid.

**141 "Sargent killed H":** Sierra Adare, *Jackson Hole Uncovered* (Lanham, MD: Taylor Trade Publishing, 1996), 24.

**141 "not to accident":** "Now It's a Foul-Play Theory," *New York Times*, November 14, 1891, 5.

**141 "for some distance":** Ibid.

**141 "with foul play":** Ibid.

**142 completely prostrated:** "Mr. Hamilton's Fate."

**142 "hard to tell":** Ibid.

**142 of Ray's death:** "Ray Hamilton's Widow," *New York Tribune*, September 16, 1890, 3.

**142 "not a lawful widow":** Ibid.

**143 "Divorced Them":** "Death Has Divorced Them," *New York Times*, September 15, 1890, 1.

**143 New York immediately:** Ibid.

**143 "business affairs,":** Ibid.

**143 one thousand dollars:** "Gov. Abbett Involved," *New York Tribune*, May 1, 1895, 1.

**144 for 'da gang.'":** Ibid.

**144 secure her pardon:** Ibid.

**144 "few chosen lawyers,":** Ibid.

**145 Keeper Patterson:** "Eva Hamilton Free Again," *New York Times*, November 26, 1890, 3.

**145 "for some time":** Ibid.


CHAPTER NINE: EVA BEGINS HER FIGHT

**146 FIGHT:** "Eva Begins Her Fight," *New York Times*, January 13, 1891, 8.

**146 November 17:** "Supreme Court, General Term—First Department," 1.

**146 Beatrice Ray:** "Supreme Court, General Term—First Department," 6.

**147 Walter Baylies:** Ibid.

**147 Gertrude Hamilton:** Ibid.

**147 "in said City":** Ibid.

**148 "County of New York":** Ibid, 13.

**148 illegal and void:** Ibid, 12.

**148 "Robert Ray Hamilton":** Ibid, 14.

**149 "in this court":** Ibid, 16.

**150 "Dutch times":** Thomas A. Janvier, *In Old New York* (New York and London: Harper & Brothers, 1900), 249.

**150 drizzly Monday morning,:** "Report of the New York Meteorological Bureau for the Month of January, 1891" (Ithaca, NY: Cornell University).

**150 "with convincing judges":** "Charles W. Fuller," *Harper's Weekly*, July 1, 1911, 33.

**150 calm and self-confident:** "Elihu Root," *New York Times*, July 30, 1899, 2.

**151 "marrow of things":** Ibid.

**151 with spectators:** "Eva Never Once Flinched," *Philadelphia Inquirer*, January 17, 1891, 1.

**151 "fact of widowhood":** "Supreme Court, General Term— First Department," 15, 16.

**151 "in this Court":** Ibid, 16.

**152 "married before":** Ibid, 17.

**152 "recognize her":** Ibid.

**152 "come to court":** Ibid, 18.

**152 "the question":** Ibid.

**152 *"prima facie* case":** Ibid.

**153 "man and wife":** Ibid, 19.

**153 "Joshua Mann":** Ibid, 22.

**153 seven years:** Ibid, 24.

**153 "Mrs. Mann":** Ibid, 30.

**154 Charles Fuller:** "Eva Begins Her Fight."

**154 fit and healthy:** Ibid.

**154 of the hearing:** Ibid.

**154 Eva entered Joshua:** "Supreme Court, General Term— First Department," 37.

**154 Eva L. Mann:** Ibid, 42.

**155 "Mrs. Swinton":** Ibid, 47.

**155 "seen here today":** Ibid, 35.

**155 "let her go":** "Eva Begins Her Fight."

**155 Surrogate's Court:** "Eva Wears a Veil," *New York Tribune*, January 15, 1891, 3.

**155 heterogeneous rabble:** Ibid.

**156 get a glance:** Ibid.

**156 case shut:** "Mrs. Eva's Dower," *New York Evening World*, January 14, 1891, 1.

**156 air of nonchalance,:** Ibid.

**156 "I believe":** "Supreme Court, General Term—First Department," 49.

**156 "little men are":** "Mrs. Eva's Dower."

**156 "man Mann?":** Ibid.

**156 "man Mann":** Ibid.

**157 Little was excused:** Ibid.

**157 caused a stir:** "She Was Known as Mrs. Mann," *New York Times*, January 15, 1891, 8.

**157 numerous objections:** Ibid.

**158 the same person:** Ibid.

**158 resting his case:** Ibid.

**158 "as possible":** "Eva Not Hamilton's Widow," *Philadelphia Inquirer*, January 16, 1891, 8.

**158 the crowd:** " 'Josh' Sues for Divorce," *New York Times*, January 16, 1891, 8.

**159 palpable:** Ibid.

**159 "been performed.":** Ibid.

**159 "previous marriage":** Ibid.

**159 "with Hamilton":** "Supreme Court, General Term—First Department," 239.

**159 fire and eloquence:** "Eva Not Hamilton's Widow."

**159 "meretricious relationship":** Ibid.

**160 stacks of papers:** Ibid.

**160 high and low:** Luc Sante, *Low Life. Lures and Snares of Old New York,* 211.

**160 professional witnesses:** Ibid.

**160 who practiced law:** Peter Carlson, "Howe and Hummel: The Grifters' Grifters." History.net, June 2018.

**161 "Dorset ram":** Richard Halworth Rovere, *The Magnificent Shysters: The True and Scandalous History of Howe and Hummel* (New York: Grosset & Dunlap, 1947), 54.

**161 Howe and Hummel office:** "Mann or Hamilton?" *Rochester Democrat and Chronicle,* January 16, 1891, 1.

**161 "joke on him":** Ibid.

**161 "to direct him":** " 'Josh' Sues for Divorce."

**161 Louis Allen:** "Mann or Hamilton?"

**162 the law involved:** Ibid.

**162 going nowhere:** Ibid.

**162 "daughter-in-law":** Ibid.

**162 "I can be sure?":** " 'Josh' Sues for Divorce."

**163 "my son's wife."** Ibid.

**163 in the week:** "Report of the New York Meteorological Bureau for the Month of January, 1891" (Ithaca, NY: Cornell University).

**163 to be closed:** "Eva's String of Denials," *New York Times*, January 17, 1891, 8.

**163 "met his death":** "Eva Poses as a Widow and Spins Explanations," *New York Herald*, January 17, 1891, 8.

**164 "not far apart":** Ibid.

**164 three years prior:** "Supreme Court, General Term—First Department," 104.

**164 possibly four:** Ibid, 105.

**164 seated before her:** "Eva's String of Denials."

**164 of marriage:** Ibid.

**165 "Joshua J. Mann":** "Supreme Court, General Term—First Department," 107.

**165 "under her care":** "Eva's String of Denials."

**165 she confirmed:** "Supreme Court, General Term—First Department," 108.

**166 St. Marks Place:** Ibid, 277.

**166 "did not wish me to":** Ibid, 111, 112.

**167 "not my people.":** Ibid, 183.

**167 "was a success":** "Eva's String of Denials."

**167 confident voice:** "Eva Never Once Flinched," *Philadelphia Inquirer*, January 17, 1891, 1.

**167 rapid-fire questions:** "Another Day of Torture," *New York Times*, January 20, 1891, 8.

**167 "not evade them":** "Eva and the Baby," *Philadelphia Inquirer*, January 20, 1891, 2.

**168 his questioning:** Ibid.

**168 "about that time":** "Another Day of Torture."

**168 "Eva and Dotty":** Ibid.

**168 Eva curtly replied:** "Eva and the Baby."

**168 Judge Ransom:** "Another Day of Torture."

**169 DOTTY:** "Supreme Court, General Term—First Department," 155, 156.

**169 "in that letter?":** Ibid.

**169 meant a wardrobe:** "Another Day of Torture."

**170 December 1888?:** "Supreme Court, General Term—First Department," 156.

**170 fishing expedition:** Ibid.

**170 "entirely outside":** Ibid, 157.

**170 "degrade me":** Ibid, 158.

**170 "Court's direction.":** Ibid, 159.

**170 "at the time?":** Ibid, 165.

**170 the witness stand:** "Another Day of Torture."

**171 "physical pain":** "Supreme Court, General Term—First Department," 166.

**171 "my testimony":** Ibid, 167.

**171 "at this time":** Ibid, 168.

**171 into the courtroom:** "Eva Makes a Confession," *New York Times*, January 22, 1891, 8.

**172 STEELE:** ibid.

**172 "under direct examination":** "It Is Not Hamilton's Baby," *Philadelphia Inquirer*, January 22, 1891, 1.

**172 "as she desired":** Ibid.

**173 "on the record":** "Eva Makes a Confession."

**173 "Hamilton":** "It Is Not Hamilton's Baby."

**173 "Yes.":** Ibid.

**173 remaining questions:** "Eva Makes a Confession."

**173 "Joshua L. Mann":** "Eva Drops Her Mask," *New York Tribune*, January 22, 1891, 3.

**173 own attorney:** "It Is Not Hamilton's Baby."

**174 About a week:** "Supreme Court, General Term—First Department," 182.

**174 "You may proceed":** "It Is Not Hamilton's Baby."

**174 in that name:** "Supreme Court, General Term—First Department," 182.

**174 in the open:** "It Is Not Hamilton's Baby."

**174 "his mistress":** Ibid.

**174 Root to take:** "Eva Makes a Confession."

**175 "win this case?":** Ibid.

**175 "to correct them":** Ibid.

**175 the objections:** "It Is Not Hamilton's Baby."

**175 "I cannot answer":** Ibid.

**176 "and Mann?":** "Eva Makes a Confession."

**176 drily concluded:** Ibid.

**176 on Manhattan:** "Report of the New York Meteorological Bureau for the Month of January, 1891" (Ithaca, NY: Cornell University).

**176 big as ever:** "She Is Not Eva Hamilton," *New York Times*, January 23, 1891, 2.

**176 Evangeline:** Ibid.

**176 "Joshua J. Mann":** Ibid.

**177 "was put forth":** Ibid.

**177 "over illegitimacy":** Ibid.

**177 "our witnesses":** Ibid.

**177 "the married men":** "She Is Eva Mann, or Steele, or Brill," *New York Herald*, January 23, 1891, 7.

**178 "been taken?":** Ibid.

**178 "the most pathetic":** Ibid.

**178 in the courtroom:** Ibid.

**178 from the bench:** Ibid.

**178 "of deep concern.":** "Supreme Court, General Term—First Department," 237.

**178 "most attractive manner.":** Ibid, 239.

**178 will and testament:** "Supreme Court, General Term—First Department," 243, 244.

**179 "from a balloon":** "She Is Eva Mann, or Steele, or Brill."

**179 of the will:** "Supreme Court, General Term—First Department," 239.

**181 "I do not know":** Ibid, 263.

**181 from his account:** "Proved to Be Dead," *New York World*, March 9, 1891, 1.

**181 "it is not!":** "Is Robert Ray Hamilton Alive?" *New York Sun,* January 25, 1891, 6.

**182 "at the ranch":** Ibid.

**182 may not know:** Ibid.

**182 near future:** "Robert Ray Hamilton Is Dead," *New York Times,* January 29, 1891, 6.

**183 of his death:** Ibid.

**183 "sent him money":** Ibid.

**183 "diseased imagination":** Ibid.

**183 named Sanford:** "Is Robert Ray Hamilton Alive?"

**183 "dead beyond doubt":** Ibid.

**183 "dower for Eva":** Ibid.

**184 western clothing:** Kenneth L. Diem, Lenore L. Diem, and William C. Lawrence, *A Tale of Dough Gods, Bear Grease, Cantaloupe and Sucker Oil,* 23.

**184 and puttees:** Struthers Burt, *The Diary of a Dude-Wrangler* (New York and London: Charles Scribner's Sons, 1924), 271.

**184 Jocko:** "Sargent Comes to New York," *New York Times,* June 10, 1891, 2.

**184 John Sargent:** Ibid.

**184 "effects with me":** Ibid.

**184 at the Windsor:** Ibid.

**185 collection of artwork:** Tom Miller, "The Lost 1878 'Working Women's Hotel'—Park Avenue at 32nd Street," *Daytonian in Manhattan,* May 14, 2012.

**185 "thoroughfares":** Ibid.

**185 until 1930:** "Historical Decennial Census Population for Wyoming Counties, Cities and Towns," U.S. Bureau of the Census, 2010.

**185 or four days:** "Sargent Comes to New York."

**185 "every direction":** "He Found Ray's Body," *Philadelphia Inquirer,* June 11, 1891, 2.

**186 "worst had happened":** Ibid.

**186 "he started across":** Ibid.

**186 "the sedgewood":** Ibid.

186 **"Alexander Hamilton":** Ibid.

187 **more than an hour:** "Ray Hamilton's Fate," *Pittsburg Dispatch*, June 21, 1891, 8.

187 **the invitation:** "Mr. Sargent Testifies," *New York Times*, June 21, 1891, 9.

188 **Ray's death:** Ibid.

188 **"the truth?":** "Ray Hamilton's Fate."

188 **"sworn to that?":** "Mr. Sargent Testifies."

189 **"very strongly":** Ibid.

189 **"being asked":** Ibid.

189 **"for pleasure?":** "Ray Hamilton's Fate."

189 **"if I only could":** Ibid.


CHAPTER TEN: EVA AT THE FOOTLIGHTS

190 **FOOTLIGHTS:** "Eva at the Footlights," *Evening Journal*, September 2, 1891, 1.

191 **Mrs. Preston:** Ibid.

191 **"the milking stool":** "Another Star Appears," *San Francisco Examiner*, September 2, 1891, 1.

191 **"mother and aunt":** Ibid.

191 **but they are not:** "The Play Is 'All a Mistake,'" *Monmouth Inquirer*, September 3, 1891, 8.

191 **take place:** Ibid.

192 **parts unknown:** Ibid.

192 **Miss Dean, vanquished:** Ibid.

192 **"public view.":** "Authority for the Announcement," *Topeka Daily Press*, May 23, 1891, 8.

193 **"upon the stage":** "The Story of His Shame," *Independent-Record*, May 25, 1891, 3.

193 **"or suggested":** "Eva's Ambition," *Buffalo Enquirer*, May 20, 1891, 1.

193 **"play for her":** Ibid.

193 **"of her life":** "The Story of His Shame."

194 **"stage arrangements,":** "Robert Ray Hamilton," *Sierra County Advocate*, May 29, 1891, 4.

**194 "been represented":** Ibid.

**194 PLAYERS:** "Eva at the Footlights."

**195 population, 2,981:** S. D. Dickinson, *State of New Jersey Compendium of Censuses 1726–1905* (Trenton, NJ: The John L. Murphy Publishing Co., 1906), 32.

**195 electric lights:** Boonton Historical Society, *Boonton. Images of America* (Mount Pleasant, SC: Arcadia Publishing, 2017), 64.

**195 "stage fright":** "Eva Mann on the Stage," *New York Sun*, September 2, 1891, 1.

**196 "highly entertaining":** "Eva at the Footlights."

**196 "fell flat":** "The Play Is 'All a Mistake.'"

**196 "who support them":** "The Shameful Exhibition," *Philadelphia Times*, September 6, 1891, 10.

**197 "American people":** "An Adventuress As a Heroine," *Scranton Times-Tribune*, September 3, 1891, 4.

**197 did not reply:** "Eva's Company Disbands," *Philadelphia Inquirer*, September 7, 1891, 2.

**197 she fainted:** ibid.

**197 for the rooms:** "Eva's Tour Ended," *Wilkes-Barre Times Leader*, September 7, 1891, 1.

**197 New York:** Ibid.

**197 "New Jersey":** Ibid.

**198 "is well named":** "All A Mistake," *Nebraska State Journal*, September 7, 1891, 4.


CHAPTER ELEVEN: MRS. GAUL'S QUEER GOINGS ON

**199 GOINGS ON:** "Mrs. Gaul's Queer Goings-On," *New York World*, December 15, 1893, 3.

**199 George E. P. Howard:** "It Was Hamilton's Body," *New York Evening World*, July 27, 1892, 5.

**199 in Wyoming:** "Ray Hamilton's Body Here," *New York Sun*, July 27, 1892, 1.

**200 Hamilton's remains:** Ibid.

**200 the situation:** Ibid.

**200 Green-Wood:** Ibid.

**200 Gramercy Park:** "It Was Hamilton's Body."

**200 in Ossining:** "Ray Hamilton's Body Here."

**201 expand them:** Paul Goldberger, *Ballpark. Baseball in the American City* (New York: Alfred A. Knopf, 2019), 17.

**201 burial landscapes:** Ibid.

**201 overshadowing trees:** Willard Glazier, *Peculiarities of American Cities* (Philadelphia, PA: Hubbard Brothers, 1885), 82.

**201 wilderness of beauty:** Ibid.

**201 478 acres:** Ibid.

**201 burial record:** "Ray Hamilton's Body Here."

**201 of the transfer:** "Ray Hamilton's Body," *Brooklyn Citizen*, July 27, 1892, 2.

**201 "information whatsoever":** Ibid.

**202 "any information":** Ibid.

**202 years prior:** Ibid.

**202 "like a leech,":** "Ray Hamilton's Body Here."

**202 Hamilton:** Ibid.

**202 "reserved generally":** "Eva Mann Appears Again," *New York Evening World*, February 14, 1893, 6.

**203 "and combative":** James D. Livingston, "Arsenic and Clam Chowder: Murder in Gilded Age New York." *The Gotham Center for New York City History*, October 15, 2010.

**203 "is ready now":** "Eva Mann Appears Again."

**203 "Hamilton":** Ibid.

**203 of March:** Ibid.

**203 "is crazy":** "Josh Mann Said to Be Mad," *New York Sun*, March 28, 1893, 7.

**204 "refuses to take":** Ibid.

**204 an asylum:** Ibid.

**204 "Hamilton.":** "Mann Said to Be Insane," *New York Times*, March 28, 1893, 10.

**204 six months prior:** "Eva Hamilton Married," *Brooklyn Citizen*, September 12, 1893, 1.

**205 black mustache:** "Eva Mann Married," *Democrat Chronicle*, September 20, 1893, 1.

**205 Twenty-Ninth Street:** Ibid.

**205 Josh Mann:** "Eva Hamilton Married."

**205 "Assemblyman":** Ibid.

**205 "Hamilton":** "Eva Mann Married."

**205 "be his wife":** Ibid.

**206 The Duke:** "Eva Ray Did Not Appear," *New York Evening World*, December 12, 1893, 2.

**206 woman of 26:** "Permitted to See Her Child," *Brooklyn Daily Eagle*, December 12, 1893, 1.

**206 Madge Irene:** "Richard the Eavesdropper," *New York Evening World*, December 14, 1893, 6.

**206 the others:** "Eva Ray Hamilton Again," *Boston Globe*, December 12, 1893, 5.

**206 to go home:** Ibid.

**207 compromising position:** Ibid.

**207 Madge Irene Gaul,:** "Eva Ray Did Not Appear."

**208 Unsavory Case:** "Mrs. Gaul's Queer Goings-On."

**208 Failed to Appear:** "Permitted to See Her Child."

**208 Writ Was Issued:** "Eva Ray Did Not Appear."

**209 Supreme Court calendar:** "Eva Mann's Appeal," *New York World*, November 7, 1893, 7.

**209 concur:** W. H. Silvernail, ed., *New York State Reporter*, Vol. 52 (Albany, NY: W.C. Little & Co., 1894), 815.

**209 "Mr. Hamilton":** "Eva Mann's Memorandum," *New York Times*, February 24, 1893, 10.

**209 R.R.H:** Ibid.

**210 "a hard pencil":** Ibid.

**210 "Hamilton estate":** "Woman Wins," *Boston Post*, July 8, 1894, 5.

**210 "for Europe":** "Eva Mann Gives a Quit Claim," *New York Sun*, July 8, 1894, 19.

**211 "has yet produced":** "Woman Wins."

CHAPTER TWELVE: SEQUEL TO TRAGEDY

**212 TRAGEDY:** "Sequel to Tragedy," *St. Paul Globe*, January 2, 1900, 13.

**212 CALLED TO MIND:** Ibid.

**213 room and board:** Kenneth L. Diem, Lenore L. Diem, and William C. Lawrence, *A Tale of Dough Gods, Bear Grease, Cantaloupe and Sucker Oil*, 17.

**213 skilled practitioner:** Cuyler Reynolds, *Genealogical and Family History of Southern New York and the Hudson River Valley*, Vol. 3 (New York: Lewis Historical Publishing Company, 1914), 1388.

**213 in Manhattan:** Ibid.

**213 scores of others:** Tom Miller, "The 1879 St. Anthony Club—No. 29 East 28th Street." *Daytonian in Manhattan*, February 21, 2014.

**214 April 11, 1877:** Reynolds, *Genealogical and Family History of Southern New York and the Hudson River Valley*, 1388.

**214 after childbirth:** Ibid.

**215 a select few:** "The Season at Newport." *New York Times*, June 24, 1878, 1.

**215 "this delicate hue":** "One of the Most Exquisite Entertainments," *New York Amusement Gazette*, September 30, 1889.

**215 social circles,:** "Schuyler Hamilton, Jr. Sued for Divorce," *New York Tribune*, September 16, 1894, 7.

**216 "support herself":** Ibid.

**216 "comes to trial":** Ibid.

**216 her husband:** Ibid.

**216 "A.L. Mason":** "New Notes from Newport," *New York Times*, April 21, 1895, 11.

**217 1801 to 1803:** "Robert Mercer and Some of His Descendants," *The Genealogical Exchange* 1, no. 1 (May 1904), 1904.

**217 "Hamilton":** "Hamilton-Mercer," *Baltimore Sun*, August 5, 1895, 8.

**218 in the cabin:** *A Tale of Dough Gods, Bear Grease, Cantaloupe and Sucker Oil*, 17.

**218 and suffering:** Ibid.

**218 "save her":** Ibid, 18.

**219 East Eighteenth Street:** Ibid.

**219 Alexandra Schuyler Hamilton:** Passport Application, Alexandra Hamilton, May 7, 1923.

**219 mental stress:** "Mrs. S. Hamilton, Jr., Dead," *New York Times*, May 4, 1899, 1.

**219 villa walls:** Ibid.

**220 lesser amounts:** "Death Due to Morphine," *New York Tribune*, May 4, 1899, 1.

**220 "to be allowed":** Ibid.

**220 the downpour:** Ibid.

**220 fell asleep:** "Mrs. S. Hamilton, Jr., Dead."

**220 the night:** Ibid.

**220 "into unconsciousness":** "Death Due to Morphine."

**220 or the maid:** Ibid.

**221 an autopsy:** Ibid.

**221 "of this annuity":** *Baylies v. Hamilton*, 36 App. Div 133, 138 (N.Y. App. Div. 1899).

**222 High Kicking:** "In a Tenderloin Cell," *Wilkes-Barre Times*, August 25, 1899, 7.

**222 uncertain age:** Ibid.

**223 "high kicking":** "Broadbrim's Gossip," *Ottawa Journal*, September 2, 1899, 9.

**223 the courtroom:** "Broadbrim's Greater New York Letter," *Fitchburg Sentinel*, August 30, 1899, 1.

**223 "the Tenderloin":** Ibid.

**223 lose his mind:** "John Sargent Insane," *New York Times*, December 28, 1899, 5.

**224 to trial:** *A Tale of Dough Gods, Bear Grease, Cantaloupe and Sucker Oil*, 18.

CHAPTER THIRTEEN: LET HIM BE FORGOTTEN

**225 FORGOTTEN:** "Let Him Be Forgotten," *New York Times*, April 22, 1891, 9.

**225 "graceful spire":** "The New Year Welcomed," *New York Times*, January 1, 1900, 2.

**225 in the belfry:** Lucie Levine, "Before Times Square:

Celebrating New Year's in Old New York," 6sqft.com, December 19, 2018.

**225 gathering place:** "The New Year Welcomed."

**225 Gilded Age:** Ibid.

**226 "Forgotten":** "Let Him Be Forgotten."

**226 "family pride":** Ibid.

**227 "to the family":** Ibid.

**227 "memorial fountain?":** "A Fountain for the City," *New York Tribune*, September 28, 1894, 9.

**227 "the fountain":** Ibid.

**228 warm morning:** "Record of Climatological Observations," NY Central Park, NOAA, 1903.

**228 "have ever met":** Frank Jastrzembski, "Schuyler Hamilton, Scion of American Heroes, Is a Civil War 'What If.'" History.net, May 4, 2020.

**228 "sustained them":** Bayard Tuckerman, ed. *The Diary of Philip Hone,* Vol. 2 (New York: Dodd, Mead and Company, 1910), 333.

**229 "Cornelia Prime":** "General Hamilton's Will Filed," *New York Tribune*, March 24, 1903, 7.

**229 "Schuyler Hamilton Jr":** Ibid.

**229 Samuel Parsons Jr.,:** *Minutes and Documents of the Board of Commissioners of the Department of Parks for the Year Ending December 31, 1903* (New York: Mail & Express Company, 1904), 186.

**230 dotting the landscape:** Sarah Bradford Landau, "The Row Houses of New York's West Side." *Journal of the Society of Architectural Historians* 34, no. 1 (March 1975), 19.

**230 other professionals:** Ibid.

**230 "second city":** Clarence True, "Riverside Drive," 1899.

**230 man and horses:** "Water for Man and Beast," *New York Times*, May 17, 1896, 25.

**230 "fountain really is":** Ibid.

**231 history of America:** Peter Pennoyer, Anne Walker, and Robert A.M. Stern, *The Architecture of Warren and Wetmore* (New York and London: W.W. Norton & Company, 2006), 37.

**231 venture in America:** Ibid, 40.

**231 "fire hydrants":** The New York Preservation Archive Project, "History," nypap.org.

**231 three laymen:** Ibid.

**232 David Farragut:** Ibid.

**232 Loyall Farragut:** New York City Public Design Commission Archives.

**236 expressive features,:** "Warrant Out for Miss Drake," *New York Times*, July 12, 1893, 9.

**236 "attraction for women":** "Edith Drake's Lovers," *Boston Daily Globe*, July 7, 1893, 2.

**236 "with mother":** "Execution of Panzini," *New York Times*, August 31, 1887, 5.

**236 New York:** Ibid.

**237 "strange exhilarations":** Ibid.

**237 and deferential,:** "New Mystery Baffles Newport," *Chicago Daily Tribune*, November 13, 1904, F4.

**237 "a mechanic":** "Warrant Out for Miss Drake."

**237 John G. Hehr:** "Edith Drake Married by Pastor Hehr," *New York Times*, July 12, 1893, 9.

**238 Boarding House:** "Banker's Daughter Lives in Slums," *St. Paul Globe*, February 21, 1904, 32.

**238 "absolutely sane":** Ibid.

**238 take care of her:** *A Tale of Dough Gods, Bear Grease, Cantaloupe and Sucker Oil*, 29.

**239 his own life:** Ibid, 32.

**239 and was killed:** "Married," *New York Times*, January 5, 1902, 5.

**239 Bright's disease:** "Death List of a Day." *New York Times*, February 14, 1907, 9.

**240 MacDonald:** "Dr. C.F. MacDonald, Alienist, Is Dead," *New York Times*, June 2, 1926, 25.

**241 "hard-working days":** Richard Zacks, *Island of Vice* (New York: Anchor Books, 2012), 92, 93.

**241 "by Roosevelt":** Jacob A. Riis, *The Making of an American* (New York: The MacMillan Company, 1901), 343, 344.

**241 "Disappears":** "Dakota Farmer Disappears," *Brooklyn Daily Eagle*, June 28, 1901, 1.

**242 "police for him":** Ibid.

**242 Morningside Heights:** "E.L. Baylies Is Dead; Was Leader in Bar," *New York Times*, April 30, 1932, 15.

**243 "for eight years":** "Eva Hamilton Dies a Pauper," *New York World*, December 7, 1904, 6.

**243 "past history":** Letter from Middletown, Ray Family Papers.

**244 "speak of it much":** Email to author. Anonymous.

# IMAGE CREDITS

1. "The Public Service of the State of New York, Vol. II," 1882. Collection of Rijksmuseum, Amsterdam, Netherlands.

2. Originally published in the *St. Louis Post Dispatch,* September 27, 1903.

3. Image courtesy of courthousehistory.com.

4. Illustration by Philippe LeBloas.

5. Photographer: Matthew Brady. Library of Congress, Prints & Photographs Division, Civil War Photographs. [Reproduction number, e.g., LC-B8184-3287.]

6. Originally published in the *St. Louis Post Dispatch,* September 27, 1903.

7. University Archives, Rare Book & Manuscript Library, Columbia University Libraries.

8. University Archives, Rare Book & Manuscript Library, Columbia University Libraries.

9. Frances Benjamin Johnston Collection, Library of Congress, Prints & Photographs Division. [Reproduction number, e.g., LC-USZ62-123456.]

10. Frontispiece, *Professional Criminals of America.* Cassell & Company, New York, 1886.

11. Originally published in *Supplement to The News.* Newport, Perry County, PA, October 18, 1889.

12. Jacob Riis, Reporters in Mulberry St., ca. 1888–1898. International Center of Photography, Gift of Alexander Alland Sr. with additional funds provided by the Lois and Bruce Zenkel Purchase Fund, 1982 (259.1982).

13. Freeport Memorial Library.

14. Monroe County Museum System: Local History Division: Photograph Collection.

15. Collection of the Jackson Hole Historical Society and Museum, 1958.0947.001.

16. Collection of the Jackson Hole Historical Society and Museum, 1958.0173.001.

17. University of Wyoming, American Heritage Center, Diem Collection.

18. Collection of the Public Design Commission of the City of New York.

19. The Hamilton Fountain Riverside Drive, New York City, September 19, 1909. Photograph from glass plate negative. Robert L. Bracklow Photograph Collection, PR 008, New York Historical Society, 66000-1186.

# SOURCES

BOOKS

Adare, Sierra. *Jackson Hole Uncovered*. Lanham, MD: Taylor Trade Publishing, 1996.

Berg, Walter G. *Buildings and Structures of American Railroads*. New York: John Wiley & Sons, 1893.

Boonton Historical Society. *Boonton. Images of America*. Mount Pleasant, SC: Arcadia Publishing, 2017.

Bradford Landau, Sarah, and Carl W. Condit. *Rise of the New York Skyscraper, 1865-1913*. New Haven, CT: Yale University Press, 1999.

Brewer, John. *The American Leonardo: A Tale of Obsession, Art and Money*. New York: Oxford University Press, 2009.

Bulkley, John McClellan. *History of Monroe County Michigan*. Vol. 1. Chicago: Lewis Publishing, 1913.

Burt, Struthers. *The Diary of a Dude-Wrangler*. New York and London: Charles Scribner's Sons, 1924.

Byrnes, Thomas. *Professional Criminals of America*. New York: Cassell & Company, 1886.

Carvalho, David N. *Forty Centuries of Ink or A Narrative Concerning Ink and Its Backgrounds*. New York: Banks Law Publishing, 1904.

Dickens, Charles. *American Notes for General Circulation*. Boston: Estes & Lauriat, 1890.

Diem, Kenneth L., Lenore L. Diem, and William C. Lawrence. *A Tale of Dough Gods, Bear Grease, Cantaloupe and Sucker Oil*. Moran, WY: University of Wyoming-National Park Service Research Center, 1986.

Fosdick, Raymond B. *John D. Rockefeller, Jr. A Portrait*. Lexington, MA: Plunkett Lake Press, 2019.

Gilfoyle, Timothy J. *City of Eros: New York City, Prostitution and the Commercialization of Sex, 1790-1920*. New York and London: W.W. Norton & Company, 1992.

Glazier, Willard. *Peculiarities of American Cities*. Philadelphia: Hubbard Brothers, 1885.

Gody, Lou. *New York City Guide. The Federal Writers Project*. New York: Random House, 1939.

Goldberger, Paul. *Ballpark. Baseball in the American City*. New York: Alfred A. Knopf, 2019.

Haines, Aubrey L., Colorado Associated University Press and Yellowstone Library and Museum Association. *The Yellowstone Story: A History of Our First National Park*. 2 volumes. Yellowstone National Park, WY: Yellowstone Library and Museum Association in cooperation with Colorado Associated University Press, 1977.

Hall, Henry, ed. *America's Successful Men of Affairs*. Vol. 1. New York: New York Tribune, 1895.

Hall, John F. *The Daily Union History of Atlantic City and County*. Atlantic City, NJ: Daily Union Printing, 1900.

Hamersly, L. R., J. W. Leonard, and F. R. Holmes. *Who's Who in New York City and State*. Cornell Library New York State Historical Literature, Vol. 6. L.R. Hamersly Company, 1914.

Hamilton, Schuyler. *History of the National Flag of the United States of America*. Philadelphia: Lippincott, Grambo & Co., 1852.

Heston, A. M. *Handbook of Atlantic City, New Jersey*. Philadelphia: Franklin Printing House, 1887.

Janvier, Thomas A. *In Old New York*. New York and London: Harper & Brothers, 1900.

Johnson, D. A. *Planning the Great Metropolis: The 1929 Regional Plan of New York and Its Environs*. London: Routledge, 2003.

Lantz, David E. *The Muskrat*. Washington, DC: U.S. Dept. of Agriculture, 1910.

Miller, James. *Miller's New York As It Is*. New York: James Miller, 1864.

Muir, John. *Our National Parks*. Boston and New York: Houghton, Mifflin and Company, 1901.

Nelson, Fern K. *This Was Jackson's Hole*. Glendo, WY: High Plains Press, 1994.

Pennoyer, Peter, Anne Walker, and Robert A. M. Stern. *The Architecture of Warren and Wetmore*. New York and London: W.W. Norton & Company, 2006.

Reynolds, Cuyler. *Genealogical and Family History of Southern New York and the Hudson River Valley*. Vol. 3. New York: Lewis Historical Publishing Company, 1914.

Riis, Jacob A. *The Making of an American*. New York: The MacMillan Company, 1901.

Rinaldi, Thomas E., and Rob Yasinsac. *Hudson Valley Ruins: Forgotten Landmarks of an American Landscape*. Lebanon, NH: UPNE, 2006.

Rovere, Richard Halworth. *The Magnificent Shysters: The True and Scandalous History of Howe and Hummel*. New York: Grosset & Dunlap, 1947.

Sante, Luc. *Low Life. Lures and Snares of Old New York*. New York: Farrar, Straus, Giroux, 1991.

Schmide, Carl E. *A Western Trip*. Detroit, MI: Herold Press, 1910.

Todd, C. B. *A General History of the Burr Family: With a Genealogical Record from 1193 to 1902*. Author, 1902.

True, Clarence. "Riverside Drive," 1899.

Tuckerman, Bayard, ed. *The Diary of Philip Hone*. New York: Dodd, Mead and Company, 1910.

Wing, Talcott E. *History of Monroe County, Michigan*. New York: Munsell & Company, 1890.

Zacks, Richard. *Island of Vice*. New York: Anchor Books, 2012.


PERIODICALS AND JOURNALS

"338-Waverly Place." *Real Estate Record and Builders' Guide* 31, no. 783 (March 17, 1883).

"Arthur Livingston Mason." *The Diamond of Psi Upsilon* 17, no. 2 (January 1931).

Bastiaens, Ida. "Is Selling Sex Good Business?: Prostitution in

Nineteenth Century New York City." *Undergraduate Economic Review* 3, no. 1 (2007).

Broder, Sherri. "Child Care or Child Neglect?: Baby Farming in Late-Nineteenth-Century Philadelphia." *Gender and Society* 2, no. 2 (June 1988).

"Catalogue of the Governors, Trustees and Officers and of the Alumni and Other Graduates of Columbia College." New York: Columbia College, 1876.

"Charles W. Fuller." *Harper's Weekly*, July 1, 1911.

Culper, Mary Shivers. "A History of Concession Development in Yellowstone National Park, 1872-1976." Wyoming: National Park Service, Yellowstone Center for Resources, Yellowstone National Park, 2003.

Honeyman, Abraham Van Doren. "Mr. Samuel E. Perry." *The New Jersey Law Journal* 38, no. 1 (1915).

Landau, Sarah Bradford. "The Row Houses of New York's West Side." *Journal of the Society of Architectural Historians* 34, no. 1 (March 1975).

"Plan 228/229." *Real Estate Record and Builders' Guide* 29, no. 731 (March 18, 1882).

"Robert Mercer and Some of His Descendants." *The Genealogical Exchange* 1, no. 1 (May 1904).

Silvernail, W. H., ed. *The New York State Reporter*. Vol. 52. Albany, NY: W.C. Little & Co., 1894.

"Social Register, New York, 1893." *Social Registry Association* 7, no. 1 (November 1892).

*The American Lawyer: A Monthly Journal Serving the Business and Professional Interests of the American Bar*. Vol. 5. Stumpf & Stewer, 1897.

*The Scrap Book*. Vol. 4. New York: Frank A. Munsey, 1907.

*The Week: A Canadian Journal of Politics, Literature, Science and Arts* 11, no. 22 (April 27, 1894).

"West End Avenue. Riverside Park in the City of New York." The West End Avenue Association, 1888.

Wolf, Jacqueline H. "Mercenary Hirelings" or "A Great Blessing"?: Doctors' and Mothers' Conflicted Perceptions of

Wet Nurses and the Ramifications for Infant Feeding in Chicago, 1871- 1961." *Journal of Social History*, Autumn, 1999, Vol. 33, No. 1.


NEWSPAPER ARTICLES (SIGNED)

Bly, Nellie. "Mrs. Eva Hamilton's Story." *The World*, October 10, 1889.

Gray, Christopher. "Streetscapes: Readers' Questions; Of Consulates, Stores and Town Houses." *The New York Times*. September 2, 1990.


NEWSPAPER ARTICLES (UNSIGNED)

"300 Mulberry St. Passes into History." *New York Times*, November 28, 1909.

"A Bogus Baby." *Brooklyn Daily Eagle*, September 4, 1889.

"A Fountain for The City." *New York Tribune*, September 28, 1894.

"A Letter From Jones, of Texas." *New York Tribune*, September 18, 1894.

"A Villainous Conspiracy." *New York Times*, September 4, 1889.

"A Woman's Ready Dagger." *New York Times*, August 27, 1889.

"Adventuress Eva Begins Her Contest." *New York Herald*, January 13, 1891.

"All a Mistake." *Nebraska State Journal*, September 7, 1891.

"An Adventuress As a Heroine." *Scranton Times-Tribune*, September 3, 1891.

"An A.S. Sullivan Fountain." *New York Times*, October 28, 1906.

"An Echo of the Hamilton Scandal." *New York Times*, November 16, 1889.

"Another Day of Torture." *New York Times*, January 20, 1891.

"Another Star Appears." *San Francisco Examiner*, September 2, 1891.

"Authority for the Announcement." *Topeka Daily Press*, May 23, 1891.

"Baby Beatrice in Atlantic City." *New York Times*, October 1, 1889.

"Banker's Daughter Lives in Slums." *St. Paul Globe*, February 21, 1904.

"Broadbrim's Gossip." *Ottawa Journal*, September 2, 1899.

"Broadbrim's Greater New York Letter." *Fitchburg Sentinel*, August 30, 1899.

"Caught Again." *Buffalo Evening News*, September 20, 1889.

"Condensed Dispatches." *Burlington Daily Free Press*, January 9, 1890.

"Dakota Farmer Disappears." *Brooklyn Daily Eagle*, June 28, 1901.

"Death Due to Morphine." *New York Tribune*, May 4, 1899.

"Death Has Divorced Them." *New York Times*, September 15, 1890.

"Death List of a Day." *New York Times*, February 14, 1907.

"Details of Hamilton's Death." *Philadelphia Inquirer*, September 17, 1890.

"Died." *New York Herald*, October 5, 1875.

"Divorce by Drowning." *Evening Leader*, September 15, 1890.

"Dr. Norvin Green's Death." *New York Times*, February 13, 1893.

"Edith Drake's Lovers." *Boston Daily Globe*, July 7, 1893.

"Edith Drake Married by Pastor Hehr." *New York Times*, July 12, 1893.

"E.L. Baylies Is Dead; Was Leader in Bar." *New York Times*, April 30, 1932.

"Elihu Root." *New York Times*, July 30, 1899.

"Eva and the Baby." *Philadelphia Inquirer*, January 20, 1891.

"Eva Asked for Morphine." *New York Times*, September 6, 1889.

"Eva at the Footlights." *Evening Journal*, September 2, 1891.

"Eva Begins Her Fight." *New York Times*, January 13, 1891.

"Eva Drops Her Mask." *New York Tribune*, January 22, 1891.

"Eva Hamilton at Bay." *New York World*, September 19, 1889.

"Eva Hamilton Dies a Pauper." *New York World*, December 7, 1904.

"Eva Hamilton Free Again." *New York Times*, November 26, 1890.

"Eva Hamilton Makes Answer." *New York Times*, December 28, 1889.

"Eva Hamilton Married." *Brooklyn Citizen*, September 12, 1893.

"Eva Hamilton's Debut on the Stage." *Keyport Weekly*, September 5, 1891.

"Eva Has Her Champions." *New York Tribune*, January 20, 1891.

"Eva L. Mann Is Now Mrs. Archie Gaul." *New York Tribune*, December 14, 1893.

"Eva Makes a Confession." *New York Times*, January 22, 1891.

"Eva Mann Again." *Boston Globe*, September 12, 1893.

"Eva Mann Appears Again." *New York Evening World*, February 14, 1893.

"Eva Mann Compromises for $10,000." *New York Times*, July 8, 1894.

"Eva Mann Gives a Quit Claim." *New York Sun*, July 8, 1894.

"Eva Mann Married." *Democrat Chronicle*, September 20, 1893.

"Eva Mann on the Stage." *New York Sun*, September 2, 1891.

"Eva Mann's Appeal." *New York World*, November 7, 1893.

"Eva Mann's Half Profits." *New York Sun*, September 8, 1891.

"Eva Mann's Memorandum." *New York Times*, February 24, 1893.

"Eva Never Once Flinched." *Philadelphia Inquirer*, January 17, 1891.

"Eva Not Hamilton's Widow." *Philadelphia Inquirer*, January 16, 1891.

"Eva Poses as a Widow and Spins Explanations." *New York Herald*, January 17, 1891.

"Eva Ray Did Not Appear." *New York Evening World*, December 12, 1893.

"Eva Ray Hamilton." *Pittsburg Press*, March 23, 1890.

"Eva Ray Hamilton Again." *Boston Globe*. December 12, 1893.

"Eva Steele's Career." *Philadelphia Inquirer*, August 30, 1889.

"Eva Wears a Veil." *New York Tribune*, January 15, 1891.

"Eva Would Be a Star." *San Francisco Examiner*, May 19, 1891.

"Eva's Ambition." *Buffalo Enquirer*, May 20, 1891.

"Eva's Company Disbands." *Philadelphia Inquirer*, September 7, 1891.

"Eva's Poor Memory." *New York Tribune*, January 17, 1891.

"Eva's Prison Career." *Allentown Critic*, April 8, 1890.

"Eva's String of Denials." *New York Times*, January 17, 1891.

"Eva's Tour Ended." *Wilkes-Barre Times Leader*, September 7, 1891.

"Execution of Panzini." *New York Times*, August 31, 1887.

"Finding Ray Hamilton's Body." *New York Tribune*, September 17, 1890.

"Frisky Mrs. Hamilton." *National Police Gazette*, September 14, 1889.

"From Hovel to Wealth." *New York World*, September 22, 1889.

"General Hamilton's Will Filed." *New York Tribune*, March 24, 1903.

"General Schuyler Hamilton Dead." *New York Times*, March 19, 1903.

"Globe Museum." *New York Evening World*, October 4, 1889.

"Gov. Abbett Indignant." *New York Times*, March 27, 1890.

"Gov. Abbett Involved." *New York Tribune*, May 1, 1895.

"Hamilton." *New York Tribune*, March 20, 1903.

"Hamilton-Mercer." *Baltimore Sun*, August 5, 1895.

"Hamilton at Mays Landing." *New York Times*, September 13, 1889.

"Hamilton's Fate." *Northumberland County Democrat*, September 19, 1890.

"Hamilton's Friends Indignant." *New York Times*, January 30, 1891.

"Hamilton's Sad Tale." *Philadelphia Inquirer*, September 7, 1889.

"Hamilton's Story Is Told." *New York Times*, September 7, 1889.

"He Asks a Divorce." *Philadelphia Inquirer*, October 4, 1889.

"He Found Ray's Body." *Philadelphia Inquirer*, June 11, 1891.

"He Is Officially Dead." *Helena Independent*, October 19, 1891.

"He Wants a Divorce." *New York Times*, January 14, 1890.

"Held for the Grand Jury." *New York Times*, September 8, 1889.

"Home and Other Matters." *Wyoming Democrat*, January 17, 1890.

"In a Tenderloin Cell." *Wilkes-Barre Times*, August 25, 1899.

"In the Toils." *New York Evening World*, September 4, 1889.

"In the Woman's Power." *Washington Post*, September 7, 1889.

"Is Robert Ray Hamilton Alive?" *Burlington Free Press and Times*, January 27, 1891.

"It Is Not Hamilton's Baby." *Philadelphia Inquirer*, January 22, 1891.

"It Was Hamilton's Body." *New York Evening World*, July 27, 1892.

"It Was Ray Hamilton." *New York Sun*, October 15, 1891.

"John Sargent Insane." *New York Times*, December 28, 1899.

"Josh Mann Said to Be Mad." *New York Sun*, March 28, 1893.

" 'Josh' Sues for Divorce." *New York Times*, January 16, 1891.

"Joshua Wants Divorce." *New York Tribune*, January 16, 1891.

"Killed Her With a Dagger." *Daily Chronicle*, August 28, 1889.

"Let Him Be Forgotten." *New York Times*, April 22, 1891.

"Mann or Hamilton?" *Rochester Democrat and Chronicle*, January 16, 1891.

"Mann Said to Be Insane." *New York Times*, March 28, 1893.

"Military Order, Loyal Legion." *New York Tribune*, March 20, 1903.

"Mr. Hamilton Sues for Divorce." *New York Tribune*, October 4, 1889.

"Mr. Hamilton Testifies." *New York Tribune*, September 7, 1889.

"Mr. Hamilton Visits His Wife." *New York Times*, September 28, 1889.

"Mr. Hamilton's Fate." *Philadelphia Inquirer*, September 16, 1890.

"Mr. Hamilton's Plight." *Philadelphia Inquirer*, August 28, 1889.

"Mr. Hamilton's Sad Death." *New York Times*, September 16, 1890.

"Mr. Sargent and the Dog." *Philadelphia Inquirer*, June 12, 1891.

"Mr. Sargent Testifies." *New York Times*, June 21, 1891.

"Mrs. Eva Hamilton . . ." *Rochester Democrat and Chronicle*, March 24, 1890.

"Mrs. Eva's Dower." *New York Evening World*, January 14, 1891.

"Mrs. Gaul's Queer Goings-On." *New York World*. December 15, 1893.

"Mrs. Hamilton Convicted." *New York Times*, September 20, 1889.

"Mrs. Hamilton Gets Her Trunks." *New York Times*, August 16, 1890.

"Mrs. Hamilton in Jail." *New York Tribune*, August 28, 1889.

"Mrs. Hamilton Indicted." *New York Times*, September 17, 1889.

"Mrs. Hamilton On Trial." *New York Times*, September 19, 1889.

"Mrs. Hamilton Still in Jail." *New York Tribune*, August 31, 1889.

"Mrs. Hamilton Weeps." *Philadelphia Inquirer*, September 19, 1889.

"Mrs. Hamilton's Petition." *New York Times*, March 12, 1890.

"Mrs. Hamilton's Visitors." *New York Times*, October 2, 1889.

"Mrs. S. Hamilton, Jr., Dead." *New York Times*, May 4, 1899.

"Murder Intimated." *Philadelphia Inquirer*, September 6, 1889.

"New Mystery Baffles Newport." *Chicago Daily Tribune*, November 13, 1904.

"New Notes from Newport." *New York Times*, April 21, 1895.

"Newport Cottage Rents." *New York Times*, February 12, 1893.

"Not Hamilton's Child." *New York Tribune*, September 4, 1889.

"Not Ray Hamilton's Wife." *New York Tribune*, January 23, 1891.

"Now It Is Eva Hamilton." *New York Times*, November 30, 1890.

"Now It's a Foul-Play Theory." *New York Times*, November 14, 1891.

"Nurse Donnelly Exhibits." *Philadelphia Inquirer*, October 1, 1889.

"One of the Most Exquisite Entertainments." *New York Amusement Gazette*, September 30, 1889.

"Permitted to See Her Child." *Brooklyn Daily Eagle*, December 12, 1893.

"Proved to Be Dead." *New York World*, March 9, 1891.

"Put Away for a Time." *New York World*, September 20, 1889.

"Ray Hamilton. A Large Lot of His Real Estate in Brooklyn Sold To-Day." *Standard Union*, December 11, 1895.

"Ray Hamilton's Body." *Brooklyn Citizen*, July 27, 1892.

"Ray Hamilton's Body Here." *New York Sun*, July 27, 1892.

"Ray Hamilton's Fate." *Pittsburg Dispatch*, June 21, 1891.

"Ray Hamilton's Widow." *New York Tribune*, September 16, 1890.

"Ray's Body to Be Disinterred." *Philadelphia Inquirer*, September 18, 1890.

"Recent Newport Happenings." *New York Times*, June 3, 1894.

"Richard the Eavesdropper." *New York Evening World*, December 14, 1893.

"Robert Ray Hamilton." *Sierra County Advocate*, May 29, 1891.

"Robert Ray Hamilton Is Dead." *New York Times*, January 29, 1891.

"Robert Ray Hamilton's Story Is Told." *Baltimore Sun*, September 7, 1889.

"Samuel B. Clarke Lawyer, Dies at 76." *New York Times*, February 9, 1929.

"Sargent Comes to New York." *New York Times*, June 10, 1891.

"Says Hamilton Left Her." *New York Evening World*, September 25, 1894.

"Schuyler Hamilton, Jr. Sued for Divorce." *New York Tribune*, September 16, 1894.

"Schuyler Hamilton Married." *New York Times*, August 15, 1895.

"Sentenced to Prison." *Philadelphia Inquirer*, September 20, 1889.

"Sequel to Tragedy." *St. Paul Globe*, January 21, 1900.

"She Is Eva Mann, or Steele, or Brill." *New York Herald*, January 23, 1891.

"She Is Not Eva Hamilton." *New York Times*, January 23, 1891.

"She Was Known as Mrs. Mann." *New York Times*, January 15, 1891.

"Siren's Checkered Life." *Rochester Democrat and Chronicle*, October 10, 1889.

"Solitary and Gloomy." *New York Times*, September 2, 1889.

"Some Men of New York." *Pittsburg Press*, May 12, 1890.

"Still Bleeding Hamilton." *New York Times*, September 27, 1889.

"The Baby Gets an Annuity." *New York Times*, November 18, 1890.

"The New Year Welcomed." *New York Times*, January 1, 1900.

"The New York Correspondent." *Wyoming Democrat*, January 17, 1890.

"The Play Is 'All a Mistake.'" *Monmouth Inquirer*, September 3, 1891.

"The Season at Newport." *New York Times*, June 24, 1878.

"The Shameful Exhibition." *Philadelphia Times*, September 6, 1891.

"The Story of His Shame." *Independent-Record*, May 25, 1891.

"To Annul the Marriage." *New York Times*, September 5, 1889.

"To Trenton Via Elizabeth." *New York Times*, October 6, 1889.

"Two Years in Prison." *Baltimore Sun*, September 20, 1889.

"Very Costly Infatuation." *New York Times*, August 30, 1889.

"Wanted a Warrant for Eva." *New York Times*, March 25, 1892.

"Wants a Divorce." *New York Times*, October 4, 1889.

"War of the Gauls." *New York World*, December 14, 1893.

"Warrant Out for Miss Drake." *New York Times*, July 6, 1893.

"Was She Hamilton's Wife?" *New York Tribune*, January 13, 1891.

"Water for Man and Beast." *New York Times*, May 17, 1896.

"Woman Wins." *Boston Post*, July 8, 1894.

## WEB SOURCES

Berman, Marc. "Atlantic City's Famous Rolling Chairs Celebrate 125th Anniversary Today." www.nj.com/atlantic-city-entertainment/2012/06/acs_famous_rolling_chairs_cele.html, June 11, 2012.

Carlson, Peter. "Howe and Hummel: The Grifters' Grifters." history.net, June 2018.

Jastrzembski, Frank. "Schuyler Hamilton, Scion of American Heroes, Is a Civil War 'What If.'" history.net, May 4, 2020.

Levine, Lucie. "Before Times Square: Celebrating New Year's in Old New York." 6sqft.com, December 19, 2018.

Lewis, Jone Johnson. "1848: Married Women Win Property Rights." thoughtCo.com.

Livingston, James D. "Arsenic And Clam Chowder: Murder in Gilded Age New York." www.gothamcenter.org, October 15, 2010.

Miller, Tom. "The 1879 St. Anthony Club—No. 29 East 28th Street." daytonianinmanhattan.blogspot.com, February 21, 2014.

"San Diego History Center Timeline." sandiegohistory.org.

"The Extent of the Industry." brickcollecting.com.

———. "The Lost 1878 'Working Women's Hotel'—Park Avenue at 32nd Street." daytonianinmanhattan.blogspot.com, May 14, 2012.

———. "The Lost Windsor Hotel." daytonianinmanhattan.blogspot.com, November 19, 2012.

The New York Preservation Archive Project. "History," nypap.org.

Warnes, Kathy. "William Clark Sterling, Sr., and Sterling State Park." monroemichigan.wordpress.com.

Zacks, Richard. "Teddy Roosevelt's Battle With the Deeply Depraved New York of Yore." thirteen.org, March 5, 2012.


## STATISTICAL DATA AND REPORTS

Billings, John S. "Vital Statistics of New York City and Brooklyn." Washington, DC: Bureau of the Census, Department of the Interior, 1894.

Dickinson, S. D. *State of New Jersey Compendium of Censuses 1726-1905*. Trenton, NJ: John L. Murphy Publishing, 1906.

"Estimated Median Age at First Marriage: 1890 to present." U.S. Census Bureau, Current Population Survey, March and Annual Social and Economic Supplements. www.census.gov/data/tables/time-series/demo/families/marital.html.

"Historical Decennial Census Population for Wyoming Counties, Cities and Towns." U.S. Bureau of the Census, 2010.

"Maine, Divorce Records, 1798–1891." Augusta, ME: Maine State Archives.

*Minutes and Documents of the Board of Commissioners of the Department of Parks for the Year Ending December 31, 1903*. New York: Mail & Express Company, 1904.

*Minutes of Votes and Proceedings of the One Hundred and Four-teenth General Assembly of the State of New Jersey*. Trenton, NJ: MacCrellish & Quigley, 1890.

*N.W. Ayer & Son's American Newspaper Annual*. Philadelphia: N.W. Ayer & Son, 1889.

"Record of Climatological Observations." Atlantic City, NJ. NOAA, 1889.

"Record of Climatological Observations." NY Central Park. NOAA, 1903.

"Report of the New York Meteorological Bureau for the Month of January, 1891." Ithaca, NY: Cornell University.

*Sixth Annual Report of the Bureau of Statistics and Labor for the Year 1888*. Albany, NY: The Troy Press, 1889.

Steadman, Francis Dennis. *Architects in Practice, New York City, 1840-1900*. New York: Committee for the Preservation of Architectural Records, 1980.

"Supreme Court, General Term—First Department." New York: The Evening Post Job Printing House, 1893.

*The Industries and Advantages of the City of Trenton, N.J. 1889*. Trenton, NJ: John L. Murphy Publishing, 1889.

COLLECTED PAPERS AND RECORDS

Anna T. Swinton, Pub. L, No. Box 365, Folder 3428 (1889), New York Municipal Archives.

Passport Application, Alexandra Hamilton, May 7, 1923.

Ray Family Papers, 1794-1889. New York Historical Society.

# ACKNOWLEDGMENTS

While the idea for this book began on a stroll through my neighborhood on the Upper West Side of Manhattan, it is only with the diligence of librarians and archivists that Ray and Eva Hamilton's story can be fully told. In particular, I owe a debt of gratitude to Julianna Monjeau, New York Public Design Commission; Matthew Laudicina, New York State Library, Albany; Nora Haskell, Jackson Hole Historical Society and Museum; Nora Plant, American Heritage Center at the University of Wyoming; Lynn Raume, Monroe (MI) County Museum; Carl Farrell, Hamilton (NJ) Historical Society; and Jocelyn Wilk, Butler Library, Columbia University.

Additionally, the staff of the New York Public Library, New York Historical Society, New York Municipal Archives, New York City Parks Department, Norwalk (CT) Public Library, Freeport (NY) Memorial Library, the International Center for Photography and the Avery Architectural Library, Columbia University, have all been of enormous help in providing material that has found its way into this book.

I am especially grateful to my editor at Kensington Books, Michaela Hamilton, for her willingness to take a chance on an author with only a minuscule collection of published work—none of it in book-length form. Michaela's enthusiasm for the story that I wished to tell was evident from our first conversation and has remained unfaltering from my initial proposal to publication day. Without a doubt, her knowledge and love of history informs these pages.

And a sincere thanks to everyone at Kensington for their thoughtfulness and creativity in turning an MS Word document into the finished product you hold in your hands.

It is customary in these book acknowledgments to thank

one's agent for their unwavering support and hard work on the author's behalf. Although this book has come about without benefit of an agent, I have to thank my attorney, James Gregorio, for shepherding this writer through his first book contract.

During the fall of 2020, in the depths of the Covid pandemic, I had the good fortune to be introduced to a talented author, Adin Dobkin. Adin read my manuscript in its entirety, offered a thorough, and honest, critique of where it was at the time, and prodded me to explore the overall organization of the book and how to best amplify its most salient points. As a result of Adin's encouragement to look anew at what I had written, the book attained a vitality that it hadn't had previously. I am most appreciative of his insight.

My friend of thirty-plus years, Frank J. Oswald (aka the Archduke of Alliteration), is a creative soul to his core and an incredibly talented writer and wordsmith. I was fortunate to have Frank review my manuscript in its nascent form and offer his always-thoughtful, distinct point of view, suffused with his usual wit and candor.

A history buff and my best friend of a lifetime, John McDonough, was the first person (other than my wife) to read my first attempt at writing this book. While that version was abandoned long ago, John's encouragement throughout the entirety of the project has remained steadfast. And my childhood buddy, Marty Meyer, a forty-year resident of the Tetons, set me straight on the flora, fauna, and geological features of Jackson Hole, for which I am most appreciative.

And a special thanks to my sisters, Adele Corbin and Susan Luebbe, and my brother, Tim Shaffer, for their love and support not only of this book, but for all that their little brother has attempted to accomplish in life.

For twenty-five years, my daughter, Caroline, has provided me with an endless reserve of love and humor—all desirable qualities to have by one's side anytime, but they are especially nice to have nearby while researching and writing a book.

And most importantly, I thank my wife, Christine, the most accomplished writer in our family. She has read every false-start, every draft, every re-write, and for three years has offered not only insightful commentary and suggestions, but stellar proofreading skills as well. Beyond that, though, there were times throughout my research and writing that I questioned my resolve to see this book through to completion. Christine's unwavering love, support, and belief in my ability to do Ray and Eva's story justice sustained me when I wasn't so sure this book would happen. For this, I am forever grateful.

# Index

Abbett, Leon, 114, 116, 143–44
Ackert, Alfred, 57
Adair & Aldred, 199–200, 201
Adams, Llewellyn, 153
Adams, Samuel, 153
Aeschbacher, Christian, 134,
    180
*All a Mistake (The Habbertons;*
        play), 190–98
    performances, 194–96
    the plot, 191–92
    preparations, 192–94
    reviews, 196–98
Allen, Louis, 160–62
*Allentown Critic,* 115
Ammidon, Royal, 157
Anchor Brick Company, 113–14,
    213
Arthur, Chester A., 34, 151, 187
*Aspen Daily Chronicle,* 32
Associated Press, 1–2, 25
Astraphobia, 219–20
*Atlanta Constitution,* 48
Atlantic City, 14, 16–18, 20–23.
        *See also* Noll Cottage
Atlantic City Hall, 25–26
Atlantic City Police
        Department, 24–25
Atlantic County Jail, 27–29, 30–
        31, 37, 39–40, 52–53,
        66, 84, 89
Atwood House, 33
*Austin Statesman,* 32

Baby (horse), 130, 132
*Baltimore Sun,* 48, 217
Bank for Savings, 154–55
Bausch, Jacob, 220–21
Baylies, Edmund L., 146–47,
        151, 200, 210, 227, 231,
        242
Baylies, Nathalie, 103, 147,
        221–22
Baylies, Walter, 147
Beatrice. *See* Hamilton, Beatrice
Bellevue Hospital, 95–96
Bellevue Hospital Medical
        College, 203
Bernice, Pennsylvania, 18, 19,
        111
Biddle, William, 24–25, 27
Bieri, Gottlieb, 134, 180
Bigelow, John, 233
Blackwell, Elizabeth, 20
Blackwell's Island, 96
Blake, Esther, 162
Bly, Nellie, 95–103
Boll, P., 64

Boonton Opera House, 195–96
*Boston Daily Globe,* 48
*Boston Post,* 210–11
Bowery Theatre, 56
Brandreth, Franklin, 105–6
Brandreth, Ralph, 105–6
Breast feeding and alcohol consumption, 72
Bright's disease, 239
Broadway Theater, 193
Brooke, Charles W., 203, 204–5, 210
Brooklyn Bridge, 12–13, 200
*Brooklyn Daily Eagle,* 241–42
Brooklyn Institute of Arts and Sciences, 231
Brown, W, J., 39
Burr, Aaron, 2, 8, 226
Burr, Edson
　marriage ceremony of Eva and Ray, 8–10, 151–52, 176
　will hearing testimony of, 151–52, 159
Burr, Josephine, 9–10
Byrnes, Thomas F., 34–47
　arraignment of Swinton and Mann, 59–60
　background of, 34–35
　Eva's seeking of a pardon, 114–15
　hiring of, 34–36
　investigation of, 34–47, 51–52, 149
　Swinton's confession, 42–47, 49, 51
　update on, 240–41

Calvary Episcopal Church, 10, 200, 228–29
Camden & Atlantic Rail, 27–28
Canyon Hotel, 124
Cararet, Victoria, 222–23

Carnegie, Andrew, 107, 141
Carnegie Endowment for International Peace, 240
Carter & Ledyard, 231
Carvalho. David N., 181
Cedar Park, 217
Century Club, 232
Cherry, Wendell, 26
Chestnut Street Theater, 196
*Chicago Daily Tribune,* 183
*City of Berlin,* 50–51, 168
City Real Property Investing Co., 231
Civil War, 10, 34, 122, 214, 217, 228
Clarke, Samuel B.
　arraignment of Swinton and Mann, 57, 62
　background of, 34
　Byrnes's investigation, 34, 35–36, 37, 51
　Eva's contesting of divorce, 110–11, 112
　Ray's death, 143
　Ray's will hearing, 187
　Vollmer's removal of belongings from Noll Cottage, 54
Cliff, Annie, 64
Coal mining, 11
Code, Henry, 199–200
Cole, Arthur, 197–98
Cole, Clarence, 68
Collect Pond, 41
Collens, Carrie, 100–101
Collens, Kate, 100–101
Colter Bay, 124
Columbia Law School, 11, 34
Columbia River, 123
Columbia University, 11, 213
Conant Pass, 127

Conspiracy theories, 1
  about Ray's death, 139–42,
    181–84
Cook, Walter, 233
Côte d'Azur, 217
Couch, David W., Jr., 143, 179–
  80
Crane, Edwina, 123
Crane, Leander, 123
Crosby, Howard, 27, 40, 69, 73–
  74
Crowley, Sergeant, 41
Custer, George Armstrong, 104–
  6
Czolgosz, Leon, 239–40

Dana, Paul, 117–18
DeForest, Henry, 106
Delmonico's, 87, 120
Díaz, Porfirio, 95
Dickens, Charles, 42
Dinard, France, 217–18, 219
Diven, George M., 111–12
Dixon, James, 155
Dodge, John, 126
Donnelly, Mary Ann, 242
  appearance at Globe
    Museum, 88–89
  Byrnes's investigation of
    stabbing, 34–47
  drinking of, 20–21, 22, 70,
    72–73, 89, 108
  hiring of, 13–14
  stabbing of, 20–25, 26–27, 40,
    102–3, 108, 114
  trial testimony of, 69–74
  as wet nurse of Beatrice, 13–
    14, 17, 23, 72–73, 84
Dower rights, 49, 142, 147, 172,
  177, 179, 209, 227
Drake, James, 236, 237–38
Drake, Mary, 236
Drake Mastin & Co., 236

Droley, John, 64
Dye, William, 180

Eagle Rock, 181
Earle, Arthur, 185
Earle, William, 185
Edison, Thomas, 240
Egg Harbor City, 28
11th New York Infantry
        Regiment (Zouaves), 34
Erie, Lake, 104–5
Erie Railroad, 8
Eustis, John E., 229
Eva. See Hamilton, Evangeline
        Steele "Eva"
Evers, Julia, 157

Farragut, David, 232
Farragut, Loyall, 232–33
Fish, Hamilton, 33
Fish, Stuyvesant, 213
Florence, Billy, 56–57, 98
Florence Apartments, 219–21
Flowerden, Frederick, 207–8
Follett, David L., 209–10
Foster, George V., 220
Foster, Stephen, 95
"Four Hundred," 3, 118
Foyle, William, 111–12, 153
Fuller, Charles W.
  Eva's appeal, 189, 190, 199,
    202–3
  Eva's divorce and, 108–9,
    111–12
  Eva's pardon, 114, 116 144–
    45, 146
  Eva's play, 193
  Ray's will, 147–49
  Ray's will hearing, 149–52,
    149–79, 190
    Burr's testimony, 151–52
    closing arguments, 176–
      78, 177–78

Fuller, Charles W. (*cont.*)
  Ray's will hearing
    Eva's arrival in court, 153–54
    Eva's testimony, 164–76
    Kemp's testimony, 155
    Little's testimony, 156–57
    personal testimony, 157–58
    proof of death, 183–84
    Sargent's testimony, 187–89
    witnesses, 159–76

Gardiner, Charles W., 193, 194–95, 197
Garfield, James A., 34, 151
Gaul, Alice, 206–9
Gaul, Archie (Edward Hilton), 204–9
Gaul, Madge Irene, 206–7
Gaul, Richard, 206–7
Gaul, Robert, 206–9
Gilbert, Dr., 45
Gilded Age
  newspapers of, 1–2
  prostitution in, 19–20
Globe Museum, 88–89
Golo Club, 104–6
Gould, George, 118
Gould, Jay, 34, 107, 118
Gramercy Park, 10, 228
Grand Central Terminal, 231
Grand larceny, 57, 58–59, 61
Green, James O.
  background of, 136
  inventory of Ray's body, 134, 180–81
  Ray's will and, 180–81, 188–89
  search and discovery of Ray, 131, 132–34, 140
  telegram to Schuyler, 136, 138–39
Green, Norvin, 136, 138–39
Green-Wood Cemetery, 200–202, 212, 221, 229
Gremeret, Annette, 236

*Habbertons, The* (play). See *All a Mistake*
Hagerty, Mary Ann, 162
Hamilton, Alexander, 2, 10, 186, 226, 227, 228, 229
Hamilton, Alexandra Schuyler, 219–20, 221
Hamilton, Beatrice
  arraignment of Swinton and Mann, 56–62
  birth certificate, 36, 44
  Bly's story about Eva and, 101–2
  Byrnes's investigation of, 36, 37, 51–52
  Donnelly as wet nurse of, 13–14, 17, 23, 72–73, 84
  Eva's alleged pregnancy and birth, 46–47, 49–52
  Eva's visit with, 90–91, 243–44
  formal separation of Eva and Ray, 18
  Ray's will and, 146–47, 221–22
  Ray's will hearing, 151, 155, 172, 173
  Rupp's care of, 52, 66, 76, 85, 87–88, 90–91
  in San Diego, 13–14
  solicitations of care for, 63–64
  Swinton's confession, 42–47, 49
    Baby No. 1, 43–45, 200
    Baby No. 2, 45–46, 200

Baby No. 3, 46–47, 52
update on, 243–44
Hamilton, Charles Apthorp, 10
Hamilton, Cornelia Ray, 9, 10,
    29, 229
Hamilton, Emma Gray
    Hebbard, 239
Hamilton, Evangeline Steele
    "Eva"
    *All a Mistake (The
        Habbertons),* 190–98
    alleged pregnancy and birth
        of Beatrice, 46–47, 49–
        52. *See also* Hamilton,
        Beatrice
        Swinton's confession, 42–
        47
    appearance of, 9, 18
    Archie Gaul and, 204–9
    arrest for high kicking, 222–
        23
    arrival in New York City, 19–
        20
    at Atlantic County Jail, 27–
        29, 30–31, 37, 39–40,
        52–53, 66, 84, 89
    Bly's story about, 95–103
    Byrnes's investigation, 34–47
    death of, 242–44
    death of Ray, 142–43
    early life of, 3–4, 11, 13, 18–
        19, 97
    European trip of, 50–51, 168
    family background of, 9, 11
    first trial of, 25–28
    indictment of, 66–67
    Joshua and. *See* Mann,
        Joshua, Eva and
    names and identities of, 3
    post-conviction life of, 90–93
    prostitution of, 19–20, 111

    Ray and. *See* Hamilton,
        Robert Ray, and Eva
    Ray's will and, 147–48
        final settlement, 212–13,
        227–28
    Ray's will hearing, 149–89
        appeal, 189, 190, 199, 202–
            3, 209–11
        bookkeeper's testimony,
            154–55
        Burr's testimony, 151–52,
            159
        closing arguments, 176–78
        Eva's arrival in court, 153–
            54
        Eva's testimony, 164–76
        General Hamilton's testi-
            mony, 162–63
        Kemp's testimony, 155
        Little's testimony, 156–57
        Ransom's decision, 178–79
        Sargent's testimony, 187–
            89
        Steele's testimony, 153
    in San Diego, 12, 13–14
    seeking of a pardon, 114–17,
        143–45, 146
    stabbing of Mary Ann
        Donnelly, 20–25, 40
    at Trenton State Prison, 93–
        95, 114–17, 142, 145,
        148
    trial of, 67–85
        closing arguments, 81–82
        conviction, 83–84, 86–87,
            89
        Crosby's testimony, 69,
            73–74
        Donnelly's testimony, 69–
            74
        Eva's testimony, 76–80
        jurors, 68–69

Hamilton, Evangeline Steele
    "Eva" (*cont.*)
  trial of
    jury deliberation, 82–83
    Ray's testimony, 74–75
    Rupp's testimony, 75–76
Hamilton, Gertrude Ray, 147,
    214, 221–22
Hamilton, Gertrude Van
    Cortlandt Wells, 214–17
  Ray's will hearing, 151, 154,
    158–59
Hamilton, Jane Bryd Mercer,
    216–18, 219–21
Hamilton, John Church, 10
Hamilton, Louisa, 29, 242
Hamilton, Robert Ray
  appearance of, 8–9
  arraignment of Swinton and
    Mann, 57–60
  arrest of, 24–26
  Beatrice's alleged birth and,
    46–47, 49–52
  Beatrice's care and, 63–64,
    66, 87–88, 90
  burial at Green-Wood
    Cemetery, 199–202, 212
  conviction of Eva, 86–87
  death of, 130–42
    conspiracy theories, 139–
      42, 181–84
    notifications of, 134–39
    search for, 131–34
    warnings against making
      a solo trek, 130–31
  early life of, 3–4
  Eva and. *See* Hamilton,
    Robert Ray, and Eva
  family background of, 3, 9,
    10–11, 29
  in Jackson Hole, 119–33
  jailing of Eva, 27–29, 33–34,
    89–90

Last Will and Testament of,
    143, 146–49, 179–80
Last Will and Testament
    hearing, 149–89
  bookkeeper's testimony,
    154–55
  Burr's testimony, 151–52,
    159
  closing arguments, 176–78
  Eva's arrival in court, 153–
    54
  Eva's testimony, 164–76
  General Hamilton's testi-
    mony, 162–63
  Kemp's testimony, 155
  Little's testimony, 156–57
  proof of death, 179–89
  Ransom's decision, 178–79
  Sargent's testimony, 187–
    89
  Steele's testimony, 153
  meeting with father, 106–8
  at Noll Cottage, 33–34, 37, 65
  Vollmer's removal of be-
    longings from, 53–55
  post-trial life of, 86–90, 103–9
  real estate holdings of, 12–13,
    121, 125–31, 146–47,
    148
  in San Diego, 12, 13–14
  stabbing of Mary Ann
    Donnelly, 23–25
  Byrnes's investigation, 34–
    47
  trial of, 25–28, 29
Hamilton, Robert Ray, and Eva
  arguments of, 17–18, 20–21,
    74–75
  in Atlantic City, 14, 16–18,
    20–23
  Byrnes's investigation of
    stabbing, 34–47

divorce, 92, 95, 108–9, 110–
    12, 116, 140, 142, 149
first meeting, 20
indictment of Eva, 66–67
marriage ceremony, 8–10,
    11–12, 151–52
news stories about, 2–4, 32–
    33, 42–43, 48–49, 60,
    67, 89–90, 109, 110,
    117–18, 142–43, 212–
    13, 235
    Nellie Bly story, 99–100
in San Diego, 12, 13–14
separation agreement, 18,
    22–23, 74
trial testimony, 74–75
Hamilton, Schuyler
    background of, 9, 10, 29
    death of, 228–29
    on Eva's conviction, 86–87
    Sargent and, 184, 186
    scandal of son Ray and Eva,
        29–30, 64–65, 119, 194
    son Ray's death, 138–39
    son Ray's interment at
        Green-Wood, 200
    son Ray's marriage to Eva,
        14–15
    son Ray's meeting with, 106–
        8
    son Ray's will testimony,
        162–63
    at Windsor Hotel, 106–8,
        138–39, 184, 194
Hamilton, Schuyler, Jr., 10,
    213–17, 219–21
    Anchor Brick Company, 113–
        14, 213
    appearance of, 213–14
    brother Ray's death, 136–39
    brother Ray's interment at
        Green-Wood, 200

brother Ray's marriage, 14–
    15
brother Ray's will and estate,
    146, 151, 154, 158–59,
    159, 163, 180, 182, 187,
    221–22
divorce from Gertrude, 215–
    16
Emma Gray and, 239
Jane Mercer and, 216–18,
    219–21
in Newport, 214–16
Hamilton, Schuyler, III, 147,
    214, 221–22
Hamilton, Violet, 147, 214, 221–
    22
Hamilton Building, 187
Hamilton Fountain, 4–5, 147,
    226–35, 239, 245–46
Harriman, E. H., 34
Harriott, Charles, 154–55
Harvard Law School, 34, 35
Hastings, Hugh, 29
Hawk, Samuel, 107
Hayward, Harry, 206–8
Hehr, John G., 237
Hemenway, William, 122
Heppenheimer, William C., 144–
    45
Hickey, Sergeant, 39, 41
Hill, Harriet, 9–10
Hoe, Richard March, 117
Hoe, Robert, II, 117
Hoffman, William, 116, 144
Hoffman House, 120
Hogan, Edward, 56–62
Holland, John, 131–34, 140,
    180–81
Hone, Philip, 228–29
Hotel Beresford, 236
Howard, George E. P., 199–200
Howe, William, 160–61

Howe & Hummel, 160–61, 202–4
Hudson, Shepherd, 90–91
Hudson River, 7–8, 113
Hummel, Abraham, 160–61, 203–4

Ingersoll, Daniel, 75
Ingraham, George L., 203
Ingraham & Allen, 33
Irving, Albert W., 25–27, 54–55

Jackson Hole, Wyoming, 119–33, 218–19
Jackson Lake, 119–20, 124, 129, 130, 212–13
Janet R., 44–45
Jerome, William T., 57–62
Jocko (dog), 130–31
Johnson, Alfred, 89
Johnson, Enoch, 89
Johnson, Jennie, 39–40, 52–53, 89–94
Johnson, Smith, 28, 52–53, 66, 83, 89, 93–94
Jones & Rouschert, 33
Jullien, Louis-Antoine, 21

Kaintuck, Idaho, 120, 129, 130–31, 135, 136, 142
Kearsarge House, 29
Kemp, William, 44–45, 155, 166
Kennard House, 153
Kennedy, John F., 2–3
King's College, 11
Knevals, Sherman W., 151
Kunkle Post Office, 172
Kyrie, Clara, 21

Layton, A. J., 111–12
Leake, Francis, 154–55
Little, William, 156–57

Livingston, Edward de Peyster, 213
Loder, Sergeant, 27
Los Angeles Times, 33
Lowell, Cornelia, 147
Lynherr, John, 157

McAllister, Ward, 3, 118
McCartney's Hotel, 124
McCluskey, George, 51–52, 53, 84
MacDonald, Carlos, 203–4, 239–40
McGibney, Sam, 237–38
Machias Union, 123
McKinley, William, 239–40
McNaught, Bobby, 36–39, 51–52, 53, 110
Madden, George, 95–96
Mallone, Michael, 115–16
Mangin, Frank, Jr., 157
Mann, Joshua, 12, 242
    background of, 21
    Byrnes's investigation, 36–47
    confession of, 42–47, 49, 51, 59
    conspiracy charges against, 56–62, 84
    Donnelly and, 21–22
    Eva and, 21, 30–31, 111–12
        Bly's story, 98, 99–101
        Byrnes's investigation, 36–47
        the confession, 42–47, 49, 51
        divorce, 160–61, 165, 166, 202–4
        Ray's will hearing, 152–62, 164–70, 173–76
    Eva's trial, 72, 77, 79, 84
    MacDonald and, 203–4, 239–40

at The Tombs, 41–42, 55–56, 91–92

Manning, Thomas, 94

Marchant, Thomas, 201–2

Market Lake, 128, 135

Market Street Methodist Episcopal Church, 8–10

Marshall, Henry Rutgers, 232–33

Marymere, 121, 124, 125–30, 140, 141, 218–19, 222, 239

   construction of, 126–30, 212–13

Mays Landing Courthouse, 67–85. *See also* "State vs. Hamilton"

Mays Landing jail. *See* Atlantic County Jail

Meade, Mrs., 19

Mercer, Elizabeth, 217

Mercer, John, 217

Mercer, Richard Sprigg, 217

Metropolitan Museum of Art, 106, 231

Metropolitan Opera, 242

Mexican-American War, 10

Mexican dagger, 23–24, 26, 32, 68, 69, 71, 88–89

Midwives, 44–45, 51–54

Military Academy, U.S. (West Point), 29, 229

Mingos, John, 153

Mitchell, Edward, 140

Mitchell, John, 141

Mixer, Henry, 104–5

Monroe, Michigan, 103–6

Monroe Marsh Company, 104, 105–6, 124, 126, 147

Moore, Casimir de Rham

   Ray's death, 135–36, 137–38

   Ray's will testimony, 179–80

   sailing offer to Ray, 103–4

   update on, 241

Moore, Clement Clark, 103

Moore, Frank, 52–53

Moorings, The, 215–16, 236

Morrison, Lewis, 150, 156–57, 183–84

Morris & Steele, 33

Morse, Burnett, 36

Mount Auburn Cemetery, 201

Mount Olivet Cemetery, 243

Muir, John, 120–21

Murphy, James, 115–16

Murray, Joseph, 29

Nagle, John T., 200

*Nebraska State Journal,* 198

Newgate Prison, 93

New Jersey Central Railroad, 93

New Jersey Court of Pardons, 114–17, 143–45

Newport, 214–16, 221, 238

Newspapers, 1–2. *See also specific newspapers*

   Hamilton scandal, 2–4, 32–33, 42–43, 48–49, 60, 67, 89–90, 109, 110, 117–18, 142–43, 212–13, 235

   Nellie Bly's story, 99–100

New York Art Commission, 231–33

New York City

   Eva's arrival in, 19–20

   newspapers, 1–2

   population of 1890, 1

   prostitution in, 19–20

New York City Bar, 11, 26, 34, 58, 203

New York City Lunatic Asylum, 96

New York City Parks
 Department, 4–5, 229,
 245
New York County Surrogate
 Court, 146, 149–79
 Monday, January 12, 1891,
  149–55
 Wednesday, January 14,
  1891, 155–58
 Thursday, January 15, 1891,
  158–63
 Friday, January 16, 1891,
  163–67
 Monday, January 19, 1891,
  167–71
 Wednesday, January 21,
  1891, 171–76
 Thursday, January 22, 1891,
  176–79
 proof of Ray's death, 179–89
New York Evening World, 88, 90
New York Health Board, 200
New York Herald, 1, 163, 179
New York Mercantile Exchange,
 136
New York Police Department
 (NYPD), 20, 34–35, 51–
 52, 240–41
New York Public Library, 231,
 233
New York Star, 117, 119
New York State Assembly, 7, 50
New York State Supreme Court,
 92, 189, 199, 202, 209–
 10
New York Stock Exchange, 187
New York Sun, 1, 117–18, 181–
 84, 195–96, 210
New York Times, 1, 56, 87–88,
 89, 107–8, 141, 143,
 163, 167–68, 171, 183,
 216, 223, 226, 230
New York Tribune, 1, 32, 155

New York World, 1, 2, 4, 67, 82,
 95–96, 156, 192, 242–43
 Bly's interview with Eva, 95–
  103
Ninth Avenue El, 12, 230
Nobel Peace Prize, 240
Noll Cottage, 17, 20–23, 33–34,
 52, 65–66
 Rupp's closing up of, 87
 stabbing of Mary Ann
  Donnelly, 20–25, 26–27,
  71, 73–74, 102–3
 Vollmer's removal of Ray's
  belongings, 53–55
Norcross & Veale's Champion
 Hotel, 65–66
Norris Hotel, 124
Nowlin, Laura, 218
Nowlin Ranch, 218

O'Brien, Morgan J., 209–10
Ochs, Joseph, 111–12
O'Conor, John, 150, 156, 187
O'Hanlon, P. F., 220–21
Osborne, Hattie, 218

Panzini, Henri, 236
Park Avenue Hotel, 184–85
Parker, Alton B., 209–10
Parsons, Samuel, Jr., 229–30
Parsons, Walter, 19, 97–98
Passaic Bridge Post Office, 99
Paterson City Hall, 10
Patterson, Edward, 92, 203–4
Patterson, John, 94, 116–17,
 142, 144–45
Patterson, Margaret, 94
Pavonia Ferry, 7–8
Peabody, Baker & Peabody, 34
Peabody, Charles, Jr.
 arraignment of Swinton and
  Mann, 57
 background of, 34

Byrnes's investigation, 34, 35, 37, 39, 240
Eva's seeking of a pardon, 114–15
Ray's stay at home of, 37, 39, 51, 63, 104
update on, 241
Pennsylvania Railroad, 184, 239
Pennsylvania Society to Protect Children from Cruelty, 44–45
Perry, Samuel E.
first trial of Eva and Ray, 26–27
post-conviction life of Eva, 90–92
trial of Eva, 53, 68, 71–84
closing arguments, 81
conviction, 83, 84
Donnelly's testimony, 71–74
Eva's testimony, 80
jury deliberation, 82–83
Phelps, Benjamin, 151
*Philadelphia Inquirer,* 25, 82, 158
*Pittsburgh Dispatch,* 95
Plaza Hotel, 214
Post, J. Morris, 180
Prescott House, 12, 146–47, 187, 221
Proctor, Alexander Phimister, 231–33
*Professional Criminals of America* (Byrnes), 35
Prostitution, 19–20, 111
Pulitzer, Joseph, 2, 95–96, 242–43

Ransom, Rastus Seneca, Ray's will hearing, 146, 148–89
closing arguments, 176–78

the decision, 178–79, 190
Eva's testimony, 164–76
Fuller's objections, 147–49
Fuller's witnesses, 158–76
the lawyers, 150–51
proof of death, 179–89
Root's witnesses, 152–58
Ray. *See* Hamilton, Robert Ray
Reading Railroad, 93
Red Cross, 236
Reed, Alfred, 67–85
closing arguments, 81–82
conviction, 83–84, 86–87
Crosby's testimony, 69, 73–74
Donnelly's testimony, 69–74
Eva's testimony, 76–80
jury deliberation, 82–83
Ray's testimony, 74–75
Rupp's testimony, 75–76
Reeves, Samuel, 69, 83
Regnault, Marie, 236
Reilly, Edward A., 40
Rexburg, 141–42, 180
Rice, Frank H., 164–65
Riis, Jacob, 241
Riverside Drive, 4–5, 230, 232, 235, 245
Riverside Park, 230, 235
*Rochester Daily Chronicle,* 32
Rockefeller, John D., 107
Rolling Chair, 17
Rollins, Daniel G., 187
Roosevelt, James W., 213
Roosevelt, Theodore, 240, 241
Root, Elihu
background of, 34
Byrnes's investigation, 34, 35–36, 37, 51
Eva's contesting of divorce, 110–11, 112
Eva's seeking of a pardon, 114–15
Ray's death, 143

Root, Elihu (*cont.*)
  Ray's will hearing, 150–79
    bookkeeper's testimony,
      154–55
    Burr's testimony, 152
    closing arguments, 176–77
    Eva's marital relationship
      with Mann, 152–62,
      164–70
    Eva's testimony, 166–71,
      172–76
    witnesses, 152–58
  update on, 239–40
  Vollmer's removal of belong-
    ings from Noll Cottage,
    54
Root & Clarke, 34, 35–36, 51,
  54, 150–51, 187, 210.
  *See also* Root, Elihu
Ross, J. Stewart, 57, 59–62
Rovere, Richard H., 160–61
Rupp, Elizabeth
  arguments of Ray and Eva,
    17
  care of Beatrice, 52, 66, 85,
    87–88, 90–91
  stabbing of Mary Ann
    Donnelly, 22, 24, 27
  *Times* interview with, 87–88
  trial testimony of, 75–76
  Vollmer's removal of belong-
    ings from Noll Cottage,
    54–55
Rural Cemetery Movement,
  200–201

Sacred Heart Academy, 224
St. Charles Hotel, 39, 40
*St. Paul Globe,* 212
St. Paul's Episcopal Church, 214
St. Vincent's Hospital, 243
San Diego, 12, 13–14

*San Francisco Chronicle,* 49
Sargent, Adelaide Crane, 123,
  130, 131, 212–13, 218–
  19
Sargent, Alice Hemenway, 121–
  22
Sargent, Catherine, 212, 223–24
Sargent, Charles, 123
Sargent, Edith Drake, 235–39
Sargent, Epes, 121
Sargent, Henry, 121–22
Sargent, Ignatius, 122
Sargent, John Dudley, 121–23
  Adelaide and, 123, 130, 131,
    212–13, 218–19
  background and early life of,
    121–22
  death of, 239
  Edith Drake and, 235–39
  Marymere and, 121, 125–30,
    212–13, 218–19, 222,
    223–24
  Ray's death, 133–42
    conspiracy theories, 139–
      42, 181–82
    notifications, 134–39
    proof of death at will hear-
      ing, 179–82
    the search, 131–33
  Ray's solo trek, 130–31
  Ray's will hearing testimony,
    187–89
  at Swift and Co., 219, 222
Sargent, John Singer, 121
Sargent, Mary, 212, 223–24
Satterlee, Henry, 200
Schuyler, Margaret, 64
Scott, Winfield, 217
Scranton *Times-Tribune,* 197
Sepert, Roman, 180
Shack Hotel, 124
Sheridan Trail, 130, 131

Shourds, Harry, 90–91
Signal Mountain, 132
Snake River, 120, 123–24, 131–
  32, 134–35
*Social Register,* 3, 10
Sons of the Revolution, 213
South Landing, 130, 131–32,
  134–35, 185
Spier, Gilbert, 186
  Hamilton Fountain and, 227–
    28
  Ray in Jackson Hole, 121,
    128–30
  Ray's death, 135–36, 137
  Ray's interment at Green-
    Wood, 200
  Ray's will, 146–47, 151, 179–
    80, 210, 227–28
  update on, 241
Sprague, Henry, 148–49, 150–51
Spring Grove Cemetery, 201
"State vs. Hamilton," 67–85
  closing arguments, 81–82
  conviction, 83–84, 86–87
  Crosby's testimony, 69, 73–74
  Donnelly's testimony, 69–74
  Eva's testimony, 76–80
  jurors, 68–69
  jury deliberation, 82–83
  Ray's testimony, 74–75
  Rupp's testimony, 75–76
Steele, Alice, 112, 153
Steele, Joseph, 153, 165
Steele, Lida Cheever, 9, 97, 172,
  176
Steele, William, 9, 11, 97–98
Steele, William, Jr., 112, 153,
  172
Stewart's Working-Women
  Hotel, 185
Strong, William L., 240
Sullivan, Timothy, 9, 223

Sweetwater River, 12
Swift and Company, 219, 222
Swinton, Anna, 12, 242
  background of, 21
  Bly's story, 98, 99–101
  Byrnes's investigation, 36–47
  confession, 42–47, 49, 51,
    59
  at The Tombs, 41–42, 55–
    56, 91–92
  conspiracy charges against,
    56–62, 84
  Eva's trial, 72, 77, 79, 84
  Ray's will hearing, 161, 166,
    168–69
  stabbing of Mary Ann
    Donnelly, 21–22
  visit to Eva in jail, 30–31
Swinton, Frederick J., 21

Talbot, Edward J., 122
Tammany Hall, 35
Terminal City, 231
Teton Mountains, 119–20, 124
Thompson, Joseph, 26–27, 40
  trial of Eva, 68–71, 74–81
    closing arguments, 81–82
    conviction, 83–84, 86–87
    Crosby's testimony, 69,
      73–74
    Donnelly's testimony, 69–
      74
    Eva's testimony, 77–80
    jurors, 68–69
    jury deliberation, 82–83
    Ray's testimony, 74–75
    Rupp's testimony, 75–76
Thorne, William, 180
Tombs, The (Manhattan
  Detention Complex),
  41–42, 55–56, 61, 91–
  92, 108, 160

*Topeka Daily Press,* 192
Transcontinental railroad, 12
Trenton State Prison, 84, 89,
    93–95, 114–17, 142,
    145, 148
Trinity Church, 225–26, 228
True, Clarence, 230

*Umbria,* RMS, 103–4
Union Dime Savings Institution,
    154–55, 167
Union League, 33, 87, 120, 187
Unitah County Coroner, 199
University Club, 33, 87, 120,
    213

Van Brunt, Charles H., 209–10
Vanderbilt, George, 117
Van Duzer, E. C., 111
Varnum & Harris, 33
Verona Hotel, 21, 22, 37, 70, 72
Vollmer, Edward
    Eva's trial, 81
    Ray's will and hearing, 143,
        162, 179–80
    removal of Ray's belongings
        from Noll Cottage, 53–
        55
    update on, 241–42

Waldron, Edsell, 241–42
Walnut Street Jail, 93

Walter, Thomas Ustick, 28–29
Warren, Edward, 193
Warren, Whitney, 230–35
Washington Academy, 121–22
Waverly, New York, 18–19, 111
Wesleyan University, 8
Western Union Telegraph Co.,
    31, 136
*West Wing* (schooner), 104
Wetherbee, Gardner, 107
Wetmore, Charles, 231–35
Wet nurses, 13–14, 72
Whitney, William, 34
Wilson, Francis, 236–37
Wilson, James G., 228
Windsor Hotel, 106–8, 138–39,
    184, 194
Wister, Owen, 141
Worthington, Ralph, 141–42
Wright, Charles, 157
Wright, Edwin, 180
Wyoming Territory, 123–24

Yancey, John F., 124–25
Yancey's Pleasant Valley Hotel,
    124–25
Yellow journalism, 2
Yellowstone National Park, 123,
    124–25
Young, Richard, 229
Young, W. J., 111–12